The ABC of Communication Studies

David Gill
Bridget Adams

Nelson

Thomas Nelson and Sons Ltd
Nelson House Mayfield Road
Walton-on-Thames Surrey
KT12 5PL UK

Nelson Blackie
Wester Cleddens Road
Bishopbriggs
Glasgow G64 2NZ UK

Thomas Nelson Australia
102 Dodds Street
South Melbourne
Victoria 3205 Australia

Nelson Canada
1120 Birchmount Road
Scarborough Ontario
M1K 5G4 Canada

First published by Macmillan Education Ltd 1989
ISBN 0-333-46757-4

This edition published by Thomas Nelson and Sons Ltd 1992

I(T)P Thomas Nelson is an International
        Thomson Publishing Company

I(T)P is used under licence

ISBN 0-17-438522-6
NPN 9 8 7 6

Printed in China

To our students

CONTENTS

If the item you are looking for is not in the Contents list, you may find it in the index at the back of the book.

ACKNOWLEDGEMENTS

Special thanks are due to Debra Murray for her original contributions which laid such valuable foundations. Thanks too, to Paul Watt for his comments on the sociology, and to Bill Smith for his input into the sections on computers.

This expanded glossary would not have been possible without the permission of the Buckinghamshire College and the generous agreement of Buckinghamshire County Council to second David Gill to Birkbeck College, London, to study communication under Dr Viv Edwards of the Department of Applied Linguistics.

Finally, Jill Brownjohn and her colleages Penny Tucker and Jane Stokes, and the budding secretaries in the training office, should be showered with bouquets for they have struggled to decode the world's worst handwriting and transfer the strangest stuff on to the floppy discs of the new technology.

Joseph Weizenbaum's program ELIZA appeared in *Communications of the ACM* in 1965, copyright © 1965 Association for Computing Machinery, Inc., reprinted by permission.

INTRODUCTION

The title 'Communication Studies' covers a vast area of interest and embraces many different disciplines, including journalism, telecommunications, social psychology, physiology, linguistics and semantics. Teachers of Communication Studies may be language specialists, sociologists or even physicists. Not surprisingly, the language used in Communication Studies can give rise to a variety of interpretations: words like medium and channel do not mean the same to a journalist and a telecommunications engineer, yet each person has a valid and important point of view.

Within Communication Studies, concepts do not have to be rigidly and narrowly defined, but if effective communication is to take place between all the various interested people, then it is necessary to avoid woolly and sloppy use of language, understand each other's specialist terms and come to some agreement over usage in a communications context.

The aim of this book is to give outlines and clear definitions of the terms and concepts in general use in communications and media studies today, indicating where alternative uses are found. We hope to provide, for all students of communications, a stepping-stone to contemporary textbooks as well as earlier specialist articles and books. In addition we hope the glossary will serve as a handy reference work and revision aid. Although principally geared to the AEB A-level coursework, much of the material, because of its fundamental and basic nature, is suitable for GCSE. It would also be appropriate for Management, Information Technology, Informatics and other courses which include communications or media studies.

This glossary has developed out of an earlier, shorter *ABC* compiled by David Gill and Debra Murray of the Buckinghamshire College at the beginning of the 1980s, specially for A-level students, at a time when the examination syllabus was very general and most available theoretical publications were too difficult for A-level. There was a heartfelt need to collect and compare different definitions and sort out the basic concepts. Since then the subject has been more sharply delineated by the Associated Examining Board, there is an ever-increasing number of textbooks suitable for A-level and other non-advanced courses, and there are signs of a growing consensus regarding definitions.

Notes on the authors

David Gill was in charge of Communication Studies at the Buckinghamshire College from 1979 to 1987. Prior to that, he taught in secondary schools, and trained teachers at Newland Park College of Education. His academic base is modern languages, linguistics and literature. He has published eight volumes of verse, as well as articles on multicultural education. He is currently indulging his interest in cross-cultural communication by teaching abroad.

Bridget Adams is Head of Physics at the Buckinghamshire College, and a Director of Music and Cinematograph Productions Ltd. She has a background in psychology and a special interest in perception and mental processes as well as in the theories and models of communication. Her current research project is the teaching of colour-mixing for art, science and technology.

HOW TO USE THIS BOOK

Refer . . .

This book is designed to help you understand the basic language used in Communication Studies. Many of the words you will come across in this subject will be familiar already: media, code, redundancy, register; but the meanings you attach to them may be hazy or even quite wrong in the communications context. Each entry in this book begins with a definition followed by an example, some explanations and implications. We have tried to give a precise idea of the concepts the terms represent. An extended entry on communication models has been added as an appendix because we have found that this is an area of particular difficulty, and we felt it would be more useful to show how the models have developed rather than give each one a separate entry.

Expand . . .

During the course of your study you can check on ideas which may not have sunk in during class or at the first reading of a textbook. Each item ends with sign-posts to related concepts and some suggestions for further reading, thus encouraging you to expand your knowledge. You are not expected to read everything, but dipping into a wide-ranging variety of books will help give insights into this vast subject area. Don't forget the bibliographies in your library which list all the books and articles published on a given topic.

Revise . . .

As well as using this book for reference purposes, we hope you will find it helpful as a revision guide. Concepts tend to come in clusters, so we suggest that you revise them in clusters, reminding yourself how each concept is related to others. We've divided the territory of Communication Studies into six regions and have planned a route through each which should take you to the most important landmarks.

Revision Routes . . .

Route 1 gives a general overview of the territory:

categories – intrapersonal communication – interpersonal communication – group communication – organisations – medio-communication – extrapersonal communication.

Route 2 moves in for a closer inspection of the categories:

(a) intrapersonal communication – self-concept – personality – memory – thinking – emotion – motivation.

(b) interpersonal communication – perception – attitude – stereotype – belief – values – class – culture.

(c) group communication – socialisation – role – small-group network – organisations.

(d) mass communication – mediation – broadcasting – networks – news values – ideology – consensus – gatekeeper – agenda-setting – audience – effect – access.

(e) extrapersonal communication – cybernetics – computer – information technology – machine intelligence.

Route 3 guides you through various communication theories and models:

communication – models – communicator – encoder/encoding – decoder/decoding – code – medium – carrier – channel – message/text – signal – content analysis – context – constraint – feedback – purpose – effect – barrier/noise – Appendix.

Route 4 helps you revise the concept of information, the way information is acquired, stored and retrieved by the human brain and how it can be processed by the new technology:

senses – memory – information – redundancy – information technology.

Route 5 takes you through the main codes of language, non-verbal behaviour and graphic signs:

(a) language – semantics – speech – accent – paralanguage – dialect – register – style – slang – phatic communication – persuasion – rhetoric.

(b) non-verbal communication – gesture – posture – orientation – proximity – touch – facial expression – eye contact – appearance – culture.

(c) semiology/semiotics – sign – code.

Route 6 leads you through communication skills:

communication skills – perception – empathy – listening – speech – writing.

ACCENT

'Accent' refers to the sounds we utter when pronouncing our language.

If we speak in a *dialect*, then we always speak with a *regional* accent. When someone says, 'She's got quite an accent,' the speaker really means that the person is speaking with a regional accent. But, in actual fact, we *all* have some sort of accent. The other kind of accent, which is not tied to one particular part of the country, is Received Pronunciation or RP. This is essentially a Southern English accent which developed in the public schools and until comparatively recently was compulsory for BBC announcers. Sometimes called 'BBC English' or 'Oxford English', this prestige accent is generally taught to foreigners learning to speak English.

It is important not to confuse *accent* with dialect. (See DIALECT.) Briefly, dialect is a kind of language. It therefore embraces accent, grammar and vocabulary, and is a broader concept than accent.

Figure 1 Accent is one component of dialect.

The point to remember about accents is that no one accent is better or more communicative than another. Yorkshire people get along with their kinds of Northern English accent; East Enders get along perfectly well with Cockney accents; the public school children at Eton manage with Received Pronunciation.

However, common experience tells us that we react differently to different accents. We may find a particular accent hard to follow, and that affects interpersonal communication. More often than not we have quite strong feelings, amounting to prejudices, about some regional accents and perhaps RP. Northerners may find southern accents 'posh' or 'affected', while Southerners may find northern accents 'harsh', but Southerners do not think of their own speech as 'posh' any more than Northerners think of theirs as 'harsh'. It would be sensible for us to examine our linguistic prejudices to see whether they disguise other kinds of prejudice. For instance, it is perfectly possible for people to jump to the conclusion that because a person speaks with a broad regional accent different from their own that he or she is uneducated, and even unintelligent!

Illustrating the above point, Hughes and Trudgill quote an experiment carried out in South Wales, where a university lecturer, introduced as such, gave the same talk, word for word, to two parallel groups of students aged 16–18, the only difference between the two talks being the accent. In the first he used RP, in the second a Birmingham accent. The children were then asked to evaluate the lecturer according to a number of criteria. Those who heard the RP talk judged the lecturer significantly more intelligent than did the others, who heard the identical talk in the accent of England's second city.

Fortunately, nowadays there are signs of greater toleration of regional accents. TV correspondents and presenters quite often speak with accents which reveal their regional origins – for instance, John Cole, Belfast, and David Bellamy, London; and Northerners working in London and the South no longer feel the need to replace their northern vowels with southern ones (the main source of difference).

See also: Dialect.
Further reading
A. Hughes and P. Trudgill, *English Accents and Dialects,* Edward Arnold, 1979.

P. Trudgill, *Sociolinguistics,* Penguin, 1981, Ch. 2.

CCESS

In media studies, access refers to opportunities available to members of the public, organisations and pressure-groups to produce their own programmes or articles in the mass media, without having them pass through the filter of the media professionals. Access can mean making use of existing publications and networks or establishing new community-led ones.

Anybody can publish their own newspaper, provided they can find sufficient capital to get started. The difficulty is in getting and keeping a readership. There are very few left-wing newspapers, despite election figures indicating a high proportion of votes for the left. The *Daily Mirror* has survived but the *Daily Herald,* supported by the Co-operative Movement, the Labour Party and the TUC, sold up in the 1960s and was renamed the *Sun,* which, when it was bought by Rupert Murdoch, became a tabloid and firmly right-wing. The *News on Sunday,* a recent attempt by a group of Socialists to counter Rupert Murdoch's stand, collapsed in a very short space of time. There are altogether fewer newspapers than in the 1950s and certainly fewer responsible and conscionable ones willing to publish controversial material. But by the end of the 1950s it seems we were already making do with reading more and more copies of fewer and fewer newspapers. It may be that the enthusiastic people who

want to set up new papers do not target their audience correctly and lack the expertise, experience and money to make their newspapers work. And now that the actual number of copies sold is also falling it is not surprising if surviving newspaper editors are reluctant to publish material that strays far from what is usual, even if they personally approve of it. As Francis Williams says in *Dangerous Estate,* 'Newspapers exist to be read . . . They are as good or as bad as their public allow, for the greatest newspaper in the world has no future if it cannot get and hold a public'.

The situation is rather different with radio. There is a consensus in this country, backed by pirate radio stations, to have community radio. This would be cheap, relatively easy to produce, and in many cases readily supported by local shopkeepers who would welcome the advertising. However, it is prevented by the Government from coming into existence. The only permitted radio stations are those run by the BBC or IBA. Any others remain pirates and are illegal. Television too is effectively state-controlled.

In the United Kingdom, television and radio form a duopoly shared by the BBC (British Broadcasting Corporation) and IBA (Independent Broadcasting Authority). The BBC was set up by Royal Charter and operates under licence. The IBA is governed by the Broadcasting Act. Both the BBC and the IBA are legally required under the terms of their remit to provide responsible broadcasting to the public. The Government allows a certain amount of freedom, considerably more than in

France for example, but less than in the United States.

In the 1970s the media began to respond to public demand for access. The BBC began, with its television *Open Door* series, while *The Sunday Times* threw open half a page each week to three commentators not on the paper's regular staff. Since then, phone-in programmes have joined such programmes as *Any Answers* as regular, if limited, means of access. The Government responded to public pressure by requiring Channel 4, when setting it up in 1982, to present more programming for minority interests. Channel 4's *Right to Reply* allows for members of the public to enter a 'video box' to record their criticisms of ITV and Channel 4 programmes. In *Comment* a guest speaker gives a personal point of view. Monday night's *Eleventh Hour* deals with controversial topics. Groups with some programme-making experience can have access to video workshops. According to a poster published by Broadcasting Support Services, Channel 4's *People to People* 'is a series which attempts to address the issue of public access to television . . . The ways in which People to People programmes are produced vary greatly but the crucial idea at the heart of the series is programmes that reflect the ideas and experiences of the participants and not merely those of the producers . . . we'd like to hear from you.' Channel 4 also commissions independent producers to accompany a person or group in the course of their activities and allow them to put their point of view. The initiative may come from Channel 4, or from an independent producer, or from the minority group in question. Someone who has an idea for a programme can approach an independent producer or Channel 4. Despite all this, there are certain groups who feel they are under-represented on television because they lack access. Among these are ethnic minorities (West Indi-ans, Indians and Pakistanis in particular), some pressure-groups (the CND, feminists, ecologists and the National Front) and those with alternative lifestyles (gays, including lesbians, and travelling people). It is not the size of the minority which is of over-riding importance. It is the need to convince the commissioning editors that the product will help the ratings, which means appealing to a much wider audience than the minority group itself. *Pot Black* could not exist if the only viewers were avid snooker players, nor is *One Man and His Dog* only for shepherds. There are probably fewer than 15 000 active quilters in this country yet a series of three programmes on patchwork and quilting is expected to have one and a half million viewers. Even if it were allowed, genuine, unfiltered, unaided access could not hope to reach such audiences. Amateur productions that might work well on community radio will not necessarily come across on television. Professional assistance, even if it means some unwanted interference, may produce a more useful product. Pressure-groups do not want to preach only to the converted and there is no point in having access if no one is watching. On the other hand, local talent might come to the fore and community TV could serve as a training ground for both performers and producers. Material of a high professional standard has a good chance of being accepted. Drama often scores over documentary. *My Beautiful Laundrette*, a film described by Derek Malcolm in *Broadcast* magazine as 'a film about a Pakistani and a neo-Fascist bovver boy having a gay love affair' was a Channel 4 commission, subsequently taken up by commercial cinema distribution for showing worldwide. A short season of dramas by black writers and the screening of TVS's film about the lives of Nelson and Winnie Mandela were among the highlights of the 1987 autumn season on Channel 4. Jeremy Isaacs, Channel 4's chief executive until 1988, was seen as willing to take risks and challenge previously-held assumptions about broadcasting. On the subject of gays, he is quoted as saying, 'The board of this channel is perfectly happy with programmes about homosexuals and it is perfectly happy with programmes which may be of particular interest to homosexuals, but it is not happy with the notion of programmes that are so single-mindedly only for homosexuals that they appear perhaps to proselytise or ghettoise in terms of subject matter' (*Broadcast*, 18 September, 1987).

As part of their remit, the BBC and IBA must ensure that due impartiality is preserved. (Unlike newspapers, they are not permitted to express their own editorial opinions on current affairs or on matters of public policy.) The word 'due' is important. According to the IBA's Television Programme Guidelines, 'the IBA is not required to secure impartiality on matters such as drug-trafficking, cruelty and racial intolerance, on which society, even today, is virtually unanimous.' Hence some groups, such as the National Front, will not be given access to air their views, and most people would feel that this is right. Other, less extreme, but perhaps controversial groups, may find it difficult to gain access because of bias amongst the programme-makers or Government intervention (see BIAS).

It is still true to say that it is difficult to appear on television and say what you really want, however articulate you are, unless you are already well-known or have friends or associates who can make the right contacts. You will notice representative individuals appearing again and again: Mary Whitehouse to comment on pornography and the media, Bruce Kent on nuclear disarmament, Derek Hatton on the fate of Militant Tendency. *Using the Media* by Denis MacShane shows how trade unionists could make best use of the media to put their side of the case. He is sceptical about access programmes and sees them as an attempt to head off criticisms but still thinks them useful.

On the whole, such access programmes as there are, are timed to reach smaller audiences. The mass communicators keep a firm grip on the broadcasting schedules and save the peak hours or 'prime time' to entertain. The role of producer is still dominant. They decide what makes news, what is currently interesting and important, and so decide which issues and which people get nationwide publicity.

Stuart Hood, Head of Television Programmes at the BBC in the early sixties, later argued that the BBC and IBA should dismantle their duopoly. They should each split their functions into two: one organisation to run the production facilities for mass audiences; and a second to produce an interesting and varied schedule of programmes, which would include prestige programmes from production companies, and more importantly, programmes from large numbers of groups and organisations using their own equipment and putting their own point of view.

With the arrival of cable television and cheaper TV broadcast equipment, 'community television' could become a real possibility. But in 1988 it still remains only a possibility and TV is largely a linear, one-way communication process with minimal feedback. Governmental pressure, whatever party is in power, may serve to keep this medium in its straitjacket.

See also: Bias, Constraint, Feedback, Gatekeeper, Mediation.
Further reading
D. MacShane, *Using the Media*, Pluto Press, 1979.

(Further reading continued overleaf.)

S. Hood, 'The Politics of Television', in D. McQuail (ed.), *The
Sociology of Mass Communications*, Penguin, 1972.
F. Williams, *Dangerous Estate –
the Anatomy of Newspapers*,

Arrow Books, 1959.
BBC Handbook (general information; the Constitution of the BBC).
IBA Annual Report, available
from HMSO bookshops.

AGENDA-SETTING

**Agenda-setting describes the ways
in which the mass media decide
which information and which issues
are most important for the public
consumption and debate.** An agenda
is simply a list of topics in descending
order of importance to be discussed at a
meeting. If an item does not appear on
the agenda, it is unlikely to be discussed.

As regular readers of newspapers and
viewers of news programmes, we become aware that somewhere, behind the
scenes, people are deciding which stories are of over-riding interest, which are
next in importance and which are
moderately important. The reasons for
the choices may vary. Some newspapers, like the *Sun* and the *Star* carry
hardly any foreign news, and occa-
sionally BBC and ITN news bulletins
have no reports of events overseas. In
the case of the tabloid papers, there is a
firm agenda that deliberately excludes
most foreign news because the editors
perceive their readership as having
little interest in it. In any event it is
costly to maintain foreign correspondents. In the case of the broadcasting
media, they sometimes run into technical problems that prevent them from
covering events, so unless it is perceived
as very important they simply do not
include it. During the Falklands War,
the Ministry of Defence refused to allow
film from the Falklands to be shown on
television before the fighting was over,

so most of this news was reported in
greater detail on the radio. Another
thing which ensures that some events
are reported and others are not is the
ease of access to the places where things
are happening. The never-ending war of
many different factions in the Lebanon
has been, and at the time of writing, still
is being reported in some detail, because
Beirut is relatively easy to get into. The
far worse desert war between Iran and
Iraq is reported only very spasmodical-
ly, because access is difficult. A further
reason for British newsmakers not to
bother much about the Iran–Iraq war is
that no British people are involved in it
or in danger from it.

The media, in short, are bound to be
selective in the events they turn into
news (we do not believe that a day can
pass without something important happening outside Britain). They are limited by finance, geography and by
their criteria for deciding what is newsworthy, and their *news values*, like the
British aspect mentioned above. Many
Commonwealth countries, for example,
only reach our TV screens if members of
the Royal family, or possibly a Test
Cricket team visit them. Working within these self-imposed limitations or
constraints the news media produce an
agenda for days at a time and tell us
what items and issues to attend to.
There is broad agreement too about this
agenda, as any analysis of the day's

newspaper, radio, and TV news headlines will prove. Interestingly, much of what we see and read about is 'preprogrammed' sometimes months in advance and editorial staff will be able to formulate attitudes long before an event occurs. Perhaps 80 per cent of all 'news' concerns events which are known to be going to happen, at least in principle, if not in detail.

Clearly the concept of agenda-setting is closely related to that of gatekeeping. The difference is in the way the editorial role is perceived. Setting an agenda suggests an active editorial policy that determines what sort of information is to be printed or broadcast. Journalists are despatched to cover certain kinds of event. Gatekeeping, on the other hand, suggests a more passive role for editors, who are bombarded with information from outside sources, and only allow a certain amount through for publication or broadcasting. But how they operate the 'gate' must depend on editorial policy, in other words on the agenda they have set, or have been set.

See also: Constraint, Gatekeeper, News values.
Further reading
D. McQuail and S. Windahl, *Communication Models for the Study of Mass Communications*, Longman, 1981, pp. 62–4.

ALGORITHM

An algorithm (the name is a corruption of Al-Khwarismi, a ninth-century Islamic mathematician) is a series of instructions or steps in a logical procedure and may be in the form of written sentences, mathematical expressions, flow charts or computer programs.

In Communication Studies, flow charts are particularly useful for setting out on the page the various steps in an act of communication such as establishing telephone contact with a friend (see Figure 2).

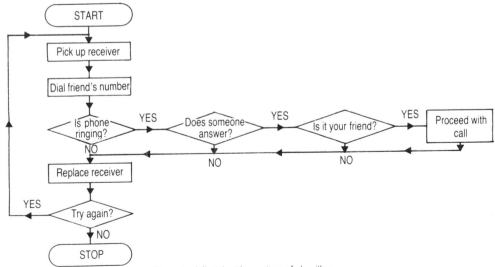

Figure 2 A flowchart is one type of algorithm.

To construct a flowchart like the one in Figure 2, you need to follow some guidelines or conventions such as the following:

1 A different shape of box is used for different kinds of procedure. Some possible shapes are shown in the diagram.

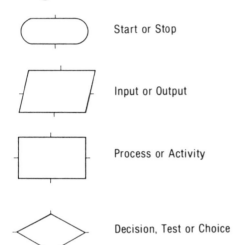

Start or Stop

Input or Output

Process or Activity

Decision, Test or Choice

2 Logic always flows downwards.
3 At a decision, the 'YES' always goes to the side and starts a new downward path.
4 Branches join back into paths between boxes and not into boxes.

Notice the regularly-repeating patterns as you step through the alternatives. This is not absolutely essential but makes a flowchart easier to read than one in which the logic keeps changing direction. If your first attempts at drawing flowcharts do not produce a steady flow through the steps but seem to go round and round obscurely, try rewording any decision boxes so that the YES and NO responses are reversed. For example, in the flowchart above, if the first decision is worded 'Is the phone engaged?' a less tidy flow is obtained. Try it and see!

See also: Communication, Models.

APPEARANCE

By 'appearance' we mean the way we look, the way we dress, do our hair, paint our faces and decorate our bodies generally. We deliberately or unwittingly create impressions on other people, and this is non-verbal signalling.

Why do you wear clothes? Not just to keep warm and decent, though comfort and modesty are important, but to express your personality. Everybody has a *self-image* (which is part of *self-concept*), a picture of the sort of person they think they are, and many people have an ideal self, the kind of person they would like to be. It can be part of the process of establishing oneself as an independent young adult, this vision of an ideal self. You may find that there are certain individuals you admire, a few people you know personally, a few people you feel you have come to know through the mass media. Many years ago, young people used to base their ideal selves on characters in history or fiction, but today the models are more likely to be film and TV stars, rock musicians or sporting personalities. One method of showing your attachment to the admired person is to wear his or her style of clothes. A huge fashion industry has come into being to pander to these ever-changing needs.

The teenage search for identity often involves a separation from the family and the joining of an outside group. Clothes help to establish and maintain such group identities. Mods, for instance, began with a number of fastidious young men dressing in a particular way and visiting various cult tailors in London. Mod music, the parkas and the mirror-bedecked scooters came later. Clothes are informal badges of identity, while uniforms serve the same purpose in a more formal way.

A uniform is a costume which is totally determined by people other than yourself; it suppresses individuality and emphasises the function or duty of the wearer. It signifies an authority which the person inside may or may not feel: there are probably many insecure soldiers and policemen. School uniform, designed to encourage conformity to school norms, sometimes arouses intense dislike in pupils, and girls express rebellion by wearing their compulsory hats at a rakish angle and boys by wearing their ties knotted around their stomachs.

The Germans have a proverb: 'Clothes make people'. We also say 'Fine feathers make fine birds'. Although extreme statements, they are based on the truth that clothes create a powerful impression, which can, at one and the same time, be quite misleading. Since people tend to conform to social stereotypes (such as City businessman in pinstripe suit with bowler hat and umbrella, the council workman in blue denims and donkey jacket), it is possible for the social climber, confidence trickster, or indeed any outsider who wants to join a group, to choose the appropriate outfit to create the right image for his or her purposes. Whatever clothes we wear, we must agree with Desmond Morris: 'It is impossible to wear clothes without transmitting social signals'.

One of these social signals is that of status. Clothing has always served to display status. There was no confusing peasants with aristocrats in the Middle Ages. In the upper reaches of society there were constant attempts to regulate clothing by law. Morris quotes a fifteenth-century clothing reform act which ran:

> no knight under the rank of a lord . . . shall wear any gown, jacket, or cloak, that is not long enough, when he stands upright, to cover his privities and his buttocks, under the penalty of twenty shillings . . . No knight under the rank of a lord . . . shall wear any shoes or boots having pikes or points exceeding the length of two inches, under the forfeiture of forty pence . . .

A more recent trend has been for high-status males to borrow clothing styles from humble occupations, such as jerseys from fishermen and denim jeans from American cattlemen.

Finally, it is now fashionable to talk about the language of clothes, where people choose items of dress (words) and combine them according to certain aesthetic rules (grammar) to make statements (sentences). The analogy may be taken further. It is well-known (see STYLE) that we adopt different styles of speech, depending on the circumstances, e.g. familiar with friends, more formal in public. Something equivalent happens with dress. We dress casually for leisure, more formally for public and solemn occasions. It would be improper to wear T-shirt and jeans to a funeral, and inappropriate to wear evening-dress to a barn-dance. At an interview, you stand a better chance of being selected if your clothes indicate that you speak the same language as the interviewer.

See also: Non-verbal communication, Self-concept.
Further reading
D. Morris, *Manwatching*, Triad Panther, 1978.
A. Lurie, *The Language of Clothes*, Heinemann, 1981.

ATTENTION

'Attention' is the active selection by the brain of certain stimuli from the environment, to the exclusion of all the others. Those stimuli which the brain does select are, at the moment of selection, more important than the rest, for the person's wellbeing.

For example, if you are at a party, where many conversations are going on within earshot, you will try to exclude the noise by attending closely to the person you really want to communicate with. But if you are just looking for somebody interesting to talk to, you may find yourself taking part in one conversation and trying, at the same time, to listen to another one which sounds more promising. The brain, generally speaking, does not cope well with divided attention of this kind.

The length of time that you focus on some topic, activity or experience is your *attention-span*. Young children tend to have very short attention-spans. Many 'A'-level students find it difficult to attend for many minutes at a time to a lecturer, however riveting, and switch their attention to more exciting sources of information (the amusing habits of the lecturer, their friends in another part of the classroom, their own thoughts). Most adults do not fare any better. Experienced public lecturers and programmers aim to present new information in slots of 10 to 12 minutes interspersed with less demanding and more entertaining material. Periods of intense study are better divided into short bursts, alternating with physical activity.

We are all aware of things 'catching our attention', of visual details swimming in and out of our consciousness, of sudden sounds, unexpected smells, intense headaches and cramps, and yet the mechanism of this *selective attention* is still not well understood. Recent theories, following Broadbent's *Filter Theory* (1958), suggest that the brain lacks the capacity to process all the signals that bombard it via the senses at any one instant, so to avoid overloading, it has the means to switch from some signals to deal with others. But for the brain to know which signals are going to be important and which are not, presupposes that it must carry out some kind of analysis of *all* signals *before* filtering some signals through for processing. Comparison with computers suggests that the brain may be sampling cyclically, taking small amounts of information from many areas in turn.

We pay attention to signals that fall into three broad categories: the unusual, the dynamic and the intense. The unusual can be anything out of the ordinary that stands out from its background for some reason, like a warning notice, a man wearing pyjamas in the street, a couple riding a tandem, the sound of brass-band music out-of-doors, the pungent smell of burning plastic. We pay attention to anything that moves, appears, especially if suddenly,

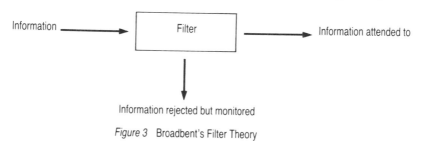

Figure 3 Broadbent's Filter Theory

varies in intensity and pitch (flashing lights, two-tone ambulance sirens), and sometimes we pay attention when a background noise stops (a pendulum clock, for instance). Intense stimuli, of course, make us attend: sudden loud noises, large objects, bright lights, powerful smells and heavy blows. And when signals are repeated, like the sound of a dripping tap, the sight of election posters in windows, the sensation of gnats biting your legs, then you initially focus sharply on them until the sensation is repeated indefinitely when it fades into the background as you become desensitised.

Getting attention and *paying attention* are essential behaviour in interpersonal communication. To start any conversation you need to attract another person's attention. It is no use approaching a shop-assistant from behind (like one old lady I know) and announcing a list of things you want to buy. First, you must make sure they are listening to you. At the counter in the post-office, it is inadvisable to launch into a complicated request if the post-mistress is head-down, filling in a form. She will find it impossible to finish her writing and listen to you at the same time. Once you have gained a person's attention, you, as a communicator, need to know how to keep it. This is crucial if you regularly communicate with a group of listeners. To hold attention, teachers learn to vary their voices, their presentation methods, activities for students to take part in, and so on; entertainers do not survive unless they are continuously

and diversely funny or clever. Conjurors, on the other hand, need to deflect people's attention away from the place where the trick is actually performed. This is done through a combination of amusing patter and distracting gestures.

Every baby knows how to attract attention: by exaggerating the signals. Getting attention continues to be an important need throughout life, though yelling is not always the best way! If you want to get attention you might brighten up your clothes, dye your hair or behave in a provocative manner. Talking loudly, behaving eccentrically, 'making a spectacle of yourself', are all obvious ways of letting people know that you are there and want attention.

Advertisers, in order to get you to pay attention to their message, exploit all these attention-grabbing stimuli in the form of imagery. The most effective ads are the dynamic ones (TV commercials). Movement, colour, sex-appeal, celebrities, as well as magical transformations (more conjuring tricks!) and surprises, all help to keep our minds open to receive the message. (See Dyer.)

See also: Non-verbal communication, Perception, Senses.
Further reading
N. Moray, *Listening and Attention*, Penguin, 1975.
G. Dyer, *Advertising as Communication*, Methuen, 1982.

TTITUDE

An 'attitude' is often defined as a tendency to react favourably or unfavourably towards certain stimuli, such as individuals, national

or racial groups, customs and institutions. As such, attitudes cannot be directly observed, but must be inferred from the way people behave, both verbally and non-verbally.

It is important to distinguish between *attitude* and *opinion*. An attitude is made up of three elements:

1 feelings, which may be favourable, unfavourable or indifferent toward the person or object in question. These feelings lead you to judge (or evaluate) the person or object positively or negatively;
2 knowledge or belief – what you know or believe about the person or object;
3 behaviour – whether you move towards the person or the object, or move away (avoidance).

So, for example, when a girl examines her attitude towards her boyfriend, if her feelings are strongly in his favour and whenever he appears she is glad to see him and likes to be close to him, this means that she assesses him positively. She may *know*, moreover, that he is considerate, interesting and amusing, and what is more, is interested in her. She may take steps to be with him more often and encourage activities which bring them closer together, even tell him she enjoys his company, showing by *behaviour* that her assessment is positive. Her *opinion* of him, which she might express to a third person, would be an expression (verbal or non-verbal) of those feelings and beliefs of which she is aware. In short, opinions have two components: the conscious aspects of feelings and beliefs; attitudes have three components: feelings and beliefs (which can be at least partly unconscious) and behaviour.

Like beliefs and values, attitudes are learned: from childhood experiences in the home, from friends, from isolated but indelible experiences, and from the groups you belong to. It is these *reference groups* that have the strongest influence on your attitudes. Also people tend to be judged by the company they keep. According to Stimulus-Response (S-R) Theory, attitudes, like all things learned, are created and modified by rewards and punishments. Once attitudes are formed, most people like to keep them stable. This you can do by entering only those situations where your attitudes and your associated beliefs and values do not come under attack. You can choose friends who, by and large, share your views, you can read a paper that reflects your political outlook (and so reinforce your attitudes), and you may even reject leaflets, switch off party political broadcasts, avoid doorstep missionaries, if you think they are going to challenge your beliefs.

The behaviour described above is a typical attempt to keep some degree of consistency amongst different attitudes; it is psychologically comfortable to have them *in balance*. If something happens to challenge your attitude (say, a politician you detest says or does something you judge to be sensible) then you are left feeling uncertain, trying to square his or her recent good sense with the past wickedness. You may, of course, either play down the good in order to save your image of a detestable person, or revise your attitude towards her (She's not so awful after all). This kind of oversimplification is referred to as 'pigeon-holing'.

David Berlo outlines how attitudes affect communication. If communicators have positive attitudes towards themselves (see SELF-CONCEPT), this self-confidence is going to help them communicate successfully (pleasantly, persuasively, etc.) with others. Their attitude towards their subject-matter is no less important. (Any teacher, for instance, who shows little interest in his or her subject, is likely to bore the class.) And finally, the communicator's attitude towards the listener is of consequence since the more the communicators can show they care about the listeners, the readier the latter will be to accept the messages.

Social scientists have shown that for communicators to produce changes of attitude in their audiences they must be perceived as expert and trustworthy (credible), they must be attractive and able to demonstrate a familiarity with the audience's general background and interests.

There are many studies on the effects of mass media advertising and propaganda. From these it appears likely that advertising may change our attitude towards something fairly trivial (for example, which margarine to buy) but what is less clear is whether the voting habits of a lifetime can change after watching party political broadcasts.

See also: Belief, Effect, Persuasion, Propaganda, Rhetoric, Self-concept.
Further reading
D. K. Berlo, *The Process of Communication*, Holt, Rinehart & Winston, 1960, pp. 45–8.
G. Myers and M. Myers, *Dynamics of Human Communication*, McGraw-Hill, third edition 1980, Ch. 4.
R. Dimbleby and G. Burton, *More than Words*, Methuen, 1985, pp. 70–78.

UDIENCE

'Audience' refers to individuals or assembled groups of people who receive messages, especially through the mass media. Originally, the term was used to mean a group of people gathered to hear a speech, lecture or debate, but later the meaning was extended to cover readers of books and the viewers of television. (The authors feel the audience for books and newspapers is better described as a 'readership'.)

In Communication Studies, the term *'audience'* may correspond to 'destination' used by Shannon and Weaver (*The Mathematical Theory of Communication*), or any term such as 'receiver', 'addressee', 'communicatee' or 'consumer' that indicates the target at which the message is aimed.

One can hardly overestimate the significance of this concept. David Berlo says, 'If we limit our discussion to effective communication, the *receiver* is the most important link in the communication process.' (*The Process of Communication*) So we need to examine the part played by the listener or receiver in face-to-face situations, and see what social scientists have to say about the nature of mass audiences.

The receiver's role in interpersonal communication

In early communication theory, there was a tendency to play down the activity of the receiver in the communication process. Shannon and Weaver saw the communicator's task as one of transmitting a signal as effectively as possible, reducing *noise* in the *channel* to a minimum. They paid less attention to the receiver who has to attend to, decode and interpret the signal. Later writers, still within the *Process School* of communication, argue that the receiver is just as important as the communicator. Take a look at Wilbur Schramm's model in the Appendix, and you will see that both people within the communication relationship share and use the same code signal (S) and that the arrows are running to 'signal' from both the sender and the receiver, like this:

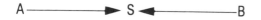

A ⟶ S ⟵ B

This is to show that the receiving role, which involves processing the message, is just as active as the communicator's role of making up the message. 'The message, once created, once sent, is on its own, and nothing happens until someone acts on it.' (*Men, Women, Messages and Media*, p.301)

This brings us close to the thinking of the *Semiotic School* according to which 'the message is a construction of signs which, through interacting with the receivers, produce meanings.' (Fiske, *Introduction to Communication Studies*, p. 3) These scholars are particularly interested in the 'text', a word which they prefer to 'message', and the way the receiver 'reads' it. They are also interested in the fact that receivers from different social and cultural backgrounds are likely to find different meanings in the same text. For example, many working-class viewers of Alf Garnett, the racist bigot in *Till Death Us Do Part*, loved him for the very attitudes his creator, Johnny Speight, was mocking.

It is essential for communicators to know their audiences

The more you know about your audience, the receivers of your messages, the more you can do to communicate efficiently. David Berlo suggests that we need to know the receiver's *attitudes*, his or her level of knowledge, listening and comprehension abilities, social and cultural background. Most of the time we do not know any details, but we can try to make reasonable guesses rather than judge only by our own standards. This will influence us in the code we choose (a language that the person will understand) and the way we use it (for example, an informal style for entertainment). The content of the message, moreover, should have considerable relevance to the receiver's needs! Of course, the receiver may put up all sorts of psychological barriers, hostile attitudes and prejudices that can frustrate your efforts to get through.

When you come to do your A-level Communication Project, you will need to think about all those factors that influence the *audience*, and therefore their response to your message. Here is how one student went about it. She found her audience in a Slimmers' Club, to which she herself belonged. Thus for a start she had the advantage of working with a ready-made group. She felt that she could help them by warning them about the dangers of eating food especially marketed for slimmers. The number of chemical additives and colouring agents struck her as dangerous to health. By talking to her fellow-slimmers she found out about their health-worries, gained some impression of their intelligence and level of education, and made up her mind not to be patronising (she was the youngest member of the group, as it happened). She produced a powerfully persuasive booklet on a subject which engaged the audience's interest because it met their needs and was attractively presented. Everybody understood the message, nobody felt patronised and four out of ten women decided to give up slimming foods and go for the alternative suggested. This impressive effect was achieved by an understanding of the audience's needs plus persuasive treatment of the message.

The mass audience and its characteristics

A mass audience may run into millions of members. For instance, in 1969, as many as 30 million British viewers watched the Apollo moon-landing on TV. The sheer size of such audiences and the amount of time that they spend on newspapers, radio and television, particularly television, raises many important questions about the role played by the mass media in our society.

It is often asked why certain popular newspapers, like the *Sun* and the *Daily Mirror* or certain TV programmes, can command and sustain such huge audiences. Put another way, what is it that people get out of newspapers which carry hardly any news, and TV series like *Dynasty* and *Dallas*, that have little connection with our own unglamorous lives? One of the answers commonly suggested is that we wish to escape from our workaday world with all its problems into a fantasy world where our wishes (to be rich, beautiful and powerful) are vicariously fulfilled. Despite the evidence that some people all the time and most people some of the time use the mass media for escapist purposes, members of mass audiences can and do fulfil other needs – for example, aesthetic ones when listening to music; or educational ones, when watching a science programme or listening to a broadcast talk by a philosopher or economist.

Can we be more precise about the composition of mass audiences? Sociologists have done much to analyse newspaper readership or TV programme ratings by age, sex, and class. By studying the BBC's Continuous Survey of Listening and Viewing, comparing use of radio with TV, they discover, for instance, that of the whole population, the under-fifteens listen least and view most, while the 15–19 year-olds listen most and view least.

Audience research is one method by which a mass medium tries to visualise its large, remote, fragmented, anonymous clientele. Other methods may be less scientific: a belief in its exclusiveness prompted *The Times* to advertise itself under the slogan 'Top People Take the Times'!

How do mass audiences relate to the media? A good deal of research has been done on the *effects* of mass media messages, during the course of which social scientists have explored the way information flows from the media into society. Some research into the performance of the mass media in the 1940 US presidential election campaign led Lazarsfeld and others to conclude that a mass audience consisted of more or less isolated individuals at the mercy of their newspapers and radio programmes, the chief media of the time. Later on, this view of mass audience gave way to the idea that within society there are some people who play a more important role than others in voicing opinions, airing issues and with influencing their fellows. Any media influences get filtered through these very sociable 'opinion-leaders' to the less active members of the population. See Figure 4.

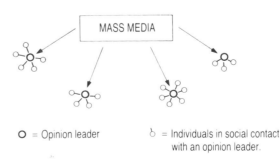

O = Opinion leader   ♂ = Individuals in social contact with an opinion leader.

Figure 4 Two-step flow model

It is not always possible to predict audience reaction accurately. This was demonstrated by David Morley, investigating audience response to the BBC's *Nationwide* programme. The aim of this programme was to represent the national community of individual citizens, i.e. anybody and everybody, to its mass audience. Different sections of the audience reacted in quite different ways. In particular, young black viewers found the programme boring with nothing to say to them. As far as they were concerned, it showed a Britain full of 'middle-class shoppers and businessmen'. It is now generally agreed that audiences do not just absorb media messages like sponges, nor are they helpless sitting targets for any propaganda that comes their way. They interpret what they see, and not necessarily in the way they are expected to.

See also: Class, Communication, Effect.
Further reading
J. Fiske, *Introduction to Communication Studies*, Methuen, 1982, pp. 18–20.

ARRIER/NOISE

A 'communication barrier' is anything the prevents the message from the communicator reaching the receiver. Usually, three different types of barrier are described: mechanical, semantic and psychological. It is possible to add a fourth: organisational. Where some meaning gets through and is perceived with varying levels of difficulty, we refer to the interference as 'noise'.

A *mechanical barrier* is some fault in or interference with the communication channel. Claude Shannon and Warren Weaver of the Bell Telephone Company used the term 'mechanical noise' specifically for faults in telephone and telegraph systems that led to poor reception. The meaning has since been extended to include all forms of disturbances in communication channels. So apart from the 'snow' on the TV screen, jamming of radio broadcasts, crossed lines on the telephone networks (all problems of engineering), mechanical noise would, for instance, cover the following factors that might ruin a good conversation: interruption by somebody else, noise from overflying aircraft, ambulance sirens, pneumatic road-drills, visual distractions causing loss of attention, physical discomfort causing the same, speech defects and impaired hearing in the participants. (See also CARRIER.)

A *semantic barrier* involves problems of meaning at each end of the communication process, inadequate or inappropriate or erroneous encoding on the part of the sender, and inadequate or erroneous decoding on the part of the receiver. If, for whatever reason, two people engaged in conversation cannot attach the same meanings to the signs being used, they are not going to understand each other. They will experience a barrier between them that has to do with the limitations on their knowledge and not with things like interruptions and deafness.

Semantic problems arise where people either do not share the same code or have very different commands of it. A few examples will show the possibilities. A couple of Japanese tourists greet you in London with '*Ohaiyo gozaimas!*' You might assume they are saying 'Hello' or 'good morning' (which they are) but thereafter you are unlikely to follow a word, until they point to a photo of Westminster Abbey in their tourist guide-book. A language is a code, and if you do not share it, it is useless for communication. Fortunately, in this case, there is a code of pictures, and when you point your finger down Whitehall towards the Abbey, you are using one of the signs from your gestural code which the Japanese visitors *will* understand.

Leaving problems of communicating with non-English speakers on one side, we can get into difficulties if we find ourselves using different varieties of English. These may be regional dialects, subcultural slang or specialist registers. Not only do dialects have their own words and idioms, but they also have their own accents: taken together, they may cause the dialect-speaker some problems of communication once away from their own region and social context. Similarly, the doctor who uses medical jargon and the Heavy Metal fan who uses rock-music slang are going to run up against incomprehension when communicating with people outside their professional and social circles.

In all kinds of ways, using words carelessly or ambiguously can lead to misunderstandings and hence poor communication. They can also lead to unintended humour, like this letter from a travel agent:

Dear Sir/Madam
With reference to your letter re Majorca tour, the flight you mention is completely booked, but we will inform you immediately someone falls out, as usually happens.

The third type of barrier is *psychological*. How we perceive other people determines the way we approach them and how we communicate with them. But our perception, in turn, is influenced by our attitudes, beliefs and values. And if these attitudes are negative – for instance, if we are prejudiced (and prejudices are strongly felt, deeply ingrained attitudes) against punk rockers or policemen or Arabs, then our feelings are going to affect the way we react to them and are likely to make us misinterpret what they say to us. In a multiracial society which pays lip-service to equal opportunities, black people often wonder whether they are seriously listened to at job-interviews where the interviewers have preconceived ideas about them.

Our attitudes are likely to have a marked effect on the way we handle information in a typical work-situation, where we are slotted into some sort of hierarchy. We have people below us, people alongside us, and people above us. Research suggests that we may not pay much attention to people some way below us, whose status is perceived to be low. If we dislike the people above us, we may hoard or secrete information rather than pass it up the line. In any case, if we are ambitious – and therefore anxious to impress our superiors – we will omit or distort information that might put us in a bad light. Being in a hierarchy and therefore more or less in competition with our fellow-workers may well breed mistrust and this in turn produces all kinds of behaviour likely to impede efficient communication.

The fourth barrier to communication has to do with the structure of *organisations* themselves. In essence, one mark of a good organisation is that it has clearly-defined and smoothly-operating channels of communication between its different members and between its various departments. Experience and research suggest that the more levels there are in the hierarchy, the less two-way communication there is going to be. Such 'pyramids', it is often argued, need to be reorganised or flattened. Secondly, if an organisation is widely dispersed with departments in different parts of the country, the most widely-separated members are least likely to be

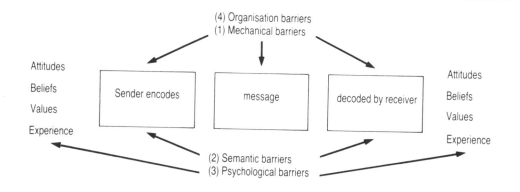

Figure 5 Model to show four types of communication barrier

in touch with each other. Colleges on split-sites often have problems of communication and morale. Thirdly, communications can be slowed down or blocked altogether if no arrangements are made for people to replace absentees (sickness, leave, etc.). Imagine what would happen to the work of a hospital or a factory if the main switchboard operator was away sick and not replaced! Networks can only operate if they link people together.

One good reason for studying communication is that you become aware of the barriers and 'noise', and can devise ways of overcoming them, at least as far as interpersonal communication is concerned. More effective communication means development of communication skills, attention to feedback, and building more redundancy into your language.

See also: Carrier, Channel, Communication skills, Feedback, Organisations, Perception, Redundancy, Semantics.
Further reading
D. Dimbleby and G. Burton, *More than Words*, Methuen, 1985, pp. 78–84.

ELIEF

Beliefs represent our view of existence. They stand for what we hold to be true or probable; they are what we agree with. Our beliefs range from things we believe to be absolutely true, through to things we are not sure about, to things we definitely believe to be false. Beliefs are invisible. Only when people express them or act in particular ways can you tell what their beliefs are.

Belief, in this broad definition, includes *knowledge*. A belief may arise from enduring and consistent evidence from our senses or experience that something is true, or where there is general agreement. We can say that we *know* that London is the capital of Great Britain or that Tuesday follows Monday, or that $2 + 2 = 4$. Fundamental convictions are, of course, difficult to change, and you may remember that in George Orwell's *1984* the hero, Winston

Smith, had to be tortured into agreeing that $2 + 2 = 5$.

Some of your fundamental beliefs may not be shared by others. You may be totally convinced that you cannot spell or do Maths or sing, and so prevent yourself from making progress in these skills. But it is only when your personal experience is backed by gloomy opinions from everybody who matters that you can honestly say: 'I *know* I can't do it.' (And even that does not rule out the possibility that you will be able to do it in the future.)

As you grow up, understanding the world becomes less simple. You need help in knowing what to believe. Do you believe in the Genesis story of the creation of the world, or do you believe in evolution? Do you believe that technology will save or destroy the species you belong to? Do you believe in getting married? And so forth. You may search for authorities – people whose opinion you respect. At first these are found in the family and later at school and in the groups you belong to. *Authority* beliefs, unlike the *central* beliefs described in the second paragraph, are open to question. You expect to have them challenged by other authorities.

We act on our beliefs. Our religious and political beliefs lead us to behave in particular ways and use particular registers of language. For example, we can go to church and talk about sin and salvation, or take part in street demonstrations and talk about apartheid and nuclear disarmament. They colour the way we interpret events. A person with Conservative beliefs would regard the Labour Party's promise to abolish private schools as an attack on his cherished beliefs in free enterprise and freedom of choice for parents. A Socialist, on the other hand, would welcome a measure that conformed to his or her belief in equal opportunities in education for all members of society. But if we profess one thing, and do another (like professed vegetarians who slip off to the Berni Steak House) then of course, we are hyprocrites.

Clearly your beliefs have a bearing on your communication with other people. If others share your belief in a particular brand of Christianity, or are fellow-Muslims or fellow-Sikhs, if they also think that David Bowie is the greatest pop-star as you do (perhaps!), then you are likely to find them easy to talk to. Conversations with people whose opinions differ from your own may be more difficult. You may conceal your views to avoid possible conflict, or you may provoke an argument, which can be very stimulating, so long as people keep their tempers.

> **See also:** Attitude.
> **Further reading**
> M. Myers and G. Myers, *Dynamics of Human Communication*, McGraw-Hill, third edition 1980, Ch. 4.

IAS

'Bias' is the term applied to the media when they give an 'unfair' advantage to one side in a dispute, either by misrepresenting, underplaying or ignoring alternative points of view.

In practice you will perceive that national newspapers have a political point of view and will therefore be *biased* (note the spelling!) in their editorials and opinion columns. So we expect *The Times*, under Rupert Murdoch, to show something of a Conservative bias, just as we expect the *Daily Mirror* to see matters from a Labour Party point of view. Furthermore, this political bias spills over into news-reporting, so that the distinction between reporting and opinion-moulding is often blurred, especially in the tabloids. So obvious is the bias in the newspapers that it causes little concern (you just buy a paper whose bias you approve of!), except that non-Conservatives deplore the fact that the large majority of national papers take a Tory line.

The broadcasting organisations, on the other hand, are supposed to be impartial. Both the BBC and the IBA are state-controlled to the extent that they have charters to guide their output. Impartiality is written into their charters. What is meant by this was published in the Annan Report (1977): 'Due impartiality' means taking into account a full range of views and opinions but also giving prominence to mainstream opinions, and recognising that the climate of opinion is constantly changing. But this impartiality is far from absolute as the following excerpt makes clear:

The broadcasters are operating within a system of parliamentary democracy and must share its assumptions. They should not be expected to give equal weight or show an impartiality which cannot be due to those who seek to destroy it by violent, unparliamentary or illegal means. (p. 268)

How impartial or unbiased are the BBC and IBA? The question is impossible to answer; it is, however, certain that many groups of people like trade unionists, feminists, politicians of the Left and Right, feel that the TV media are biased against them. Trade unionists in particular have long felt hard done-by in this respect, and monitoring efforts by such bodies as the Glasgow University Media Group have tended to confirm their sense of grievance. A biased representation of an industrial dispute can be very subtle, as John Hartley demonstrates in *Understanding News*: he shows how *News at Ten*, covering Mrs Thatcher's visit to Cardiff on 11 December 1980 (a critical time since thousands of steelworkers were facing redundancy), turns a story of political opposition into one of violent disorder. This was achieved through the use of particular camera shots selected, sequenced and provided with a suitable voice-over, all of which encouraged the viewer to 'read' the event in a certain way.

Those groups or individuals who believe that the media are biased against them, may believe that there is a *conspiracy* among broadcasters to misrepresent or exclude them. Stuart Hood, a left-wing writer on the mass media, discounts the idea of a conspiracy to misrepresent or ignore the workers' case in industrial disputes, and suggests that the bias has more to do with the kind of people the TV staff are: middle-class, with secure jobs, team spirit and a sympathy with the established order of things. In other words, the bias is largely unconscious.

In Communication Studies, we know that it is quite impossible to report totally objectively about any event. Even live coverage of a Wembley Cup Final has the camera filming only part of the game at any one moment: some players will be off-camera but may be moving into significant positions for the future of the match. Again, the newspaper reporters' perceptions will limit what they see. They only have the time and opportunity to witness a certain amount and interview a few people. Their reports, already highly selective, then have to be edited by people who were not present at the original event. When they finally reach their audiences, they will not be accurate reflections of the event. As a final comment on the problem of objectivity, for years the police and CND have been counting the numbers of people taking part in anti-nuclear protests. Theoretically it should be possible to count people filing past a lamp-post; but the police and CND have never once agreed in their rough estimates.

See also: Acccess, Consensus, Perception.
Further reading
J. Hartley, *Understanding News*, Methuen, 1982, Ch. 4.
S. Hood, 'The Politics of Television' in D. McQuail (ed.), *The Sociology of Mass Communication*, Penguin, 1972.

BROADCASTING

Broadcasting is the transmission of radio and television programmes that are intended for general public reception, as distinguished from private signals that are directed to specific receivers.

The term 'broadcasting' is derived from the practice of sowing seed by scattering it over the soil in a broad sweep. Anybody with the right radio or TV receiver within range of the transmitter is free to pick up broadcast signals. To talk about broadcasting is to talk about powerful organisations like the British Broadcasting Corporation (BBC) and the Independent Broadcasting Authority (IBA), communicating with mass audiences and supplying them with most of their daily news, other information and entertainment.

Broadcasting should be distinguished, as the above definition suggests, from narrowcasting. Where broadcasters transmit simultaneously to large, scattered audiences, narrowcasters send their messages to small, specific groups of receivers. Closed Circuit Television (CCTV) used in large stores or overflow meetings is one example. Citizen's Band (CB) radio is another. The radio networks used by the Army to coordinate military manoeuvres are also an example of narrowcasting.

After Marconi's first transatlantic broadcast in 1901, developments in radio moved quite swiftly. Sound broadcasting services began around 1920 and TV broadcasting began in the 1930s. The British Broadcasting Company began life in 1922 to broadcast 'news, information, concerts, lectures, educational matter, speeches, weather reports, theatrical entertainment . . .'. But by 1925 it had become a public corporation answerable to Parliament and controlled by a Board of Governors appointed by the government. The first Director-General, Lord (John) Reith, established a strong tradition of public-service broadcasting. The IBA broke the BBC's monopoly of television in 1954, the new channel being funded by the advertisers who saw in television a powerful new publicity medium. In the 1970s BBC radio was joined by the IBA's commercial radio stations.

The question of who controls broadcasting is an important one in view of its reach and impact: almost every family in the country has a radio and/or a television set. No broadcasting agent in the world is absolutely independent of government or commercial pressures. Different systems of control have emerged in different countries. In many communist and Third World countries the state controls the broadcasting media through a special committee responsible to the government. The BBC and IBA are also state-controlled. The BBC, as mentioned above, is a public corporation, bound by the guidelines of its charter, publicly financed, and overseen by its governors. (See also ACCESS.) Within these limitations it has editorial control and is theoretically free to broadcast information embarrassing to the government of the day. However, the government seeks to control as much output as it can and has been known to put pressure on the Chairman of the BBC to withdraw certain programmes. Then there are partnerships between government and private interests (Radiotelevisione Italiana) and purely private companies like the American radio and 'Pay-TV' cable companies, whose revenue comes from advertising and subscriptions.

The story of technical development in broadcasting may be found in a good encyclopedia. Suffice it to say that in 1986 our four national TV channels are being joined by many more brought to us from the USA and elsewhere by means of satellites orbiting the Equator and relaying signals across the globe. The large dish-shaped aerials that receive satellite signals are beginning to appear on our rooftops. At the same time, Britain is following America in cable television, thus increasing the number of possible viewing channels to 20 or more. The government has already given private companies the go-ahead but the public's response to being wired up and paying subscriptions for new channels, which would specialise in sport, feature films, news programmes, etc. has been less than enthusiastic. The invention of the home video recorder now means that viewers may preserve any programme they want, and both the BBC with CEEFAX and the IBA with ORACLE provide an information service which only throws up on the screen the particular information the user asks for by keying in a page number.

See also: Access, Bias.
Further reading
'Broadcasting' in *Encyclopaedia Britannica: Macropaedia.*

AMPAIGN

A campaign is an organised attempt over a longish period, and often making use of the mass media, to persuade the public to change its mind and act in favour of a particular political party, issue or commercial product or service.

Many organisations start up campaigns. Some may be funded by the government, like the Christmas 'Don't drink and drive' campaign. Others may be organised by political parties, especially in the run-up to a General Election. Others may be pressure-group campaigns, like that of the Campaign for Nuclear Disarmament, the British Union Against Vivisection or parents and educators concerned about the effects of television on children.

Apart from national campaigns, many take place locally. You are almost certain to find campaigns going on in your neighbourhood against the closure of a school or a hospital, or perhaps positive campaigns to improve road safety or to open an arts centre. Your local newspaper will report the progress of such campaigns and should be a useful source of information about the campaigning methods used.

Since campaigns are designed to change public opinion, they have to be carefully planned and conducted over quite a long period of time: months, sometimes years. Campaigners make use of the available mass media, usually the local newspapers and, if there is one, the local radio. They issue press-releases, ask for interviews, advertise public meetings and write letters to editors. If they are shrewd, they will organise events that will provide the sort of pictures which are welcomed by newspapers and are tempting to TV news programmers (see also ACCESS).

If the mass media are unhelpful, it is important to remember that they are not the only means of communication you have. You can still approach the public directly through leaflets, petitions, street demonstrations and 'happenings'.

On the commercial side, advertisers are constantly running campaigns to launch new products or sustain interest in old ones. But how can we know how effective such campaigns are? Sometimes 'post-sell' research in specific areas or among specific groups of customers subject to an advertising campaign has demonstrated a corresponding rise in sales, though generally it is difficult to prove such precise effects.

See also: Access, Effect, Persuasion, Propaganda.
Further reading
G. Dyer, *Advertising as Communication*, Methuen, 1982, Ch. 4.

CARRIER

A carrier is a physical entity (either a material substance or an energy wave) that carries signals along communication channels. (One non-human carrier is the pigeon.)

In many cases it is possible to discriminate clearly between *carrier*, *channel*, *medium* and *signal*, but it is difficult to be precise in some situations unless you keep pedantically to strict scientific or engineering terminology. The term 'medium' has at least two meanings, (1) the general sense for a physical or technical means of transmitting a signal used when comparing the communication styles of theatre, cinema, newspapers and television, or voice and writing, and (2) the limited sense of the material medium through which the signal is carried, e.g. air (see MEDIUM). The term 'channel' also has several different usages. In this section we have limited ourselves to the precise technical definition of channel as a means of directing the signal, and to the second meaning of medium. We give an indication of how the two meanings of the word medium apply, but see MEDIUM and CHANNEL for the important distinction between medium and channel.

Face-to-face

When two people are talking together the intervening space is filled with air. Both sound and light waves can be carried through the medium of the air so the participants can use any forms that can be seen or heard (provided that neither is blind or deaf). Without being too technical, it is difficult to distinguish between sound waves and the medium they travel in. It is probably reasonable to say that the carriers of speech signals are the sound waves, which in turn are carried by the air. For light, no physical medium is required so we need only say the carriers of visual signals are the light waves themselves. There are no physical channels constructed in the air (no wires) and the only channelling that is necessary is to make sure that the two participants are *facing* each other clearly. This is why we refer to such situations as *face-to-face* and not, say, nearby. If the participants turn away from each other and communicate by sound alone then there is no channelling. Sound waves travel in all directions and can be picked up without channelling, provided the communicators are within hearing distance and there are no barriers in the way. (Note, however, that sound travels well through solid objects and can be channelled along rods, pipes and strings, e.g. on board ship for communication between decks or in prison where inmates can tap messages to each other via the radiator system.)

Using the telephone

For telephoning, the intervening medium can comprise air, land, sea or space, depending on how far apart the communicators are situated. For short distances, either electric cables are laid and these constitute the channels in which electric current is flowing, or laser beams are channelled along optical fibres. For longer distances, radio waves are used as carriers. Radio, like light, requires no material medium and the radio waves are channelled by being focused into beams directed at the radio receiver. The carriers (electric current, laser beams or radio waves) are travelling all the time, whether a message is being passed or not. Information is imposed on the carriers by modulating (altering in some way) the carriers, so producing the signal.

To complete this sequence, we must add the stages from speaker to telephone mouthpiece and from telephone earpiece to listener. To use the telephone, the speaker must produce sounds coded into a recognisable language. These sounds are carried by sound waves to the microphone which encodes them into electrical impulses (the signal) ready for carrying by electric current. If radio waves are to be used (say, for international calls) there must be a further encoding into radio modulations, and so on. At the receiving end of the system the vibrating plate in the earpiece decodes the electrical pulses into sound which the listener can hear and interpret.

Writing a letter

When writing a letter, your immediate carriers are your sheets of notepaper which are modulated by your writing to produce a signal (or text). However, your letter relies on other carriers and channels to overcome the intervening distance between you and the person you are writing to. So the medium may be land, sea or air. The main channels that have been fashioned or mapped out are roads, railways, shipping lanes and flight-paths. The main carriers along these channels are post-office workers, vans, trains, aeroplanes, etc. The sequence is complete when the light waves pass from the written page to the reader's eyes.

Distortion and noise (see also Barrier/Noise)

All physical channels and carriers are subject to distortion. The encoding of sound into electrical impulses and decoding back to sound is not always accurate. Your voice on the telephone does not sound the same as it does face-to-face. With a poor telephone line or a faulty handset the distortion can be significant.

Engineers distinguish between three main types of 'noise'. Least disturbing is low-level background noise such as crackle or hiss. If signals from another channel start to get noticeably mixed up with the main channel this is referred to as *interference*. Interference may be intermittent and is more insistent and more of a nuisance than is background noise. In good weather, signals from European radio stations often interfere with our reception of local radio. One reason we are restricted to certain types of CB radio in this country is that some bands of frequencies interfere with hospital heart 'pacemakers'.

Most noticeable is *breakthrough* where an intelligible, meaningful message from another channel comes through clearly as in 'crossed' telephone lines or when police messages break through on VHF radio.

Distortion and noise apply equally to visual channels.

Summary
Face-to-face
Medium (1) = voice and NVC (presentational; see MEDIUM).

Medium (2) = air.

Channeling = orientation face-to-face.

Carriers = sound and light waves.

Signal: strictly speaking, this is the modulation of sound and light waves, i.e. changes in the patterns of light and sound which reach our senses and are then perceived as audible and visible signs and signals.

Using the telephone
Medium (1) = telephone system (mechanical).

Medium (2) = land, sea, air, space.

Main channel = electric cable, optical fibres, or focusing of radio waves.

Main carrier = electric current, lasers or radio waves.

Signal = modulation of electric current, lasers or radio waves.

Writing a letter
Medium (1) = writing (representational).

Medium (2) = land, sea, air.

Main channels = transportation routes.

Main carriers = transportation vehicles.

Sub-carriers = sheets of paper.

Signal = text consisting of written signs.

A similar analysis can be used to compare mass media, which can all be seen as mechanical media used for extending the range of the presentational and representational means via the relevant channels and carriers.

See also: Barrier/Noise, Channel, Code, Medium, Signal.

CATEGORIES

The usual categories of communication are intrapersonal, interpersonal, medio, mass, group and extrapersonal: they are mainly based on the numbers of people involved but also on types of networks used. They are not mutually exclusive and it is not always possible to classify a particular event as belonging to one rather than another but they help to divide up the vast area of communication into more manageable parts.

(a) *Intrapersonal communication* is communication *within* the individual self and to the self. This includes such activities as thinking, recollecting, imagining and calculating, which are all conscious; and dreaming, which is unconscious. Communication is a closed circuit, as in Figure 6.

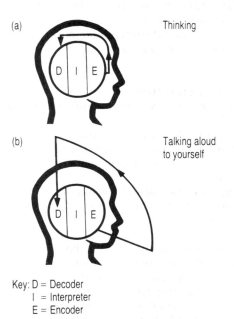

Key: D = Decoder
I = Interpreter
E = Encoder

Figure 6 Osgood's communication model (see Appendix)
Adapted from D.K. Berlo, The Process of Communication

The closed circuit can take in something of the outside world, when we talk to ourselves or write for ourselves in diaries.

(b) *Interpersonal communication* is communication *between* people. Typically this refers to two people communicating with each other face-to-face, e.g. two neighbours chatting over a fence, a lecturer interviewing a candidate for a college place, a political canvasser trying to persuade a householder on the doorstep. Our interest here, in this *social* activity, is in the kind of speech and non-verbal language that people use to share their meanings about the common world they live in. What actually happens in the dialogue (or interaction) depends on many different factors, some in the physical environment, but most in the individuals themselves. See INTERPERSONAL COMMUNICATION for more details.

In the case of telephone conversation, where the participants cannot see each other and cannot read each other's nonverbal signals, we can still say that the communication is between person and person. And the same would go for communication by letter. However, the term medio-communication has been invented for these instances.

(c) *Medio-communication.* This recent term recognises that there is an important difference in structure between a mass medium like radio and the telephone or postal service. The latter are certainly used by large numbers of people, and on the basis of numbers alone, they could be called *mass* media. However, the press, radio and TV are *broadcasting* media and the communication is essentially one-way, whereas telephone and postal networks allow millions of interpersonal exchanges to take place at the same time.

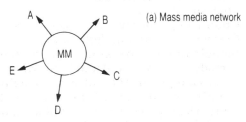

Figure 7 (a) A,B,C,D,E are members of one family living in different towns. They all have TV sets and watch *Eastenders.*

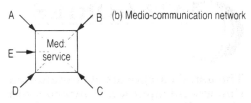

Figure 7 (b) A,B,C,D,E all have telephones. Any one of them can reach any other member through the telephone exchange.

(d) *Mass communication* is essentially communication broadcast by public or commercial companies for the benefit of very large numbers of receivers. Mass meetings, political rallies, rock festivals all draw huge crowds and, strictly speaking, could be regarded as media of mass communication. However, the term is generally applied to such mass media as newspapers, magazines, cinema, radio, TV, book publishing (especially bestsellers) and the record and cassette industry. Audiences run into millions and are not known to the organisations that produce the reading, viewing or listening matter. The control and influence of the mass media is a matter of real academic interest and public concern.

(e) *Group communication* is communication within groups of people, and the study of the way groups communicate with other groups. It is normal to divide *groups* into *small groups* like families, friends, working-parties and committees, and *large groups* like business organisations and trade unions. Like individuals conversing in pairs, members of small groups communicate, as a rule, face-to-face. But being a member of a group means that you may have one or more special *roles*; e.g. oldest child in the family, classroom clown, committee chairperson; and this will affect your communication behaviour.

Large groups, broadly speaking, fall into two categories; those random ones that meet to be entertained in the theatre or informed at a public meeting (in other words, audiences), and those permanent ones that work together in an organised way for a common purpose. A good deal of research has been done into the structure of organisations and the part played by communication in making them efficient.

(f) *Extrapersonal communication* means communication with the non-human. It includes communication with animals and communication with 'intelligent' machines like computers. It also includes communication in more debatable areas of experience, e.g. with spirits, with God, and with possible extra-terrestrial beings.

See also: Broadcasting, Extrapersonal communication, Group communication, Interpersonal communication, Intrapersonal communication, Mass communication, Medio-communication, Networks, Role.

ENSORSHIP

Censorship is the process used by authorities, usually political, to control the flow of information, whether between private individuals or between the mass media and the public.

Most countries have some form of censorship, since, in the eyes of the authorities, some information will always be regarded as dangerous. Military secrets, they argue, should not be made public, lest they should fall into the hands of potential enemies; films dealing with sex in explicit and unorthodox forms may be censored or banned outright to protect members of the public. In totalitarian states, the authorities suppress any information directly critical of the regime, and therefore likely to create opposition to it. However, democracies as well as dictatorships recognise that free communication brings about changes, and that these changes may not be in the interests of the ruling groups. Censorship, then, is a kind of political and moral filter set up by the authorities to ensure that seriously disturbing information does not reach their mass audiences. The extent of censorship varies according to the nature of the regime.

Censorship in the UK is principally concerned with two kinds of information: mass media productions that may scandalise and possibly corrupt sections of their audiences, and facts that governments for reasons of 'national security' (and they are the judges of this) wish to conceal from the electorate.

Public entertainment has been censored here for 400 years, but it was in 1737 that Parliament appointed the Lord Chamberlain to censor stageplays. He could ban plays he thought politically dangerous and even close down theatres. His powers were abolished in 1968, but plays today are still subject to the Obscenity Laws.

In the early days of the cinema, the guardians of public morality saw in the film a much more powerful threat to moral standards. The film industry itself, for its own protection as much as for the protection of society, set up the British Board of Film Censors in 1912. It continues to this day to give certificates to films, licensing them for certain categories of audience. However, local authorities have the right to ban the showing of a film in their district, even though the censor has passed it. Film censors make their cuts according to standards they believe to be widely acceptable at the time. Up to the early fifties, for example, no nudity or sex appeared in films shown in this country, but during the sixties, the censors, sensitive to the more permissive atmosphere, allowed full frontal nudity, first without, and then with pubic hair, and then sexual scenes of increasing explicitness. The presentation of violence, long the subject of censorship, grew more sensational too. John Trevelyan, who was censor during the period, argues in the postscript to his book *What the Censor Saw* that the purpose of film censorship should be 'the protection of children and young people and not the protection of adults or of the film industry'.

The government itself acts as a censor, since much of its business is carried on in secret. Historians have to wait 30 years before they are permitted to read government records, and some 'sensitive' files remain sealed for much longer, e.g. all post-war documents mentioning activities of MI5 and MI6. Any attempt to publish classified material (there are four classes of secrecy: restricted, confidential, secret and top secret) may be punished under the Official Secrets Act. Moreover, the government gives instructions to the press in the form of D-notices as to which kinds of information they should refrain from printing. The twelve D-notices are mainly concerned with defence and security matters, e.g. the whereabouts of nuclear weapons stockpiles and those bunkers scattered about the country designated as Regional Seats of Government in the event of nuclear war.

The anxiety shown by the authorities when some civil servant (or rather ex-civil servant) breaks the secrecy rules was clearly demonstrated in the Peter Wright case. To prevent Peter Wright, a former Assistant Director of MI5, from publishing *Spycatcher*, which contained some embarrassing revelations about MI5 actions to undermine Harold Wilson's Labour Government, the Government took out High Court injunctions against the *Guardian* and *Observer* newspapers, forbidding publication of extracts, and sent a top civil servant to Australia to get a legal ban on publication there. Meanwhile, the book has been published in the USA, but the government's efforts to uphold the secrecy of the secret service continue.

Censorship is much more thorough-going in one-party states. In the Soviet Union, for instance, Glavlit, the censorship organisation, is said to employ 70 000 people. This huge, nationwide enterprise censors all newspapers, journals, books, even children's picture-books, the aim being to make certain that the Communist Party's ideology and view of international affairs are faithfully communicated to the public: there is room for minor criticism, but none for fundamental criticism of the Soviet system.

What do Soviet writers do if they feel that their work will fall foul of the censor? They have various choices. They can tone down the message. Of this, Alexander Solzhenitsyn, the famous dissident writer, wrote the following in his *Open Letter* to the Fourth Congress of the Soviet Writers' Union:

> Many members of the Writer's Union . . . know how they themselves have bowed to the pressures of the censorship and made concessions in the structure and concept of their books – changing chapters, pages, paragraphs, or sentences, giving them innocuous titles – just for the sake of seeing them finally in print, even if it meant distorting them irremediably . . .

Some writers opt out of official publication altogether, and circulate their work secretly in typescript, or, at some risk, arrange to have their novels published abroad. If the present liberalising trends continue in Russia, it is possible that Soviet readers will at last have the opportunity of reading such banned works as Boris Pasternak's *Dr Zhivago*, Alexander Solzhenitsyn's *Gulag Archipelago* and Vasily Grossman's *Life and Fate*.

When the rights and wrongs of censorship are debated, we generally think of self-expression in some public medium, like the films and books mentioned above, but censorship can also interfere with interpersonal communication. It is normal practice in wartime for the military authorities to censor the letters that members of the armed services send home to their families and friends. Civilian prisoners' letters are also vetted, and boarding schools have been known to censor pupils' letters home!

See also: Access, Bias, Gatekeeper.
Further reading
J. Trevelyan, *What the Censor Saw*, Michael Joseph, 1973.
Index on Censorship (Writers and Scholars International). Any number of this journal will reveal censorship in action in quite a range of countries.

HANNEL

'Channel' is the physical means of directing communication between the communicator and the receiver or audience. The term is used in at least three distinct ways:

1 In a precise technical way together with the concept of 'carrier' in the physical sciences, and by communication technicians.

2 In a general non-technical fashion to indicate the most important characteristic in a communication process.

3 In a limited way, by some writers, to refer to the receiver's senses.

We deal with the first use under CARRIER.

Channel, in the second, more general sense, may be used when we want to compare similar and contrasting communication routes and do not need to be precise. For example, when comparing different telephone networks we could refer to the available channels as cable, radio or laser without going into technical detail. Or we ask whether a link-up with the USA was by cable or satellite, or whether a television system is over the air or by cable. In each case, we can also refer to these different means as 'channels of communication'. We can also refer to whole systems as 'channels of communication', for example, the telephone system compared with the postal system.

When the term is used rather loosely like this, it is very easy to confuse 'channel' with 'medium'. For instance, we can talk of the channel of radio and the medium of radio. But the distinction is clear if we remember that channel is a physical characteristic, as in comparing radio waves which travel through air or space with electric current which requires cables (wireless versus wires!), whereas the medium is the communication system as in comparing the effectiveness of radio broadcasts with newspapers.

The criteria for choosing either a particular channel or a particular medium are therefore different, although they are related. Channels are chosen according to their ability to carry across the intervening space, whereas media are valued for their social, political or psychological effectiveness. In short, people such as engineers are interested in the efficiency of channels to transmit information, whilst media people are more interested in producing the messages.

Some writers use the term 'channel of communication' to refer to a receiver's senses, i.e. hearing, vision, touch, taste and smell. So a blind person can only receive information on four channels. This application, limited as it is, is nevertheless helpful when considering people with a sensory loss, and in evaluating communication skills, as our attention is drawn to difficulties not only in face-to-face encounters but also with the use of technological equipment. The equipment you have to pick up signs and signals *is* of paramount importance. You will see that David Berlo uses this definition of channel and illustrates the senses with drawings of parts of the body: the ear, eye, hand, nose and tongue.

See also Barrier/Noise, Carrier, Communicator, Medium, Signal; Appendix
Further reading
D. K. Berlo, *The Process of Communication*, Holt, Rinehart & Winston, 1960.

C LASS/SOCIAL CLASS

Class is a extremely slippery concept to attempt to define. In broad terms, it refers to a form of stratification which predominates in industrial society, and which is based on economic factors.

Karl Marx constructed a theory of social class based on the ownership and non-ownership of the 'means of production'. For example, in nineteenth-century capitalist society, the means of production (the machines and factories which produced goods) were owned by one social class, which Marx called the 'bourgeoisie'. The other main class Marx called the 'proletariat', these being the people who did not own the means of production, and hence were compelled to work for the factory-owners in exchange for a wage. Central to the Marxist conception of class is the idea that it is linked with exploitation, which in turn results in class conflict.

Some modern sociologists, however, see class in descriptive terms as a way of categorising hierarchies of occupations. In this sense, a person's class is defined by his or her occupation, since it is held that what you do for a living will give some indication of your lifestyle and income. But you cannot base class on income alone. Winning a few hundred thousand on the pools will not make a farm labourer middle-class overnight!

When working out statistics according to social class, sociologists prefer to use some form of the Hall-Jones scale, which classifies society according to occupation as follows:

class 1 professional and high administrative
class 2 managerial and executive
class 3 inspectional, supervisory and other non-manual, higher grade
class 4 inspectional, supervisory and other non-manual, lower grade
class 5 skilled manual and routine grades of non-manual
class 6 semi-skilled manual
class 7 unskilled manual.

However, bodies like the Audit Bureau of Circulation who supply figures for newspaper circulations, prefer this six-point scale:

A   Upper middle-class households (2.5% of all households)
B   Middle-class households (10%)
C1   Lower middle-class, e.g. white-collar workers (23%)
C2   Skilled manual and clerical workers (33%)
D   Unskilled manual working-class (22%)
E   Families living on subsistence-level; pensioner households (9%)

So the social profile of three newspapers would look like this:

	The Times %	Daily Mail %	Sun %
AB	59	24	6
C1	32	32	17
C2	11	26	40
DE	4	18	37

(*Audit Bureau of Circulation, 1983*)

The figures represent percentages of the total circulation for each paper.

One indicator of social class is speech. Which if these two speakers is socially higher?

A: I seen it coming.
    We ain't got none.

B: I saw it coming.
    We haven't got any.

Obviously B. This is because there exist social-class dialects and social-class accents in English. By and large, middle-class people speak standard English, though sometimes with a regional accent, whereas regional dialects are varieties of English spoken by working-class people.

How important is social class in Communication Studies? First of all, we can say that at an interpersonal level, class is very much part of the *context* in which communication takes place. Your perception of another person's class-origins may affect your feelings about him or her, and as a result affect your behaviour.

You may be put off by an Etonian accent and think the person snobbish, when he may not be. Middle-class people with educated standard English may look down on working-class dialects. Likes and dislikes of the way people speak conceal deeper feelings about the way wealth is distributed in our class-divided society. Working-class people often resent middle-class affluence, status and jobs, since they did not have the same 'life chances' as Max Weber put it (that is, good health, education, housing). Again, middle-class people can despise – and fear – the people 'below' them. This is not to say that class differences make communication impossible: people of different social backgrounds can and do get on together, despite a fairly marked 'them and us' climate in British industry.

See also: Context, Perception, Speech.
Further reading
M. Slattery, *The ABC of Sociology*, Macmillan Education, 1985.

# CODE

A code is a system of signs governed by rules agreed between members of the community who use it. It is essentially used to communicate meanings over time and space.

The idea of codes lies right at the heart of human communication. In fact, without the intervention of signs and a regular way of using them, communication would be impossible. How much communication could take place without speech, body language, writing and other kinds of graphic representation? We are left with the idea of thought-transference. But even here, where people claim to have received messages that have used none of the normal media and channels, they still have to identify the message (in words or images) before being sure that they have received it. It seems that whatever mysterious channel is used in telepathy, the thoughts still have to be encoded.

Codes have developed as human beings have developed their communication skills of body-language, speaking and writing (in that order).

Each medium opened up its own channel. Spoken languages are codes that have grown up over a long period, making use of the acoustic channel. Writing, which is more recent, depends on the visual channel for its effect. But most of what we normally call codes have not evolved in communities, but have been invented for highly specific purposes. To enable blind people to read, Louis Braille invented a system of writing that blind people could read through the channel of touch. To solve a rather different problem, Samuel Morse invented a code that could be transmitted over electric telegraph wires considerable distances and at great speed. Semaphore and other flag signals convey information visually.

Codes have the following distinguishing features:

1   They must consist of more than one sign. A warning beacon fire is just a signal, not a code. But a series of smoke signals may be elements in a code. Put another way, a code is a set of signs from which individual signs can be selected. The Roman alphabet is a typical set (or paradigm), so are the numerals from 0 to 9.

2 The signs can be combined in various ways, according to rules, to form messages or texts. The name *syntagm* has been coined to describe any combination of signs. So the word 'PUSH' on a door is a syntagm made up of four signs chosen from the paradigm of the Roman alphabet. The number 10 (on the other side of the door) is a syntagm made up of two signs according to a rule about values which states that the figure 1 in that position means 10 and not 1. Both 'PUSH' and '10' convey useful information.

3 The meanings that codes convey depend upon who is using them. We simply learn them, at home, outside, at school. If you want to understand how any particular society works, you have to study the codes its members use. (See CULTURE.) Cultural differences can cause people to misunderstand the most apparently obvious signs. A German motorist on a first visit to England, may not understand why everybody is expected to drive in built-up areas at the slow speed of 30 km/h! The way we measure distance and speeds is part of our culture, so 30 in this country signifies a 30 miles per hour speed limit, whereas a figure on a continental roadsign would refer to kilometres per hour.

4 All codes have been designed to meet special social needs. Smoke-signals and talking drums were used to send coded messages over long distances more rapidly than by sending runners. The International Highway Code has been developed to regulate fast-moving traffic on busy road networks and is regularly updated to cope with changing conditions. Some codes have been invented as a way of organising and classifying data, like Linnaeus's system for classifying plants and birds.

Human need has given rise to so many codes that some form of classification is useful. We can distinguish between *presentational* and *representational* codes. (See also MEDIUM/ MEDIA) By presentational we mean codes that encoders use to present themselves to other people directly, without

1. **Logical codes**
1.1. *Codes related to language*
1.1.1. Alphabetical codes
1.1.2. Substitutes for language e.g. picture-writing
1.1.3. Codes that are closely related to speech and help with the production of meanings,   e.g. intonation, gestures
1.2. *Practical codes: signals and programmes*
1.2.1. Military signals like bugle-calls
1.2.2. Traffic control systems,   e.g. The Highway Code
1.3. *Codes which signify systems of knowledge about reality*
1.3.1. Scientific codes e.g. algebraic formulae, geometric diagrams
1.4. *Codes used to predict the future*
      The Zodiac, the Tarot pack

2. **Aesthetic codes**
2.1. *Codes that signify the rules that underlie art and literature*
      E.g. Conventions associated with rhythm, rhyme, verse-form in poetry

3. **Social codes**
3.1. *Protocols,*   e.g. What clothes you wear for various social occasions
3.2. *Rituals,*   e.g. Wedding ceremonies
3.3. *Fashions*   e.g. Consumer goods as status symbols
3.4. *Games*

Figure 8   Codes (summarised from Pierre Guiraud, *Semiology*)

producing a separate message or text. Dress is one such code. If, instead of wearing a leather jacket, jeans and trainers, you come to college in an immaculate suit and polished shoes, you have clearly intended to create a different image. Perhaps you are going for a job interview and want to give an impression of being businesslike and efficient. The message is inseparable from your clothes. Or, to put it another way, your choice of clothes *is* the message. Appearance is just one aspect of nonverbal communication that makes use of presentational codes.

Representational codes, on the other hand, are used to produce messages that have an existence separate from the encoder. These messages or texts might be a line of Braille, a page of shorthand, a poem, a radio signal in morse, or a photo-story.

One of our most versatile codes is also one of the simplest: binary. This consists of just two signs which can be expressed as YES/NO, ON/OFF, +/−, 1/0 or other pairs of 'opposites'. Samuel Morse used binary code in the form of dots and dashes; Louis Braille used it in the form of embossed dots and flat positions in a matrix. We can use binary code for counting, replacing our usual denary or 10-base number system. Binary is the code we use to communicate with computers since the 1/0 signs can be converted into +/− switching of electric charges through the Central Processing Unit. (See COMPUTER.)

Pierre Guiraud's thorough survey of codes in Figure 8 bears out the point already made that to study a community's codes is to study its culture.

See also: Computer, Culture, Decoder/Decoding, Encoder/Encoding, Medium/Media, Sign, Signal.
Further reading
P. Guiraud, *Semiology*, Routledge & Kegan Paul, 1975.
E. C. Cherry, *On Human Communications*, MIT Press, 1968, Ch. 2, pp. 30–40.

COMMUNICATION

There are almost as many definitions of communication as there are writers on the subject, but two kinds of definition predominate. The first thinks of communication as a process whereby a communicator or sender directs a message through a medium/channel to a receiver with some effect. The second sees communication as a social activity, where people in a given culture create and exchange meanings in response to the 'reality' they experience.

The aim of the Process School, as it has been called, is to separate out the different components and stages of the process in order to be able to study how the whole process works. Harold Lasswell's verbal model, 'Who says what in which channel to whom with what effect', is an early example of communication as process. Since he was particularly interested in propaganda (persuasive communication), he emphasised the idea of *effect*. Other writers find the ideas of *purpose* and *context* of fundamental importance, since most human communicators have an aim in communicating, and the social circumstances in which they communicate are bound to influence the way their messages are formulated and understood.

The process school also came to recognise the central fact that no message can be transmitted without first being converted into an appropriate code for the channel being used. So thoughts may be encoded in gestures, speech, writing, pictures, etc. depending on the availability of visual or aural channels.

It is at this point that the process school most obviously overlaps the *semiotic* school. These writers focus on the *text* (which does not have to be in writing – it can be a painting, photograph, film, dance sequence, etc.); on its signs and codes; on the people who *read* or decode the texts; and the social reality in which both texts and people exist. The study of communication leads in the end to a study of culture. For example, the Esso catchphrase 'Put a Tiger in your Tank' is a typical text of our time. We decode the tiger, a savage, exotic, powerful beast, and find an appeal there to uninhibited energy, as well as the cultural value that power and speed are good and desirable.

All accounts agree that communication is a basic human activity, a non-stop activity, since even in our sleep our mind rearranges memories in the shape of dream images. During our waking hours, we are absorbing and giving out information, both deliberately and unconsciously. We may be saying one thing but signifying the opposite with an uncontrolled facial expression. Whatever we say and however we dress, we create an impression on other people. Only the invisible will escape decoding, and it has often been repeated that 'one cannot *not* communicate'.

We have to communicate to meet all our daily needs: the need to get food and shelter, the need to cooperate with others to satisfy our desire for friendship and social success, a multitude of practical and economic needs, not to mention the need for getting and giving information, entertaining and being enter- tained, and the need to be creative artistically. In effect, communication links us with an ever-widening network of human beings, beginning with our immediate family and spreading out through our friends (with the aid of the mass media), to society and the world at large. And the way we develop as individuals depends very much on how successfully we build up these networks. Communication is not merely the exchange of 'hard facts': it is the sharing of thoughts, feelings, opinions and experiences as well.

Looked at from the point of view of the individual, communication enables you to become a useful, contributing member of society. Looked at from the point of view of a society, communication among its constituent members ensures that society survives and develops. So another way of defining communication would be to echo Colin Cherry: 'The establishment of a social unit from individuals, by the use of language or signs.' Or Wilbur Schramm: 'Communication is the tool that makes societies possible.'

For 126 definitions of communication see F. E. L. Dance and C. E. Larson, *The Functions of Human Communication* (see Further reading).

See also: Categories, Channel, Context, Effect, Medium, Models, Purpose.

Further reading

J. Fiske, *Introduction to Communication Studies*, Methuen, 1982, Introduction.

D. McQuail and S. Windahl, *Communication Models*, Longman, 1981.

F. E. L. Dance and C. E. Larson, *The Functions of Human Communications,*, Holt, Rinehart and Winston, 1976, Appendix A, pp. 171–92.

COMMUNICATION SKILLS

A communication skill is an ability to encode or decode information effectively. In the case of encoding, this means relating to the audience, taking the audience's needs into account, and using body language and speech to good effect. Or it may mean using other codes like writing, drawing, mime and dance. The most important decoding skills are listening and reading.

In everyday face-to-face communication, the most important communication skills are those which enable us to explain our needs, whether they are to do with our work or with our social life, to other people; and, in turn, to understand theirs. Throughout the day we undertake little strategies to cope with situations we meet. Exchanging greetings with your neighbour (*phatic communication*) is a simple strategy of verbal formulae, smiles and gestures that is really a ritual. We have strategies for making suggestions, objections and excuses. We have ways and means of starting up conversations, interrupting others, changing the direction of the discussion, breaking off. All of this we do more or less unconsciously, unless we are in an unfamiliar situation. To use these common strategies effectively is, nevertheless, a skill.

A second skill is to be able to present yourself effectively, which often means acting out a part. So, for example, if you have forgotten to bring in your homework at the appointed hour, you will probably exaggerate your dismay, strike your temple with your fist and denounce yourself for being so forgetful, all of which disarms your teacher.

A third skill is our perception of others. We can learn to observe people closely and objectively and be aware of ourselves as communicators as well (see PERCEPTION). Related to perception is the skill of putting ourselves in another person's shoes and seeing things from his or her standpoint. This is called *empathy* (see EMPATHY).

A fifth communication skill is to be able to respond positively to feedback. It is important enough to perceive how someone is reacting to what you are saying or doing, but it is another thing to use the feedback to steer the conversation away from embarrassment or to explore some underlying anxiety the listener may secretly wish to discuss.

A sixth skill is to be able to look attentive, give plenty of signs of encouragement and approval. This can only really go with listening, an essential decoding skill in interpersonal communication (see LISTENING).

It is obvious that many of the above skills rely upon the fundamental communication skill of speaking. To be able to explain things clearly, describe events vividly, tell a good joke, respond with wit and speed are all part of the skill of speaking that come with practice. Schools, still concentrating on reading and writing, could do more to improve oral skills by fostering group projects, classroom discussions, thinking aloud by pupils, talks and debates.

Speaking to a large audience – public speaking – needs all the virtues of sincerity, clarity, liveliness, empathy that you find in good private conversation together with greater self-confidence, more careful planning of appropriate material for the audience, and even the techniques of rhetoric (see RHETORIC).

Reading and writing are two communication skills that enable us to communicate with people at a distance and over time. We learn them systematically at school. Reading, a decoding process, is usually taught by a combination of methods, of which 'phonics' and 'look and say' are perhaps the best known. The 'phonic' method builds up words from letters and sounds, while 'look and say' gets children to recognise whole words from their shape and pronounce them. For example:

Phonic method

h – a – t → hat

'Look and say' method

Reading is more than turning marks on paper into sounds. It is, of course, perfectly possible to read aloud without understanding a word of what you are reading. Reading is a process of getting meanings out of symbols, and most of us are aware of the limits of our comprehension. At some point reading becomes specialist study. Even if you had a degree in English Literature, you might find quantum mechanics hard to read. When you do a lot of reading, as a student now and later at work, you may wish to increase the speed and accuracy of your reading. Manya and Eric De Leeuw, authors of *Read Better, Read Faster*, claim that students on their rapid reading course increased their speed, on average, by 60 per cent, and their comprehension by 10 per cent on non-literary texts.

There are many books on the art (or skill) of writing. These teach you such conventions as spelling, punctuation and grammar; and to be able to handle these is essential. But there are a hundred and one ways of writing. Most of your writing, while you are at college, will take the form of essays (for your lecturers to read), informal letters for your friends and relatives, and formal letters to strangers (e.g. part-time job applications). Where you seriously intend to communicate (and writing is a matter of greater deliberation than speaking) you need to choose the appropriate style, register and format, always remembering that it is better to make your message clear and complete rather than trying to impress your reader with clever turns of phrase, unless your main aim is to amuse. Writing is also an important form of intrapersonal communication, a useful and pleasurable way of clarifying your thoughts and experience. Whether in your diary or in the form of poetry and story you can cultivate your skill, experiment with words, and please yourself. Sooner or later, perhaps, you will contribute to poetry and story-writing as an art.

See also: Empathy, Listening, Perception, Phatic communication, Register, Style.
Further reading
R. Dimbleby and G. Burton, *More Than Words*, Methuen, 1985, Ch. 2.

COMMUNICATOR

The term traditionally refers to the role of originator or producer of messages. It is used mainly of individuals but could equally well refer to an organisation like a newspaper or a radio station. (Note that the corresponding term for a passive receiver is communicatee. With the current trend towards thinking of the receiver as equally active, both sender and receiver could be called communicator.)

There are many alternative terms, as you will see from Figure 9, a chronological table of process models.

It is worth noting here that Shannon and Weaver were originally concerned with the way in which messages sent by telegraph and telephone were liable to faulty transmission and misinterpretation. To identify where the faults were occurring they considered the source (the person) separately from the transmitter (the technical medium of telegraph and telephone). Within the individual, of course, the source and transmitter are inseparable and controlled by the same brain. And the same goes for *receiver* and *destination*.

Later writers were explicit about the fact that all messages have to be encoded in some way before they can be sent, and that in the individual this encoding process is performed by the brain. (See ENCODER/ENCODING.)

We are all communicators, and how effective we are at communicating depends partly on our communication skills (see COMMUNICATION SKILLS) and personalities. There are many other factors that will affect the success of our communicating in any given situation. These include our attitudes, values and beliefs, our experience and education, our social background and our culture. These same factors affect us equally when we are in the receiver's role.

Communicator is also a professional term for those who work in the mass media or in jobs like advertising and public relations which make use of the media. Newspaper columnists, film directors and TV producers are all communicators, since they are responsi-

c 340 BC	Aristotle	Speaker	Speech	Audience
1940s	Lasswell	Who	Says What	To Whom
	Shannon & Weaver	Source & Transmitter	Signal	Receiver & Destination
1950s	Westley & Maclean	Advocacy roles & Channel roles	Message	Behavioural roles & System roles
	Jakobson	Addresser	Message	Addressee
	Osgood	Source	Message	Destination
	Gerbner	Communicator	Signal or Statement	Receiver
1960s	Berlo	Sender	Message	Receiver
1970s	Schramm	Sender	Message	Receiver (active)
1980s	Adams	Producer	Signal	Consumer

Figure 9 Summary of process models based on 'sender–message–receiver'

ble for shaping the messages in the print and broadcasting media that reach the public. You will notice, if you look back at Figure 9, that Westley and Maclean have identified two kinds of communicator. Messages, in their view, are originated by a group of people (*advocates*) but filtered through the media by another group of people, media professionals, who act as *gatekeepers*. Advocates would be people like Bishop Desmond Tutu (using television and other media to rally world support against apartheid in South Africa), Ian Paisley (rallying Ulster Protestants against the Anglo-Irish Agreement) and Mrs Mary Whitehouse (using television to criticise scenes of violence, sex and bad taste broadcast by television). But it must be remembered that all advocates run a certain risk in using mass media for their own purposes. They are in the hands of editors and producers who have the last say in how the message is presented to the public. A strong communicator like the miners' leader, Arthur Scargill, found himself being presented in some right-wing newspapers, through carefully selected photographs and misreported speeches as another Adolf Hitler.

Perhaps the major problem media communicators have to face is that their experience of many of the audience groups they cater for is very limited, so there is a hit-or-miss element in launching new programmes. According to Philip Elliott (*Sociology of Mass Communications*, p. 253) TV producers adopt one of three attitudes towards their potential audiences. Some go ahead in the hope that the audience will follow them, others work for themselves and value the criticism of fellow producers, whilst others again concentrate on ways of gaining and holding the audience's attention. This last approach may make for dazzling television but waters down the informational content of the programme.

See also: Audience, Code, Communication skills, Encoder/Encoding; Appendix.
Further reading
P. Elliott, 'Mass Communication – A Contradiction in Terms?' in D. McQuail (ed.), *The Sociology of Mass Communications*, Penguin, 1972.

OMPUTER

A computer is an electronic device for processing data. This data has to be digital in form (i.e. sets of signs such as numbers, letters, words) so that it can be converted into binary signals suitable for on/off switching in the electronic circuits that process data with great speed and accuracy, and store data for future use.

Figure 10 shows you at a glance the computer as a processing system. In the case of the microcomputer, with which you are probably familiar, the Central Processing Unit (CPU), the various input devices (keyboard, cassette and disc) and the output devices like the Visual Display Unit (VDU) and the printer are collectively called the *hardware*. A computer will only do exactly what it is told, so programs – or lists of instructions – are written in code (see ALGORITHM) to enable it to carry out specific tasks. For example, you can turn a BBC microcomputer into a word processor by using a program such as WORDWISE, VIEW or INTERWORD. By using the code in the INTERWORD program you can lay out your writing on the screen

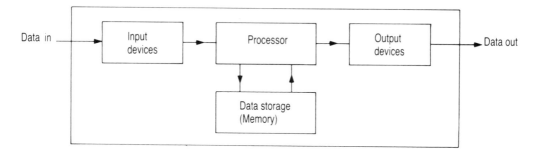

Figure 10 The computer as a processing system

just as you want it. And you can insert another program which will check through your spelling! These programs, whether on cassette, floppy disc or chip, are called *software*.

The communication process (see EXTRAPERSONAL COMMUNICATION) between you and a computer is quite complex. You may have an up-to-date voice input device and be able to talk to it, but you would be more likely, at present, to address it by means of a keyboard. But *how* do you address it? Computers do not respond to natural languages like English, in fact they can only do their job of processing data if the instructions come in 1's and 0's (binary code). Reducing your idiomatic English to binary code cannot be done in one stage. You have to learn a *high level language* like BASIC or FORTRAN, which are limited codes of English. These are translated by the computer into ASCII code (American Standard Code for Information Interchange), then into hexadecimal code (using 2 digits for the 8 used in binary), then into machine code and finally into binary. The computer delivers its response to you in the high level language on your screen or printed automatically on paper.

There is no doubt that the computer is transforming Western, and parts of Eastern society. Already we rely upon it to quite a large extent in many important spheres of activity. For example,

starting in the home, it seems, according to a recent survey, that 25 per cent of homes in the South of England have microcomputers. Although these may often be used for Space Invaders and the like, many are operated for more serious purposes as data-stores, spread-sheets and word-processors.

When you shop in a supermarket, the point-of-sale terminal that adds up and prints out your purchases, may also transmit all those details to a central computer which checks the shop's stock. In this way the manager knows when to order fresh supplies, and in what quantities.

Modern administration depends on computer records. The Inland Revenue and big employers like county councils and the banks have shifted much of their paperwork into electronic data-processing.

For over 20 years many manufacturing processes in industry have been controlled by computers. Perhaps the most dramatic are the industrial robots working in the car industry (Fiat in Italy, Nissan in Japan, Rover Group in Britain). In Japan, the Fanuc factory, itself almost totally automated (only one person on the night-shift!) makes 100 robots a month. In the textile and clothing industries as well as in architecture and building, computers are programmed to aid design-work.

Computers may be found in the

National Health Service. Here they are used to diagnose patients' complaints and so assist doctors. Plans are afoot to transfer all medical records on to computer.

The computer revolution has reached our schools. In 1984, all secondary and most primary schools had access to at least one microcomputer. So most children get some experience of computers: enough, perhaps, to overcome the computerphobia that afflicts many of the older generation; but computers have not yet been integrated into the school curriculum as essential teaching aids. Nor are they likely to replace flesh-and-blood teachers in the foreseeable future.

It is just not possible to list all the applications of computers in such a brief survey, but the military uses should be mentioned, since they are of life-and-death importance. Both NATO (North Atlantic Treaty Organisation) and the Warsaw Pact have missiles with thermonuclear warheads pre-programmed to hit targets in each other's territory with considerable accuracy. Their command, control and communication systems are also highly automated. There has been much recent talk of the 'automated battlefield' and 'electronic warfare'. However, it appears that if nuclear weapons were exploded anywhere near such computerised command systems, the electro-magnetic pulse set up would send electronic signals haywire – and rob the military commanders of *all* control!

For the social and political implications of computers and associated technologies, you should refer to INFORMATION TECHNOLOGY.

See also: Code, Extrapersonal communication, Information technology, Machine intelligence.
Further reading
(a) There are huge numbers of books on computers and computing. Do not be afraid to start with the Ladybird Book *Computers*, but graduate quickly to: Malcolm Peltu, *Introducing Computers* (National Computing Centre).

(b) On the applications and implications of computers:
C. Evans, *The Mighty Micro*, Gollancz, 1982.
P. Zorkoczy, *Information Technology: an Introduction*, Pitman, 1985.

CONSENSUS

'Consensus' means that which the majority of members of any group agrees on as true or desirable. The term is used of agreements reached in small groups like clubs, and large groups like political parties. It also applies to a whole nation.

At a small-group level, people need to reach a consensus, an attitude or course of action to which all or most members are happy to subscribe. A consensus is reached through discussion and debate, in which the more resolute members use their communication skills to convert the rest to their point of view. Some organisations will only proceed when they have reached unanimity, where *everybody* agrees. The Quakers or Friends are a case in point.

Consensus is also a term applied by

social scientists to society as a whole. It is self-evident that if a society is to exist at all, there must be a broad, general agreement among its members about the codes to be used; for example, the national language or languages, the laws and the political system. In Britain, there is a high degree of consensus in these matters. English is the official language, the laws apply equally to every citizen, and parliamentary democracy under a constitutional monarch is the method of government. On the other hand, the apartheid system in South Africa with its separate laws and territories for the different races has never achieved consensus support. It was imposed by the ruling Afrikaaner minority on the black majority, and now shows signs of crumbling.

The mass media are under some obligation to reflect the feelings, beliefs and values of the majority, but their knowledge of this consensus is largely guesswork. In the end, *they* decide what we are supposed to agree about; they set the agenda for what news and views we should consume, and the manner in which they are to be presented. They decide too which issues threaten their supposed consensus. For many years, before the bi-partisan consensus on the possession of nuclear weapons finally broke down, nuclear disarmers were represented in much of the press as harmless eccentrics, but as they made their case stick and grew in numbers, they were represented as dangerous subversives. The point to remember is that a consensus can break down and give rise, eventually, to a new consensus.

See also: Agenda-setting, Mass communication, Medium/media, Socialisation.
Further reading
T. O'Sullivan et al., *Key Concepts in Communication*, Methuen, 1983, pp. 49–51.

 **ONSTRAINT**

'Constraint' refers to any limitations inherent in any medium of communication, or in any message. These limitations, or pressures, as they are sometimes called, are experienced by both the communicator and the audience. Constraints are generally discussed in connection with the mass media.

As far as the medium of speech is concerned, we can say that it is only effective over a short distance, since there are physical constraints on the human voice. These, of course, can be overcome by other media such as the telephone and radio. Speech has other constraints. It is impermanent, easily distorted in the memory, and easily forgotten. The medium of writing makes language permanent. Again, speech is a notoriously inadequate medium for describing shapes and colours with any accuracy. Visual means such as diagrams, drawings or colour-charts, are used to overcome these constraints.

All communicators in the mass media work in a general framework of constraints. Newspaper and broadcasting journalists generally work in teams so that their freedom of expression is to some extent limited by the outlooks and values of their colleagues. Novelists and poets are not constrained in quite the same way. Since the mass media produce their messages for public consumption, communicators will pay attention to public opinion (see CONSENSUS) and that will act as a constraint on what is published or broadcast. For example, neither the BBC nor ITV has produced a programme in favour of drug-taking or the need to establish a British republic. In addition to the pressure of consensus opinion there are laws of libel as well as codes of practice (guidelines against bias, for instance) that act as constraints. And then there is a limit to the amount you can spend on making a programme, or gathering news stories: money is a great constraint too.

Each medium has its own special constraints, like that of speech mentioned above. A newspaper is subject to constraints of space (the number and size of its pages) and of time in the production process. Newspapers work to deadlines, the final deadline being just before the presses begin to roll, when only the most sensational story will oust the front-page main story. Sub-editors scribbling, or typing under pressure of time, to rewrite reporters' stories, seldom check the facts with the reporters, so the accuracy of news is bound to suffer. Moreover, reporters and sub-editors have to conform to the *house style* of their paper, which determines the way they treat their stories and pictures. That too is a constraint. And lastly, right up to the deadline for printing, the format of a newspaper acts as a limitation that can distort the message:

> The pressure to fit a story into a page design, whether in the newsroom or at the last moment by the stone-sub, is the largest single factor behind quotations or counter-balancing facts being abridged or left out. (D. MacShane, *Using the Media*, Pluto Press, 1979, p. 50)

Television is essentially a visual medium. TV programmers have developed many conventions to do justice to 'moving pictures'. They are reluctant to have people simply talking to the camera for any length of time. Instead of 'talking heads', they prefer to have the expert gardener weeding flower-beds, the philosopher strolling in the college cloisters, the performer making up in the dressing room. The speakers often disappear altogether, except for their voices which continue in a disembodied way. A convention of this kind acts as a constraint on programme-producers. Allied to this, the priority given to the pictures means that commentary must be sparing and fit in subtly with the pictures.

Like newspapers, TV has to work to deadlines. Until the arrival of video cameras (Electronic News Gatherers as they are called) TV news services needed more advance notice than newspapers to get their camera-teams out to the crisis spots. Cine-film has to be processed before being turned into television signals. Nowadays, the two-man video film crews work from TV mobile units that will transmit the news back to the TV centres. The new video technology has overcome one important constraint of cine-film.

Programme formats naturally produce constraints. News scriptwriters, for some of their bulletins, have to write commentaries for ten minutes of pictures. Three sides of typewritten A4 is not even a thumbnail sketch of world news! Again, the words have to relate to the pictures. And there is a further constraint: the last story in the *Nine O'Clock News* or *News at Ten* is almost bound to feature an animal or a member of the royal family, preferably the former ridden by the latter.

From the point of view of the receiver, different media impose constraints on the way they can be received. Television and print media completely absorb your attention. You cannot watch TV or read the paper and do your homework simultaneously. On the other hand, you may be able to listen to the car-radio and still drive safely. Radio, engaging only your hearing, leaves your other senses free, but imposes some constraint on your readiness to attend to other sounds. Personal 'walkmans' are potentially dangerous to drivers, cyclists and pedestrians as they produce a cocoon of sound which isolates the wearer from the surroundings: they create a *barrier* to communication, not just a constraint.

Of those writers who have created models to demonstrate the mass communication process, only the German,

Maletzke, appears to have included constraints from medium, message and audience on the communicator and constraints from the medium on the audience. (D. McQuail and S. Windahl, *Communication Models*, Longman, 1981, p. 40)

See also: Access, Audience, Barrier/Noise, Bias, Consensus.

CONTENT ANALYSIS

Content analysis is a research method that identifies key items in the message content of any mass medium, counts them, compares them with other items, and compares them with equivalent statistics gathered from society at large. An illustration of this is that the social scientist Sidney Head (1954) found that murder accounted for 14 per cent of all crime represented in TV drama, compared with only 0.65 per cent of all crime in society.

Content analysis is a statistical method that is best used to examine whole outputs of messages. Raymond Williams uses the technique in his book *Communication* to compare the contents of national newspapers over a period of time. The Glasgow Media Group have analysed TV broadcasts of industrial news. Other researchers have studied gender-roles and the way ethnic minorities are represented in children's literature and TV commercials.

The value of content analysis is in the comparisons that can be made within the study. When you do your own rough-and-ready analysis of news

coverage, you will probably find that quality papers like the *Guardian* carry up to three times as much foreign news as the popular tabloids. You will find too that the quality papers have quite a wide range of topics, whereas the range of the tabloids is rather limited. A thoroughgoing content analysis could pin these differences down with precision, although there can be problems when you come to decide on categories. For instance, 'Charles and Diana fly to Tokyo on state visit'. Is that home news, foreign news, political news or royal family news?

Given the raw statistics of a content analysis, what sort of conclusions may be drawn? Some may be fairly obvious, others less so: but they tell us about our cultural values. Content analysis of many science textbooks shows they have very few illustrations or examples of women in science, compared with men. This imbalance reflects our traditional view of science and helps to perpetuate it. The uncommon crime of murder (see statistics above) has always held great dramatic potential, from the Greek tragedies of Aeschylus and Sophocles onwards. It still fascinates.

Why? A recent analysis by George Gerbner of American television murders revealed that the killer was more often than not a white, middle-class, young, adult male. He concluded that the choice reflected the prestige group in society.

See also: Message/Text.
Further reading
J. Fiske, *Introduction to Communication Studies*, Methuen, 1972, Ch. 7.
G. Dyer, *Advertising as Communication*, Methuen, 1982, pp. 108—11.

ONTEXT

Context is the environment or framework within which communication takes place. It includes the time and place as well as the social relationship of the people involved. Context has a marked influence on communication behaviour.

For example, if you were invited out to a 'posh' restaurant by your fiancé(e)'s parents, the experience would be rather different from that of having a burger in Macdonald's with your mates. You might make a point of dressing neatly, you would be on your best behaviour, and your speech might be somewhat more formal than usual. You would be reacting to people who could be especially important to you, to the elegant and possibly unfamiliar surroundings of the restaurant, and to the sense of occasion (a first encounter).

Social scientists have found the following classification of social contexts useful:

formal – informal
work – social
friendly – unfriendly
equal status – unequal status

The invitation from your fiancé(e)'s parents would produce a context falling between formal and informal; it would

be social, friendly (you hope!) and the status unequal. At Macdonald's, the context would be informal, social, friendly and equal.

Every communication situation has a certain structure. A meal follows a certain pattern of events, as does a committee meeting or a game of hockey. These activities satisfy common needs and prompt appropriate (and therefore predictable) behaviour. Committee meetings give rise to speeches, arguments, note-taking, decision-making, etc.; meals to sharing food, eating and small-talk. Each situation has its roles and rules. The chairperson has the role of controller or facilitator of a committee meeting, a parent (usually) the role of food-server at a family meal. Committee meetings are run according to rules, often formalised in a constitution; meals follow conventions of soup first, main course, second helpings, sweet, etc.

Physical settings are crucial in influencing communication behaviour. For a good party, food and drink is not enough: soft lighting, music, comfortable furniture make all the difference. Similarly, it is unsatisfactory to run an art class in a dim, cluttered storeroom: for painting you need lots of space and a good north light, in short the right conditions and the right atmosphere. Churches may lead you to talk in hushed whispers; noisy engine-rooms and factories force you to shout or resort to gestures.

Any change in the context will modify people's behaviour. This may be seen when parties become overcrowded and overheated, and fights break out. It may be seen in the experimentally verified fact that cheerful interior decoration makes people feel friendlier towards one another.

Some people manipulate the context to their own advantage. By wearing dark glasses you can be one up on the other person because you are denying them a source of feedback. You can arrange the furniture so that you have the light behind you and the other has the light in his or her eyes. And you can make sure that you have the bigger chair.

Time is also a crucial part of the context. If you were to ring up a friend at 2 a.m. to ask to borrow a record, you might get a less than enthusiastic response. Nor is first thing on Monday a good time to beg favours.

No one should underestimate the power of the setting to influence communication. But whatever the physical surroundings, other people are part of the context. Your own personality and experience will affect your performance and you will take account of the nationality, age, sex, relationship and social status of others. You will notice whether they are attractive, nervous or confident, forbearing or overbearing. All these factors and many others will affect what you say and how you say it (style and register) as well as how much of the conversation you command.

Within the overall communication situation (some communication models put an envelope labelled 'context' round it) whatever talk (or silent communication) takes place, is going to depend upon people understanding the context in which words and gestures are used. Clearly the sentence 'Give him a sock' would mean one thing to children when discussing self-defence amongst themselves, and another when sorting out clothes with one of their parents.

See also: Interpersonal communication, Register, Role, Proximity, Style.
Further reading
M. Argyle and P. Trower, *Person to Person*, Harper & Row, 1979, Ch. 5.

ONVENTION

A convention is a rule of social behaviour or artistic practice common to a culture or subculture.

For example, it is a convention in this country to wipe your shoes on the doormat before entering a house. Most British people do this because they have been taught to do so since childhood. In Japan, the convention is to take your shoes off altogether and change into slippers. To walk about indoors in outdoor shoes is deeply shocking to the Japanese. In short, different cultures have created different sets of conventions, and within main cultures subcultures distinguish themselves through their own special conventions. If you like, another way of thinking about culture is to see it as a collection of conventions.

Every aspect of our daily lives is governed by conventions. We have special modes of address when greeting people; we have certain rules of behaviour when acting as hosts or guests; we have table-manners and etiquette; every conversation we have follows certain conventions of eye-contact and turn-taking. Some of these rules are explicit and have been written down (there are books about etiquette); others, like much of our body-language, are implicit. Since the main message of conventional behaviour is 'I belong to the same culture as you do', it is largely a *phatic* form of communication. In fact, conventional behaviour seems so natural and normal that it is only when somebody breaks a convention that you really become aware of it. And breaking conventions is a way of drawing attention to yourself, because by doing so you are in a small way putting yourself above a social 'law'. If a man kept his hat on in church he would certainly offend members of the congregation, and in some churches, a women offends if she does not cover her head. If you wore your shoes in a mosque, you would soon be asked to take them off!

All the productions of the mass media are governed by conventions of form and style. Conventions of headlines, layout, journalese and news values determine the front page of a newspaper.

Conventions govern the live coverage of sports on television. For instance, at the moment of delivery, the bowler is always filmed from behind or from in front, but never from the side. TV commentary is spasmodic (the pictures do much of the talking), whereas radio coverage of the same match requires almost continuous talk. In television there is a strong convention against 'talking heads'. Producers prefer to use an interviewee's comments as a 'voice-over' and have the camera following the speaker through the garden, driving to work, climbing a steeple, or whatever. Because television is a visual and kinetic medium, it must provide interesting pictures all the time to attract and hold attention. In its first year of broadcasting, Channel 4 broke this convention and invited people who had something important to say to 'speak to camera' for half-an-hour at a time. It was a refreshing change to hear ideas being developed at some length on a TV channel.

Every art form has its conventions, as you will understand if you are studying English Literature, Art or Music. Poetry, for example, is written in a variety of rhythms and uses conventions of stanza, form and rhyme. In representational painting, foreground figures are larger than background figures, to give the illusion of perspective. And some cartoonists tend to draw hands with only three fingers (See Figure 11).

See also: Code, Culture, Phatic communication, Redundancy.

Figure 11   Some cartoonists draw hands with only three fingers (*Punch*, 1 July 1987)

CULTURE

Culture is a collection of beliefs, values and ways of doing things which are typical of a particular community and which are expressed and perpetuated through various codes.

The community in question may be a nation, so that it is possible to talk about American culture or Japanese culture. Or the community may be even larger and comparisons may be made between European culture and African culture. Since religion has proved such a vital factor in determining what we believe, how we worship and behave, it is also possible to refer to Christian, Jewish, Muslim and Hindu cultures, among many others.

Within British culture, for example, one can find several other applications of the term *culture*. There is *popular culture* or *mass culture* which refers to the commercial forms of art and entertainment (such as pop and rock music, TV soap operas, paperback romances, tabloid newspapers) that engage a mass audience. There is *high culture* (being a *cultured* or *cultivated* person), which since Victorian times has been regarded as the pursuit of spiritual perfection through encounters with the finest products of the arts ('serious' music, 'great' novels, 'magnificent' paintings). These cultural differences correspond more or less, though not absolutely, with differences of social class.

Britain is now, as a result of post-war Commonwealth immigration, a *multicultural* society. One of the most fascinating but sometimes painful social processes to observe has been the way settler groups with their own cultures have struggled to relate to the dominant British culture. Early attempts by black people to be *assimilated* into British culture were often frustrated by unwelcoming attitudes on the part of the white majority.

Nevertheless, many first-generation settlers became *integrated* to the extent that they learnt English, voted in elections, paid their taxes, sent their children to school, etc. But it soon became clear to these *ethnic minority groups* that to abandon their own cultures could leave them floundering with an uncertain identity. So the current trend is for Sikhs, Muslims, Hindus, the Greek Orthodox Christians from Cyprus, and others to maintain their respective religions which are central to their communities, to encourage the learning of their mother-tongues, and to preserve their customs and ceremonies. Under the more enlightened local education authorities, an effort is being made in schools to encourage children to value their own cultures, and to understand and respect those of all their classmates. This is called *multicultural education*.

To clarify the idea of culture in our original definition, compare some typical features of British culture with those of the Japanese, using Figure 12.

It is obvious that where people from different cultural backgrounds meet each other, there are going to be all kinds of communication problems. These may be quite fundamental if neither speaks the other's language. But even if they are able to use a common language, difficulties occur as a result of the different cultural assumptions that the speakers make. This fascinating area of Communication Studies is called *cross-cultural communication*.

Cross-cultural communication

How close would you stand to a chance acquaintance? Probably no closer than

Cultural feature	British	Japanese
1 When you greet someone	you shake hands	you bow from the waist. The degree of the bow depends on the relationship of the two people and the context in which they find themselves.
2 On entering a house	you wipe your shoes on the door-mat	you take your shoes off. Slippers are provided.
3 When you take a bath	you fill a body-length bath with hot water and wash yourself *in* the bath.	The bath is a waist-high tub. You soap and rinse yourself *beside* the bath. then soak in the clean tub water.
4 Your staple diet	is bread, potatoes, meat and cooked fish.	is rice, noodles and raw fish.
5 Your religion	is most likely to be Christianity.	is most likely to be Shintoism or Buddhism.
6 Your writing	uses the 26 characters of the Roman alphabet.	consists of ideograms (from Chinese) and some extra syllabic characters.
7 Gardens consist of	flower-beds, lawns, shrubs and trees. Many are geometrically shaped.	trees, shrubs, rocks, pools that imitate natural landscapes. Not many flowers.

Figure 12 Comparison of typical cultural features (Britain and Japan)

four feet. Arabs and Indians prefer to stand closer than that. So what is a comfortable distance for an Arab to chat with an acquaintance, might be distinctly uncomfortable for you. People such as diplomats, who have many contacts with foreigners, need to be aware of these *proxemic* differences, so as not to cause offence by backing away or coming up too close!

It is now clear, thanks to the work of Desmond Morris and others, that very many of the gestures that people use either belong specifically to that culture or have a meaning which is specific to that culture. For example, Japanese people point to their noses to mean 'me'. That is a typical Japanese gesture. But the temple-screw is one of those common European gestures, except that it means 'He's crazy' in Britain and quite the opposite in Holland: 'He's very intelligent'. And the hitch-hiker's erect thumb might catch a lift in France or Germany, but it would attract a stream of abuse in Israel, where it is an obscene gesture.

More subtle problems may arise where, for instance, a settler group actually speaks the national language of their new home. They will have difficulties with accent, stress and intonation, through what is called *mother-tongue interference*, and as a result they will unwittingly give out the wrong signals and create wrong impressions. John Twitchen, in his film *Crosstalk* made for the BBC series 'Multi-racial Britain' showed the main differences between Asian-English and English-English and how they could lead to mutual irritation. Indian languages like Panjabi and Urdu, for example, have little stress, and this carries over into the English spoken by Asians where they may fail to make the clear difference between 'last week' and 'this week'.

For their part, Asians find that the

high pitch and stress used by English people when they are trying to explain or emphasise is too emotional and impolite.

See also: Code, Gesture, Language, Non-verbal communication, Proximity.
Further reading
M. Argyle and P. Trower, *Person to Person*, Harper & Row, 1979, Ch. 1.
E. T. Hall, *The Hidden Dimension: man's use of space in public and private,*, The Bodley Head, 1969.
D. Morris, *Manwatching*, Triad Panther, 1978.

CYBERNETICS

Cynbernetics is the study and use of information to control energy systems. The word is derived from the Greek 'kubernetes' meaning 'steersman', and which is also the root of our word 'govern', hence control.

A steersman controls the path taken by a boat, by means of *feedback*. Information from a compass, the set of the sails, the direction of the wind and so on, is used to make continuous small corrections to the tiller or wheel in order to keep the boat on course. A skilled helmsman hardly needs to think but responds automatically with smooth, sometimes minute, muscular movements. The helmsman's senses (sight, hearing, sense of movement and balance) constitute an *information system* which carries reports and instructions, whereas the muscles and the steering machinery are an *energy system* for carrying out work. *Cybernetics* is concerned with the way information systems regulate energy systems.

Any self-regulating system must have built-in feedback, like a thermostat in a heating system. You adjust this to switch off at, say, 70°F and switch back on again when the temperature falls to 65°F. This is a continuous process and is called a closed loop, using feedback through the thermostat to achieve control.

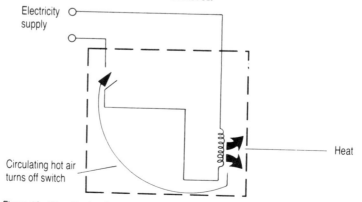

Electricity supply

Circulating hot air turns off switch

Heat

Figure 13 'Negative feedback' in a thermostatically-controlled heating system

Cybernetic processes may be natural, human, mechanical or social, anything from a child riding a bicycle to a whole political system. The sheer scope of the concept can be appreciated when you think of the role played by feedback in communication. As human beings we are all cybernetic systems. Walking along a path, we may come to a closed gate. Our eyes perceive the gate and the fact that it is shut. Our brain sends an instruction to our hands to take hold of the handle and open the gate. And so we react successfully to our environment. The cybernetic system might include other human beings, since all face-to-face communication makes use of feedback; or it might include a machine like a bicycle or a computer.

Perhaps the experience of communicating with machines is the aspect of cybernetics that affects us most. Whether driving a car or operating a computer we are using machines to extend our own abilities (to travel, to process information). And for some very complex tasks, like programming spacecraft, computers are used to cope with any emergencies that may occur in flight: machines control machines.

Once you bring together a high level of understanding of the way manufacturing processes work and advanced computer technology, the way is open for automation. For some time continuous processes like the production of petroleum and chemicals have been controlled automatically, and now computers are being harnessed to cybernetic processes in every area of industry and administration: Rover Group cars are made by robots, and cash dispensers in the street give you warm bank-notes in response to a keyed-in number.

See also: Computer, Extrapersonal communication, Feedback.

D ECODER/DECODING

A decoder is a sense organ or receptor, or a technical device which converts a signal (which is by definition 'coded') into a form that a receiver can understand.

So, as far as human beings are concerned, the eyes serve as decoders of visual information brought to them by light waves, the ears decode sound waves, the nose and tongue decode chemical messages, while the whole body is responsive to touch. As a result of recent advances in brain research we know which areas of the sensory cortex decode messages from the various senses. And it seems that the left hemisphere of the brain processes language information, since those who suffer damage in that area (the condition is called *aphasia*) find that they can hear words but not understand them.

Decoding information is a skill and as such can be improved with training. All sighted people can see objects and people in their environment, identify them and react to them appropriately (for example, avoiding a moving car, spotting a friend in a crowd). But birdwatchers, navigators, detectives and scientists are trained observers in their particular areas. If the information is in a form like writing, then everyone has to make a systematic effort to learn the code, and reading is one of the most important skills taught at school. Many people assume that listening is an automatic process rather than a skill to be learnt and refined, but listening too is explicitly taught in some schools. To read a novel with real understanding, or to listen to a talk or a symphony with comprehension and pleasure are highly active forms of decoding.

Communication models, like those of Osgood and Schramm, separate the decoding function of the sense organs from the interpreting function of the brain. There is good reason for doing this, since it is possible to hear words and not make sense of them (oriental languages baffle most Westerners) and one of the reasons why we ask new acquaintances to repeat their names is that proper nouns can be very unusual. Similarly we can be stumped by close-up photographs of what turn out to be familiar objects.

Some writers, however, use the term *decoding* to include the interpreting function of the brain. Your brain, they argue, cannot tell you what is there without comparing it with what it knows already. We fail to decode at all, if we have nothing to compare the data with (some ancient writings have still to be deciphered), or we decode wrongly because our code does not correspond exactly with the code used in the message. Margaret Abercrombie gives an interesting example of *aberrant decoding* when she suggests that the

prehistoric cave paintings apparently depicting gracefully running animals really show dead animals lying on their sides. If this were a correct interpretation, it would indicate that our romantic culture has led us to misinterpret the food carcases painted by the hunters of the Old Stone Age.

Wilbur Schramm and many other writers, especially those of the semiotic school, stress that decoding is just as active as encoding, that listening is as painstaking as speaking, reading as writing. For communication to take place effectively the receiver (listener or reader) must bring attention and thought to the task. However, at the highest level, the encoding skills seem to be rarer than the decoding skills. For every good novelist there are hundreds of good readers; for every good poet, tens of sensitive poetry-readers; for every composer, thousands of listeners; and so on. It is hard to see that decoding can be such a skilled and creative process as encoding; but opinions differ.

In the world of telecommunications the techical decoding devices would include the telephone earphone, the radio loudspeaker, the cathode-ray tube with its assembly of three electron guns in the colour-TV receiver, the telex machine and computer output devices.

See also: Code, Encoder, Listening, The senses.

 IALECT

'Dialect' is a term used to distinguish different varieties of a language in all its aspects, including accent, vocabulary and grammar. So Sussex, Yorkshire, Belfast, New-castle and Standard English are some of the dialects of English.

Standard English differs from the other English dialects in that it is bound to no particular region. It developed from dialects spoken in and around London in the fourteenth century and came to be the language spoken by the educated upper classes and a model for all who wished to speak and write well.

In fact, it is the kind of English now taught and tested in schools. It is worth remembering that the prestige accent (see ACCENT), Received Pronunciation, is used by only a minority of speakers of Standard English. Most people in Britain, in practice, speak Standard English with a regional accent.

Regional dialects differ from Standard English in grammar and vocabulary, and they differ in many respects from each other. In East Anglia, people say 'he go' and 'he eat', whereas in Berkshire they say 'he goes' and 'he eats' (like Standard English) but also 'we goes' and 'they goes'. All regional dialects make use of multiple negatives, such as 'I ai*n't* going *no*where', and 'I do*n't* want *no*thing'.

Compare also such relative clauses as:

'That was the man what done it'
              as done it'
              at done it'
           'done it', etc.

The Standard form is:

'That was the man who did it' or 'that did it'.

All dialects have their own interesting local words and expressions. 'Tek thi clogs off!' (Lancs) would mean 'Don't make so much noise!' The expression is still used, even though industrial workers no longer wear wooden clogs. Durham miners eat 'bait'; Notts miners eat 'snap'; Northerners have 'jam butties', Liverpudlians have 'sarnies', Southerners have 'jam sandwiches'. Creole-speakers will 'nyam' their food. Interestingly, Jamaican Creole has over 400 words from African languages, i.e. fufu (yam), banjo, zombie, etc.

Many people speak both dialect and Standard English, depending on who they are with. However, according to sociolinguists (scholars who study the way factors like social class affect the use of language), the lower you are in the social scale, the broader your dialect is likely to be. See Figure 14.

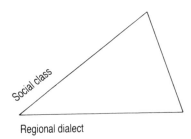

Figure 14   Diagram showing relationship of dialect and social class

Dialect can affect communication in two opposite ways, depending on the conditions where it occurs.

Dialect is part of a community's identity, so people who share a dialect feel a sense of solidarity, and good feelings make for good communication: in this sense, dialect is positive. In the face of outsiders, dialect can be used as a protective wall. West Indian teenagers, one group who feel alienated from mainstream society, have created their own brand of Creole which serves them as a secret language.

Dialect can also work in a negative way. It is sometimes quite difficult to decode the combination of accent, intonation, vocabulary and grammar that make up an unfamiliar regional dialect. If you are a dialect-speaker yourself you may well have felt frustrated at not being able to make yourself understood. A countryman at the Worcester Assizes was talking about a field of mole-hills:

Judge: What are these oonty-toomps you keep mentioning?
Witness: What be oonty-toomps? They be the toomps the oonts make.
Judge: But what are oonts?
Witness: Why, them as make the toomps.

Many West Indian children felt this frustration when their parents brought them to Britain in the sixties: they thought they were speaking English, but their English teachers could hardly follow them. There is a further point: despite a lot of interest in regional dialects and deliberate attempts to preserve them, many people regard them (quite wrongly) as sub-standard forms of English. Dialects are spoken mainly by working-class people, so they are badges of working-class identity; they can and do trigger off social snobbery in people who regard themselves a cut above the working-class. When dialects affect people's percep-tions of their users like this, interpersonal communication can lead to all kinds of misjudgements and misunderstandings.

See also: Accent, Class, Language, Perception.
Further reading
A. Hughes and P. Trudgill, *English Accents and Dialects*, Edward Arnold, 1979.
P. Wright, *The Language of British Industry*, Macmillan, 1974.

EFFECT

All messages produce some kind of reaction, however small, from the people who receive them, and influence their thinking and behaviour. Messages also have an influence on the people that produce them.

Effects are related to purposes in many communication situations. By sending out signals we can inform, instruct, persuade, entertain, cooperate with, and befriend other people and do much more. At an interpersonal level much of what we say and write is designed to affect the thinking and behaviour of others. These effects may be quite small, like persuading your parents to let you stay out late; or very important, as when you pluck up courage to say that you want to break off a relationship. These examples suggest that the sender of the message has a purpose which she or he hopes to achieve by producing an effect on the receiver.

However, if we look more closely at the sender's motivation we need to ask whether the sender is acting solely for the benefit of the receiver, or only for the benefit of the sender, or for the benefit of both. If the communication benefits the sender, then we can say that it has an effect on the sender. A boy might want to break with his girlfriend for his own satisfaction (he has found someone else) but equally he may see that since they do not really get on, it would also be in her interests to separate. People who write books learn from the experience and gain financial reward and can only guess at the effects the books have on the readers. So we find that senders' purposes are a mixture of wanting to achieve effects on the receivers and on themselves. Moreover, the receiver may have strong motivation for seeking out and paying attention to certain communication signals. By attending to other people's signals, we can learn, acquire new attitudes, perform tasks, laugh, cry, and influence the sender. A good listener knows she or he is having a beneficial effect on the speaker. It is only because readers want to go out and buy books that writers can make money. We can send out or attend to signals equally actively, and achieve effects on either the sender or receiver or both. This inter-relationship of effects is shown in Figure 15 where sender and

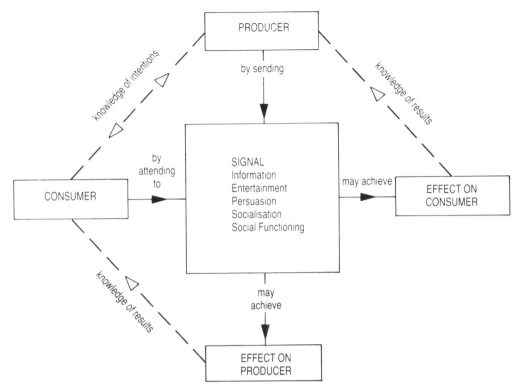

Figure 15 Purposes and effects model (after Adams)

receiver are labelled Producer and Consumer respectively, to emphasise their active roles.

The question of mass media effects has been the subject of much research. Advertisers and broadcasters have developed techniques to discover what consumers want and what effects have been achieved: they include market research, opinion polls and surveys of behaviour. Academics, disturbed by the possible corrupting effects of the all-persuasive mass media, and especially television, have studied both short- and long-term effects.

The earliest view of the part played by the mass media in society used the idea of the hypodermic syringe. Mass media were seen as simply injecting the patient (the public) with doses of bad behaviour. The more people were ex-posed to crime films, the more the crime rate was supposed to rise. But pre-war studies in America found little causal connection between film-going and delinquency. The hypodermic-syringe-effects model, which proved hard to support with evidence, gave little credit to people for any kind of critical response or any other sources of information. They were supposed to be isolated, passive and totally vulnerable.

Not surprisingly, this view of media effects was soon to be challenged. According to Katz and Lazarsfield (*Personal Influence*) the effects of mass communication take quite a different route. Ideas and attitudes are said 'to flow *from* radio and print *to* opinion leaders and *from them* to the less active sections of the population' (p. 32).

Katz and Lazarsfield's ideas led to

further research into the reasons why people, and not only the so-called opinion leaders, attended to the mass media. The answer appeared to be that they had various psychological needs which had to be satisfied. For example, some people admit to watching *Coronation Street* because they are lonely and need companionship. This uses-and-gratifications theory assumes that people know what they need and select what they think will satisfy their needs. People, in other words, are free agents and not mindless victims of the media.

However, the very latest research has been coming to the conclusion that the media, *in the long term*, do have strong influence after all. Many writers now see that the media do gradually shape our view of the world for us through their imagery. To take an example, David Glover argues that women's magazines mould and reinforce women's views of themselves and their place in society (p. 31). Similarly, men's magazines mould and reinforce men's views of themselves. Cultural effects theory, of which this is an instance, suggests that media effects depend on both the images projected and the cultural background of the audience. When David Morley researched into the reception of *Nationwide*, the BBC TV current affairs programme, he found that groups of bank managers accepted the content of the programme, though they didn't like the style, while groups of shop-stewards liked the style but criticized the assumptions behind *what* was being said. Young blacks found the programme boring because it seemed to be about a foreign world of middle class shoppers and businessmen.

See also: Audience, Mass communication, Medium/Media, Purpose.
Further reading
D. Glover, *The Sociology of the Mass Media*, Causeway, 1984, Ch. 1.
G. Dyer, *Advertising as Communication*, Methuen, 1982, Ch. 4.

EMOTION

An emotion is any experience of strong feeling, usually accompanied by physical changes in the circulation of the blood, breathing, sweating, blink-rate, etc. and is also often accompanied by intense and impulsive actions.

So the emotion of anger might include a rush of blood to the head, heavier breathing, perspiring, the clenching of the fists and grinding of the teeth, giving way to shouting, stamping, hitting out or throwing things. An emotion, then, describes an intense state of that inward arousal, which probably accompanies all human behaviour. Emotions relate to actions in the following ways:

1   When we perceive a danger, we are motivated to escape, and with that motivation comes the feeling of fear.
2   We can act first in order to arouse a feeling we like, like diving into a swimming-pool on a hot summer's day because we know we are going to enjoy the experience.
3   Emotions, on the other hand, can produce actions. We feel miserable so we curl up in a corner and mope. Emotions can be a very great stimulus to action – witness the many social reformers who have been fired by righteous indignation! On a more personal level, you know that a degree of anxiety helps you get your homework done and perform better in exams.

Tony Lake has a helpful way of describing the functions of our feelings. He says that each person has so many resources to call upon, either bodily (strength, agility, etc.), behavioural (feelings, memory, skills, intelligence) or social (other people). Now the feelings act as a kind of FT share index, measuring the total value of our resources at any one moment. So if the value seems to be falling, then we experience negative feelings like pain, fear, anger, frustration, inferiority, misery, and so on. But when the value of our resources seems to be going up, we experience positive feelings of pleasure, even excitement, when we discover that our love for another is returned.

Our feelings and emotions are an integral part of interpersonal communication: they influence what we say and how we say it. An emotion of disgust would make you choose strong words – 'How could you be so horribly revolting! Put it outside, for God's sake!' And the emphasis and intonation would be exaggerated too (see PARALANGUAGE). At the same time, your emotion of disgust would encode itself in all kinds of body language like wrinkling up your nose, turning away your head, and so forth.

Communication is essentially about the sharing of meaning. It is worth remembering that a lot of meaning is in fact feeling, and it is feelings that strengthen or destroy our relationships with others. For instance, somebody who treats you in an off-handed way may not actually say very much which is openly contemptuous, but you sense the hostility and have got the message: 'I don't like you'. As far as you are concerned, that is the meaning (though that may not have been the intended meaning at all). Creating human relationships means sharing our feelings, which means expressing them through all our means of communication. This is not so easy as it might seem at first sight, since people have all sorts of inhibitions that prevent them from confessing their needs and revealing the more guilt-ridden chapters of their experience. It is often quite difficult for us to express sympathy, to find the right words, the right touch. And yet sympathy allows us the pleasant sensation of feeling concern for others. More important than sympathy is *empathy* (see EMPATHY), which means trying to feel your way into somebody else's consciousness and perceiving and experiencing the world from that person's point of view. It is, in Tony Lake's phrase, 'to take our own needs into another person's inner world to be shared and met.'

See also: Empathy, Non-verbal communication, Paralanguage, Perception.
Further reading
T. Lake: *Relationships* Michael Joseph, 1981.

EMPATHY

Empathy is the ability to feel as other people do, by imaginatively entering their minds and seeing the world from their point of view. This is not quite the same as sympathy.

To sympathise is to feel for somebody, usually to feel sorry for somebody in trouble. To empathise is to go one step further and feel just as the other person does. Empathy is a special kind of perception which helps us to attune ourselves to others and so communicate with greater sensitivity.

Myers and Myers stress the importance of *empathetic* listening, which means listening to others with a genuine concern for their feelings and problems. 'It is listening to a person without passing judgement on what is being said, and mirroring back what has been said to indicate that you understood what feelings the speaker was putting across.' (p. 173). By not judging, and by showing that you sympathise with the other person's feelings, you are being supportive rather than threatening. As a result, the speaker will feel able to talk more freely.

Carl Rogers, the American psychologist, suggests that we can improve our empathy when in an argument by ruling that each person may only speak for himself after having 'mirrored' back the other person's ideas and feelings to that person's satisfaction.

Imaginative people – for instance, novelists, and playwrights, with the task of creating a whole spectrum of different characters (think of Dickens and Shakespeare) – use the power of empathy: so do people working in the caring professions, like psychotherapists, social workers, teachers and nurses.

If you are egocentric (concerned exclusively with yourself), then empathy will come hard, since it implies a genuine interest in the way others experience pain, frustration and disappointment as well as relief and joy.

See also: Perception, Listening.
Further reading
G. Myers and M. Myers, *Dynamics of Human Communication*, McGraw-Hill, third edition 1980, Ch. 7.

ENCODER/ENCODING

A device, either physiological or technical, which transforms a message from a source into a suitable form (code) to be transmitted to a receiver who then decodes it.

The code in which the message is expressed for communication purposes is a system of signs and rules that govern the way the signs are combined to produce meanings. It may be language (speech or writing), body-language, American Sign Language, or some code like Morse, that requires an electrical or physical channel. Communication will only take place effectively if the communicator encodes the message in a code which the receiver is expected to share: two English people chatting in English, two CB radio-buffs expert in their CB code, two West Indians speaking Creole dialect, and so forth.

In the case of interpersonal communication, the encoder is part of the brain (the cortex) that controls the vocal mechanisms, hand and wrist muscles and other muscles to transform impulses and feelings into utterances, gestures and writing. So when Alex has an impulse to greet Barbara, that part of his brain called the Speech Centre encodes the signal in a nerve code so that it is able to travel from the brain to the muscles that control the speech organs. This nerve code consists of short bursts of electro-chemical energy that shoot along the nerve fibres at a fixed speed of about 400 feet per second. Each impulse lasts only one-thousandth of a second. However, the frequency of the impulses does vary, depending on the urgency of the signal. Alex's brain sends a complex pattern of nerve signals to the muscles controlling the lungs and diaphragm, the vocal cords, the mouth, tongue and other speech organs, which together produce vibrations in the air which Barbara has no difficulty in decoding as 'Hello, Babs.'

When you talk to yourself, plan a trip in your head, or daydream, the encoding process is still going on, even though you have no intention of communicating with anybody else. You can easily verify this by listening to yourself thinking or singing silently. The brain is able to encode and decode without being stimulated to activate the voice and the ears.

Those means of communication that depend on technology also encode messages in a variety of ways, the most widespread making use of electricity. Let's look briefly at three 'electric' media in historical sequence:

1 The electric telegraph used to encode messages in the digital code of Morse, transmitting long and short pulses of electricity down a wire by means of a switch. Electric currents were made to activate bells, buzzers or needles on a dial to enable the person at the other end (the next station on the nineteenth-century railways, where it was widely used) to decode the message.

2 The telephone, patented by Bell in 1877, used – and still uses – a carbon microphone as an encoding device. Your voice causes a diaphragm in the mouthpiece to vibrate. These vibrations in turn compress to varying degrees a cell of carbon granules. The electric current that flows through the cell then varies with the variations of pressure and is *modulated*. So the pattern of sound waves is encoded in a pattern of electrical waves. These are decoded back into sound waves at the end by an electromagnet and diaphragm in the earpiece. See Figure 16.

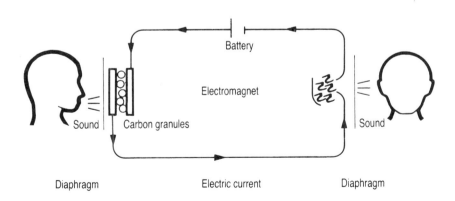

Figure 16 Model of telephone circuit

3 The encoding process in television is highly complex. Putting it at its simplest, the message that the TV camera transmits has been largely determined in the studio or an outside location. But before the action in the studio or football stadium can appear on your screen, the light waves are converted or encoded into varying electric current (the microphones are encoding sound waves into variations in electric current at the same time). These electric signals are not suitable for transmission over long distances and have to be amplified and then used to modify (or modulate) constant electromagnetic waves which are transmitted by aerial. The radio-wave signals are picked up by your receiver which decodes them back into electric current which is, in turn, decoded into light and sound waves to produce the picture on the screen and the sound accompaniment.

What underlies all these encoding processes is the fact that information cannot be transmitted in its original form. It has to be reconstructed in a different form to make use of the available channels. Sound waves are useful channels – but not for the dumb who cannot encode their thoughts in speech. Light waves are a useful channel too, but would not be used for encoding messages for the blind, who cannot receive visual information from the outside world. Electromagnetic carrier waves are a useful channel, but not if there are no radio transmitters to break down speech and music into modulated patterns, and no radio receivers to decode them.

See also: Carrier, Channel, Code, Decoder, Signal.
Further reading
How it works: Television (Ladybird Books).
Open University, *Communication: Living with Technology* Foundation Course T101 Block 2.

EXTRAPERSONAL COMMUNICATION

Extrapersonal communication is communication with the non-human. It includes communication with animals (though not between animals) and communication with 'intelligent machines' like computers. It would also include communication in the occult areas of experience like telepathy and spiritualism, as well as attempts to send signals to extra-terrestrial beings. The AEB 'A'-level syllabus confines itself, however, to people communicating with machines.

Communicating with animals

Anybody who has owned a pet knows how far it is possible to communicate with animals. Compared with dogs, cats are fairly unresponsive, and goldfish extremely so. But dogs, dolphins and chimpanzees do respond readily to human signals and are capable of being trained. Nor is the communication all one-way. Far from it. Dogs will stand by the door, signifying that they want you to take them for a walk, and cats will persuade you to feed them by wrapping themselves round your ankles in a pointed way. Our cousins, the apes, are the most intelligent of animals, next to ourselves, and several attempts have been made in recent years to teach chimpanzees to communicate with people. Early efforts to make chimpanzees talk failed since their organs are not adapted for speech. An American couple, the Gardners, adopted a young female chimpanzee and taught her American Sign Language. (See CODE.) After three years, Washoe mastered 87 signs and was using some of them in combinations, such as 'Roger tickle' ('Please, Roger, tickle me') or 'tickle Washoe', or 'comb black' (the black comb). The examples of Washoe and later lovingly-trained chimpanzees suggest that some animals, at least, can learn the basic symbolism of language and use, like young children, grammatical rules.

Communicating with the occult and telepathy

Communicating with spirits (spiritualism) is an area of experience where *medium* has another meaning from the usual one in Communication Studies. A medium is a person who is said to be sensitive to vibrations from an invisible world of disembodied spirits and able to communicate messages from the living to the dead, and vice versa. The codes used by the spirits are usually, if the reports are to be believed, speech and table-rapping. Many people, of course, doubt the existence of communicating spirits at all. In the case of telepathy (the communication of ideas by other than physical means), there is some well-tested evidence that it happens (see William McDougall, *Extra-sensory Perception*) though no one knows how. The medium and channel are in doubt,

and the whole phenomenon is a mysterious aspect of interpersonal communication.

Communicating with extra-terrestrial beings

Numbers of scientists now believe in the possibility of there being intelligent beings on planets in other galaxies where the physical conditions might be similar to ours. Already messages have been fired into space on rockets, or transmitted by radio, but so far there has been no response from the universe. Even supposing there were intelligent forms of life elsewhere in the cosmos, the likelihood of their recognising human signals and decoding them correctly would be very slight indeed. In 1973, Carl Sagan and Frank Drake of Cornell University, designed a plaque with a diagrammatic drawing, and some basic information about the earth, its position and its human inhabitants. The drawing included a man and a woman; the man's hand is lifted in greeting. All this was sent on Pioneer 10 past the planet Jupiter into outer space. But consider all the assumptions that have had to be made about possible extra-terrestrials. Their sensory equipment will need to include sight, a human sense of 'top' and 'bottom', a sense of perspective. They would need to have gesture codes (to recognise the man's hand lifted in greeting) and graphic symbols like direction arrows. What this message, which has not yet, as far as we know, been received, does show is that successful communication depends on knowing the receivers' culture, the aggregate of all codes. See Figure 17.

A shows two typical earthlings, one with his hand raised in a gesture of greeting and friendship.

B is a sideways view of Pioneer 10,

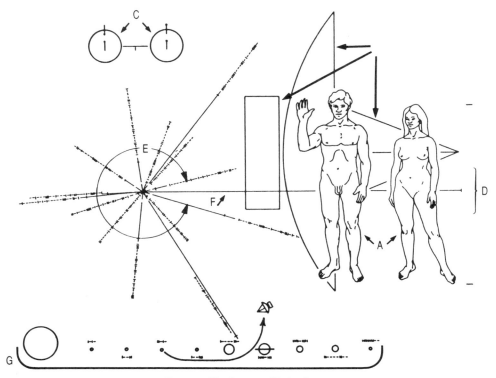

Figure 17 The Sagan and Drake plaque

scaled to show the height of the earthlings.

C represents the two states of the hydrogen atom (the most abundant element in the universe) as a unit of time (radio frequency) and distance (wavelength). As a hydrogen electron orbits the atom, it gives off a pulse of radiation with a wavelength of 21 cm. This is the basic unit of measure for the message.

D deliberately placed next to the woman, shows how the measure works. In the binary system, it is the symbol for eight. Multiplied by 21 cm, the binary symbol gives 168 cm or five and a half feet for the woman.

E with its starburst pattern, represents 14 specific pulsar stars in our galaxy. All are identifiable by the precise frequency (in binary terms) at which they give off radio signals.

F the 15th line, extends behind the earthlings to show the distance from the Earth to the centre of the galaxy.

G represents the solar system. It shows that Pioneer left from the third planet from the sun, swept past the fifth (Jupiter) and then turned away into interstellar space.

Communicating with machines

Communicating with machines is an everyday experience for most of us. If you ride a bicycle, drive a car or use a typewriter, you give instructions to a machine which responds to them auto-

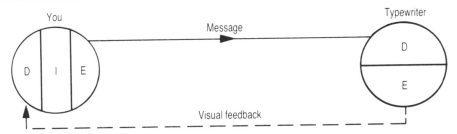

Figure 18 Communication with a typewriter

matically. Feedback from the machine is essential for you to control it successfully. We can adapt Osgood's interpersonal communication model to show what happens when you communicate with a typewriter (see Figure 18).

You think up your message, i.e. encode it in language. Whatever you type on the keyboard is reproduced on the paper. What the typewriter does is to decode the touches mechanically into printed characters. There is no interpretation. If you hit Daer Sir, the message is Daer Sir. However, spotting the mistake (through visual feedback) you can Tippex it out and retype the word correctly.

Communicating with a machine differs from communicating with another person in the following respects:

1 Unlike a person, a machine is not self-motivated. Even an automatic pilot in an aircraft or a ship has to be switched on.

2 Because a machine has no will of its own, and no temperament, you can predict the effect of your communication with 100 per cent accuracy (always supposing the

machine is in working order). You turn the steering wheel to the left, and the car turns to the left.

3 The only relationship you can have with a machine is one of controller and controlled. To control a machine you need feedback from the machine itself and from the environment. The boundary between you and the machine, where the interaction takes place, is known as the interface.

The computer is a special kind of machine, electronic, not mechanical, which has more human qualities than, say, a bicycle. Computers have to be approached through language (voice or keyboard inputs), they have memories, they hold dialogues with the computer-user through printed or spoken outputs. Their programs are sometimes so clever that people can be deceived into believing they are communicating with a person directly and not a piece of software (the Turing Test).

See also: Code, Computer, Interface, Machine intelligence.

EYE-CONTACT

Eye contact is the meeting of your eyes with somebody else's, and if this eye contact (EC) is prolonged, the term 'mutual gaze' applies.

The eyes are the most impressive part of the face, and apart from their basic function of helping us see the world about us, they enable us to react to other people and affect their behaviour in various ways. Our eyes, in short, speak volumes.

Eyes can convey a whole range of messages, in conjunction with the facial expressions. You can intimidate somebody by staring hard and coldly. At the other extreme you may exchange soft, caressing looks with somebody you are fond of. The mutual gaze of lovers is what John Donne described in 'The Extasie':

Our eye beams twisted and did thread
Our eyes upon one double string

When you look into the other person's eyes, you are paying attention to them, but if you look past them, they will feel uncomfortable and probably turn round to see what you are looking at. In fact in ordinary conversations eye-contact (EC) and direction of gaze have an essential part to play. When two people are talking together they look each other in the eye intermittently.

Each person looks at the other 25–75 per cent of the time. The length of glances varies from 3 to 7 seconds, and the couple, particularly if they know and like each other, will maintain eye-contact for as much as half the interaction time.

It has been shown experimentally that people look nearly twice as much while listening as while speaking: their glances are longer and their away-glances are briefer. The reason for this is that the listener is eager to glean visual information to supplement what is heard. A great deal can be learned from facial gestures, particularly from the eyes, eyebrows and mouth.

Similar rules govern the way we gaze when we embark on, sustain and end conversations. It is normal for person A to avert his gaze just before addressing a second person, B. At the ends of sentences or phrases, A will look up briefly, and at the end of the utterance give B a longer look. Why does A look up at tactical moments in his discourse? He is looking for feedback; he wants to know whether B is attending, whether she is still interested, and whether his words have had the hoped-for (or any

other) effects on her. At the same time A is looking for permission to continue, which B normally grants through head nods, murmurs or grunts. A's final glance signals to B that it is now her turn to speak. B will then go through a similar sequence. People who do not keep to the normal pattern may be seen as either overbearing or too forbearing.

Every eye contact and eye avoidance, in short, helps to shape and influence conversation, serving as an important second channel for feedback. This channel becomes even more important if one of the speakers has to lip-read.

As with other parts of non-verbal behaviour, gazing habits differ from culture to culture. English people may be troubled by the long looks they get from Italians, but Italians may find our reserve equally off-putting. In the multi-cultural classroom different gazing habits can create some problems. It is perfectly usual for West Indian children to avert their eyes when being told off by an adult. Their parents expect them to do it. But English teachers expect children to look them in the face when being reprimanded so they may get the impression that the West Indian child is insolent when he looks away.

The impression you make on others has much to do with the way you use your eyes. If you make a lot of eye contact, then the chances are others will think of you as a friendly, self-possessed, outgoing sort of person. Conversely, if you do not use much eye contact, through shyness, people may think you cold, evasive and indifferent – which you may not in fact be.

See also: Non-verbal communication.
Further reading
D. Morris, *Manwatching*, Triad Panther, 1978, pp. 71–6.
M. Argyle, *The Psychology of Interpersonal Behaviour*, Penguin, third edition 1978, Ch. 4.

FACIAL EXPRESSION

'Facial expression' refers to the way the face is able to express emotions, either in repose or through movement. Your face is the most communicative part of your whole person. And your eyes are the most expressive part of your face, which is why we have devoted a separate section to eye contact.

You can think of the face communicating information on three different timescales. There is what we might call the permanent face with its unchanging, or slowly-changing features, which we tend to interpret according to certain *stereotypes*. We think of people with high foreheads as intelligent, thick-lipped people as sensual and lazy, people with protruding eyes as excitable. With older people typical expressions like smiles and sneers become ingrained, so that a smiling face may mean a friendly, cheerful, easy-going character, while a tense face may well signify determined, aggressive or quick-tempered people.

Secondly, the face expresses emotions, which are patterns of expression which take a little time to develop. Even 'sudden' anger has to build up, the muscle tension increases, the blood

flows to the head, the eyes begin to bulge – and so on. Faces encode our feelings, the chief of which are contentment, surprise, fear, sadness, anger, disgust, contempt and interest. There is a typical facial expression (a sign) for every one of them. Thayer and Schiff (1969) proved what cartoonists have taken for granted for years, that people can quite easily interpret emotions from diagrammatic faces where only the eyebrows and the mouth vary. Looking at the faces in Figure 19, and the interpretations, would you agree?

Other research has shown that human-beings the world over produce the same facial expressions for the six emotions of happiness, sadness, surprise, fear, anger and disgust.

Ekman and Friesen (1971) discovered, for example, that Neolithic New Guinea tribesmen could correctly identify American facial expressions for the basic emotions.

The above evidence is interesting because it shows that not all our non-verbal codes are learned, and therefore subject to cultural variation. Some facial expressions, certain movements like the rapid lift of the eyebrows to

| Neutral | Happy | Sad | Angry | Fiendish | Angry | Sad | Happy/sheepish | Sad |

Figure 19 Test faces used by Thayer and Schiff with majority interpretations

signal alarm, or the eyebrow flash and dilation of pupils indicating sexual attraction, do appear to be inborn and universal.

Finally, your face will flash signals to accompany what you say, providing continuous feedback to your partner. Facial movements, often very rapid, are controlled by the verbal message. Such movements as smiles, frowns, nods, raised eyebrows all help to influence the course of the conversation. Your face, along with all your paralanguage, will reveal your attitude towards your part-ner as well as towards the topic you are discussing.

See also: Non-verbal communication, Feedback, Paralanguage, Stereotype.
Further reading
D. Morris, *Manwatching*, Triad Panther, 1978.
M. Argyle, *Bodily Communication*, Methuen, 1975.

FEEDBACK

'Feedback' is a term taken from cybernetics, a branch of engineering concerned with self-regulating systems. In its simplest form, feedback is a self-stabilising control system such as the Watt steam governor which regulates the speed of a steam engine or a thermostat, which controls the temperature of a room or an oven. In the communication process, feedback refers to a particular kind of response from the receiver, which gives the communi-cator some idea of how the message is being received so that he or she can modify the way in which the message is being produced.

In an engineering situation, feedback has three characteristics:

1 It responds to a situation.
2 It can modify the circumstances that cause the situation.
3 It may be either negative or positive.

Refer to Figure 20, which you have already seen as Figure 13. If the operation modifies the situation in such a way that output is prevented or reduced, this is known as *negative feedback*. In the thermostat, when the required temperature is reached, an

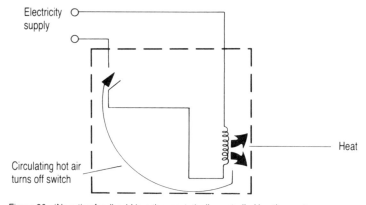

Figure 20 'Negative feedback' in a thermostatically-controlled heating system

electrical contact is broken, which switches off the heater. The temperature is not permitted to exceed a certain fixed value.

If the operation causes output to increase, this is known as *positive feedback*. If positive feedback is unchecked it can lead the system to run out of control. You probably know that if you phone in to a radio station you must turn off your radio. Otherwise the telephone picks up the sound and feeds it back to the radio station where it adds to the signal being broadcast. The signal can grow and grow until it leads to a high-pitched whine known as 'howl-round'. Controlled positive feedback is used in transistor radio circuits to amplify electrical signals.

Intrapersonal and interpersonal feedback

When you are chatting to somebody you can see yourself and hear your own voice. This helps you choose your words carefully, modulate the pitch of your voice and stop yourself from shouting. The feedback is negative if it is helping you to reduce output – that is, to lower your voice, refrain from swearing, or keep your hands still.

At the same time, your companion hears you and may react to what you are saying with head-nods, smiles, wide eyes, leaning forward. All this information about the effect of your words reaches you before it is your partner's turn to reply. It is a form of simultaneous two-way communication. This would be positive feedback if you took notice and felt encouraged to go on with your story, continue to be friendly, perhaps even increase the jokes, wave your arms to emphasise a point, laugh and move your body to a more relaxed and open position. However, if your partner frowns, looks upset and turns away with tense body movements, such negative feedback might lead you to tread more carefully or change to some other topic of conversation. In an argument, if negative feedback is ignored, signs of distress can turn into positive feedback leading to shouting and frantic gesticulating which may get out of control.

Strictly speaking, negative feedback does not imply 'bad', nor positive feedback 'good'. Negative feedback indicates that you should do less of what you are doing or change to something else. Positive feedback encourages you to increase what you are doing and this

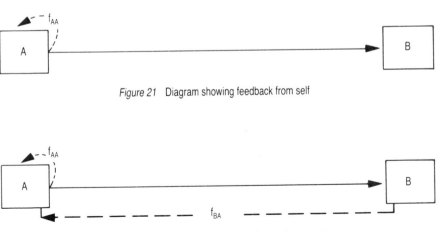

Figure 21 Diagram showing feedback from self

Figure 22 Diagram showing feedback from self and partner

can go out of control (over-excitement at a party, fighting or having a row). If you are crying, feedback from those around may cause you to dry your eyes and put on a brave face (if feedback is negative) or weep unashamedly (if feedback is positive).

The essential function of feedback is to help people check on the effect of what they are saying or doing. In addition, if you are responsive to feedback and encourage it ('Am I saying the right thing? Do you understand?'), then you help the other person to feel involved in what you are trying to communicate.

Remember, the word feedback does not apply to just any response. Consider this dialogue:

Me: Excuse me, how do I get to the Youth Centre?
You: Go straight down there and take the second road on the left, you can't miss it.

Here the answer to my question is a straight response, not feedback. I need some practical information. I'm not particularly interested in your reaction to my question, as long as you can tell me what I need to know. Your verbal answer followed my question, it didn't stop me in mid-sentence or cause me to raise my voice. Your reply does not indicate that I should change the way I am speaking. Generally speaking, interpersonal communication contains a mixture of an ordinary two-way flow of ideas and feedback. Some people are more sensitive or open to the feedback.

Feedback and the mass media

Feedback works rather differently for the mass media. It cannot be simultaneous. You can only react to a newspaper once it has been printed and distributed. You can switch off your TV set if you disapprove of a programme, or try to ring the producer, but neither response can alter the programme (which is often pre-recorded anyway) as it goes out over the air. So we have to speak about delayed feedback. Over weeks and months, newspapers study their circulation figures, and the IBA and BBC carry out detailed surveys to see how many people watch their programmes.

Some surveys consist of questionnaires distributed to representative samples of the population. Other volunteers have a device attached to their television set which keeps a record of whenever the set was on. Yet others keep a regular tally of the programmes they watch and their comments. Viewing figures, and the 'top ten' are published in trade magazines. Readers' letter-columns in the papers and 'access' programmes like Channel 4's *Right to Reply* also provide the communicators with audience reactions. All this information can be taken into account when planning future output.

Feedback is generally accepted as making a communication process more efficient. Efficiency is important for mass media like newspapers and commercial television, dependent on advertising, that have to pay their way. The BBC has to justify its licence fee. All the time it must be remembered that mass communication is essentially one-way and that any arrangements for gathering audience response (feedback loops) exist to make that output as effective as possible. Feedback that suggests changes that are not seen by the programme-makers as beneficial is likely to be ignored (see BIAS).

See also: Access, Bias, Cybernetics, Eye-contact, Mass communication.

GATEKEEPER

'Gatekeeper' is a term coined by D. M. White to designate the role played by those who decide the content of any mass-medium channel and how it should be presented. In practice, these are the editors and sub-editors of newspapers, the producers of TV and radio programmes. They are gatekeepers in the sense that they 'open the gate' to some of the information and opinions flowing into their channel, and 'close the gate' to the rest and so present a highly selective view of reality.

The role of gatekeeper has been much discussed in connection with producing the news. News is seen to flow from events which are reported by journalists and members of the public to editorial offices, where the flow is interrupted and cut down in volume by professional copy-tasters and editors and channelled into the required format, a newspaper or a news broadcast. It then reaches the public, who in turn act as gatekeepers, passing on some items by word of mouth. Dennis MacShane's model of the news production line divides the process into three stages: the first of news gathering, the second of selecting the news and the third of treating it. Most of the gatekeeping is done at the third stage, and it is not very reassuring to see that at five separate points along the line a story can be altered without the knowledge of the previous person in the chain. (See D. MacShane, *Using the Media*.)

It remains to ask what makes a copy-taster pass one news story and 'spike' another (in editorial offices there is an actual spike for unwanted stories) and what guides a sub-editor when rewriting a story that *has* been selected.

As far as selection goes, it is not just the individual taste of the gatekeeper, though personal views will have some influence in the choice. The criteria that guide decisions are what have come to be called 'news values'. In other words, what makes a good story. Many attempts have been made to list news values. MacShane's rule of thumb of newsworthiness is a useful start: a story should involve conflict, hardship, danger to the community, unusualness (oddity, novelty), scandal and individualism. From your own reading of national newspapers you will find that lead stories tend to be about politics, economics and foreign affairs in the quality papers and politics, celebrities, and human excesses like murder, rape and satanism in the tabloids. Issues tend to be personalised, not the National Union of Mineworkers versus the Coal Board but Scargill *v* MacGregor. Certain nations and groups of people are more newsworthy than others. Many British newspapers carry news about America but little about China. The Royal Family, media stars, the wealthy and the criminal get more attention than most. And since the tabloid papers see their main task as one of entertaining their readers, they choose anything sensational, glamorous, amusing, shocking. . .

Sub-editors have to make the most of the stories passed on to them and find an angle that will reflect their news values. Then they rewrite the stories in the house-style, the kind of English that the paper's readers have come to expect, and point up the interest with bold headlines, eye-catching photographs and attractive layout.

At the same time, the news processors have to bear in mind the paper's political bias, the laws of libel, the Official Secrets Acts and even constraints of taste.

It is worth adding that gatekeeping is only one function of media editors. In practice, they actively determine what events are to be covered; they commission stories; they pay their journalists to investigate possible scandals. In short, they set the agenda for what is to appear in newspapers and broadcasts.

See also: Agenda-setting, Bias, News values; Appendix (Westley and Maclean mass communication model).
Further reading
D. MacShane, *Using the Media*, Pluto Press, 1979, Ch. 4.
T. O'Sullivan et al., *Key Concepts in Communication*, Methuen, 1983, pp. 154–5.
D. McQuail and S. Windahl, *Communication Models*, Longman, 1981, pp. 100–107.

ENRE

Genre is a type of media production. Applied to literature, genres would include, broadly, such types of writing as novels, short stories, essays, plays and poetry, as well as more specific types of story such as historical romances and spy-thrillers. Among radio and television genres may be counted soap operas, police series and sitcoms (situation comedies).

When, in our study of the mass media, we look at the content of the messages being transmitted, we also need to consider the form in which they are communicated, and this means paying attention to genres. The (incomplete) list below will give you some idea of the variety of genres broadcast in the course of one evening's television:

Genre	Programme title
Soap opera	*Dallas, Eastenders*
Natural history	*Osprey Watch*
Comedy	*No Place Like Home*
Police Series	*Juliet Bravo, The Bill, The Streets of San Francisco*
Rock roadshow	*No Limits*
Quiz	*Food and Drink Summer Quiz*
Documentary	*Brass Tacks (Chopsticks, Bull-dozers and Newcastle Brown)*
Thriller	*Build My Gallows High*
News magazine	*Newsnight*
Sitcom	*Bewitched*

What is it that marks off one genre from another? There is no simple answer, but in many cases a genre has an easily recognisable content and setting: cowboys on horseback, clapboard houses, arid mountains, Indians on the skyline immediately evoke the Western, whilst tough-looking men studying dossiers, lighting cigarettes in parked cars, or driving furiously after criminals through the backstreets to a shootout in a cul-de-sac are the familiar stuff of the police series genre. But genres may also be distinguished by style. The cartoon film is a case in point. There, animation is so different from film acting as a method of representation, that style overrules content. We can refer to Hanna and Barbera'a *The Flintstones* as cartoon comedy, whereas the episodes have a lot in common with sitcoms.

As readers and TV viewers, our

knowledge of genres arouses precise expectations. When we sit down to read a 'whodunit', we look forward to being presented with a murder, a list of suspects, a trail of clues and decoys, all amounting to a challenge to pit our wits against the author's to solve the problem before the answer is revealed. *The Good Life*, with Felicity Kendall and Richard Briers, was a popular sitcom about a young couple trying to be self-sufficient, farming a suburban garden. Things often went wrong for them, but they never had to sell up (after a poor potato crop) because they couldn't afford to pay the mortgage. Realism of that kind would have been foreign to sitcom conventions.

All the same, a study of genre may show how practitioners will sometimes develop its potential until the original framework has been broken almost beyond recognition. In the case of the English novel, how much has James Joyce's twentieth-century *Ulysses* in common with Daniel Defoe's eighteenth-century *Moll Flanders*? Do they really belong to the same genre? Or again, take the Western film, a more recent genre than the novel. According to Jon Tuska, who claims to have seen 8000 of them, the Western has hardly changed at all in subject matter from the early days of *The Great Train Robbery* (1903) to *Pat Garrett and Billy the Kid* seventy years later. The classic plot is crime, pursuit and retribution. Nevertheless, he does admit there have been some radical changes in ideology and style, especially after the Second World War. In films like *Broken Arrow*, where James Stewart marries an Apache squaw and helps the Indians to defend themselves against perfidious white men, the American conscience begins to be heard. Indians are no longer yelping savages misguidedly holding up the advance of progress and civilisation, but a tragic minority culture destroyed by more ruthless forces. The simple morality of cowboy good, Indian bad, no longer applies. Not only that, but all moral certainties crumble in Sam Peckinpah's bloodthirsty films without heroes (e.g. *The Wild Bunch*). While in Sergio Leone's Spaghetti Western (another genre!) *A Fistful of Dollars*, Clint Eastwood, coolly chewing his cheroot, guns down large numbers of people. The cowboy hats and six-shooters have not changed, but the moral climate certainly has, and that says something about both the directors of such violent films and the audiences who enjoy watching them.

It remains to be said that genres have a powerful influence on the production of works of art and entertainment. Some film companies and some film directors have specialised in single genres, e.g. MGM in musicals and Alfred Hitchcock in thrillers. Many writers specialise in science fiction or historical romances. Existing genres with their familiar conventions provide ready-made moulds in which new writers and artists feel challenged or constrained to cast their own creative ideas. In communication terms we can say genres are highly redundant, because highly predictable.

See also: Convention, Redundancy.

GESTURE

A gesture is an action that communicates some meaning, deliberately or unconsciously, to the person who sees it.

This may be a deliberate hand-signal, such as a crooked finger to beckon somebody to approach; or it may be involuntary, like head-scratching, the main purpose of which is to gain relief, but which may also communicate perplexity or nervousness. In practice we decode involuntary or incidental gestures just as readily as deliberate ones. Indeed, incidental gestures are *more* revealing because unconscious and therefore uncensored.

We can also gesture with our heads, tongues, shoulders, arms, legs and feet – virtually any part of the body – though our hands are most versatile at gesticulation.

Most of our non-verbal signalling is done through facial movements. But we do use our hands to punctuate our talk in various ways. These particularly expressive gestures are called 'batons'. When you watch a political speaker in full flow you will notice the warning 'baton' as he raises his forefinger, the clenched fist as he expresses determination and the hand-chop as he polishes off the opposition. We all have our own favourite baton gestures, like the characters in Dickens's novels. Here is Mr Podsnap in *Our Mutual Friend*: 'Mr Podsnap had even acquired a peculiar flourish of his right arm in often clearing the world of its most difficult problems, by sweeping them behind (and consequently sheer away) with those words and a flushed face.'

Desmond Morris, who has classified gestures in *Manwatching*, mentions mimic gestures, which are imitations of, or mimic a person, object or action – for example, the angler mimics the size of the one that got away. There are also a good many symbolic gestures, like screwing your index finger against your temple when you believe someone has 'a screw loose'. Or you may keep your figures crossed for some scheme of your own, or to wish somebody else good luck. This protective cross goes back to Christian practice of invoking God's aid against evil. And there is a wealth of rude gestures too.

Technical gestures

Just as there are special registers of language in different professions and occupations, so there are special technical gestures used in many of these activities. TV studio managers, for instance, communicate with their performers through a set of simple signs:

(i) Manager holds forearm erect = Get ready to speak.
(ii) Manager lowers forearm to point at speaker = Begin.
(iii) Manager rotates forearm rapidly, like demented clock-hands = Not much time left.
(iv) Manager draws out hands in front of his chest = Stretch it.
(v) Slashes hand across throat = Cut! Stop at once.

This is a single code for a limited purpose. Much more elaborate gestural codes have been invented, like the American Sign Language for the deaf, for general communication purposes.

Many gestures are used simply, but there are compound gestures which are made up from many separate movements. Laughing is a case in point. Any of up to twelve different things may happen when you laugh: you utter a hooting or barking sound, your mouth opens wide, you throw your head back, you close your eyes, etc.

Gestures may help when you are abroad and do not know the language, but even in Western Europe only some of our British gestures are understood. The Germans clutch their thumbs for good luck, the equivalent of our fingers-crossed gesture. The temple-screw mentioned above means something quite different in Holland: 'He or she is very intelligent'. The hitch-hiker's erect thumb might stop a car in France or Germany but would start a stream of abuse in Israel. The further afield you travel, the less likely you are to understand the gestures. The Japanese, for example, beckon by flapping their hand up and down, its palm facing down-wards (something like our 'go away' gesture). If they make a circle with thumb and forefinger they mean 'He or she is very rich' and a Japanese pointing to his or her nose means 'me'.

See also: Facial expression, Posture, Non-verbal communication.
Further reading
D. Morris: *Manwatching*, Triad Panther, 1978.
D. Morris: *Gestures*, Cape, 1979.

GROUP COMMUNICATION

Group communication is communication within groups of people and between groups of people.

It is usual to subdivide *groups* into *small groups*, like families, friends, working-parties, committees; and *large groups* like business organisations, colleges and hospitals. Here we look at small-group communications and refer you to ORGANISATIONS for communications within larger groups.

Individuals in a small group are still communicating face-to-face, but the larger number of participants exercises a special influence on everybody's behaviour. Many studies have been carried out to discover what makes small groups work efficiently, and since much of our work is done in planning-groups, committees and working-parties, the value of such knowledge is obvious.

Groups come into being when a number of people share a common goal which they know cannot be achieved by any one of them alone. No one student could run a student union branch: the work is too complex, the responsibilities are too great. Once a common goal, a reason for having a committee, has been established, the process continues. It has been neatly summarised as 'forming', 'storming', 'norming' and 'performing'. Storming is the period where people argue about how they see the committee's function and structure. People reveal their differences, their

personalities; some may be overbearing and even disruptive. The next stage is to establish rules for meetings and a special climate of discussion. Norms are set up, a norm specifying the kind of behaviour group members may expect from any other group members. Some groups, like academic committees, expect a businesslike atmosphere and formal language. The SU Entertainment Committee would probably develop different norms, where formality was out of place. Once norms are established the group develops pressures to ensure that the norms are respected. Now the group is beginning to perform.

Robert Bales (1955) studied the performance of small, initially leaderless discussion groups. He reached the following conclusions.

1 People did not participate to equal degrees. One or two members contributed much more than the others.

2 Active participants gave information and offered opinions.

3 The less active confined themselves to agreeing or disagreeing, or asking for information.

4 Group members distinguished between the man they *liked* best and the man they thought the *most influential*.

When observing group behaviour, it is usual to analyse each member's performance under three headings:

1 behaviour which helps to complete the tasks on the agenda;
2 behaviour which strengthens the group, by making people feel good and their contributions worthwhile;
3 behaviour which disrupts the group's work.

The *best-liked* man in Bales' study scored high under the second heading ('the socioemotional dimension'). He would typically be the kind of person who related well to others, offered encouragement, resolved difficulties, relieved tensions through humour. The *most influential* man scored high under the first heading, tackling the task in hand with suggestions and views and prompting others to make suggestions.

Most groups have formal roles, defined in their constitutions. The secretary of the SU executive has to prepare agendas, write minutes, deal with correspondence, etc., while the chairperson conducts the actual meetings. Much research has focused on the leadership role in group performance, and four distinct styles have been described.

The *autocratic* style: one member, usually the chairperson, holds the floor most of the time, imposing his or her will on the others, who resent being 'steam-rollered' and lose interest in issues where their suggestions are not welcomed. A fair amount of work, however, can be achieved.

The *laissez-faire* style: the group is without a leader, decisions may be taken but no one is deputed to carry them out, meetings may be fun but little is achieved.

The *democratic* style recognises that everyone has a contribution to make. Leaders are elected for a term or the leadership role rotates among all the members. A democratic group is one that takes the decision-making process very seriously. Where unanimity is impossible, a vote is taken.

A *collective*, on the other hand, will avoid leadership roles altogether and work as a team of equals, arriving at unanimity. This entails long group-discussions, but once decisions are taken, everybody feels committed to carry them out.

Observers use sociograms (diagrams showing who communicates with whom) and analysis grids on which to record the contributions each group member makes. Parallel to this, Harold Leavitt and others have shown experimentally how people perform in small group networks with respect to efficiency and their morale (see NETWORKS).

> **See also:** Organisations, Networks, Role.
> **Further reading**
> J. Gahagan, *Interpersonal and Group Behaviour*, Methuen, 1978, Ch. 6.
> R. Dimbleby and G. Burton, *More Than Words*, Methuen, 1985, Ch. 3.

IDEOLOGY

Ideology is a collection of ideas about what is important to any community or nation.

We all have, as individuals, our own beliefs about society, our own set of values and our own norms of behaviour. It is easy enough to say: I believe that my parents are old-fashioned, I think meat-eating is wrong, I would always trust a stranger. These are personal guidelines, the beginnings of a personal ideology. However, the term *ideology* is not used in quite this way. This is because it has its origins in Marxist thought, and Marx was interested in the conflict between social classes. According to him, your social class determines the way you think and feel. 'It is not the consciousness of men that determines their being, but on the contrary, their social being that determines their consciousness.' Under bourgeois capitalism, the ruling class communicates its way of thinking (its ideology) to the rest of society in various indirect ways, through an education system and through mass media which have a degree of independence. In the Soviet Union, where the dominant ideology is Marxism-Leninism, the state-controlled media and education system ensure that the groundwork principles of Soviet society are perpetuated.

Most of us in Britain are not aware of there being a dominant ideology. In fact, ideology consists of knowledge that is so taken for granted (it seems so natural) that we seldom bother to question it. For instance, it is generally assumed that the communist societies of Eastern Europe are so different from the democratic capitalist countries of Western Europe or the USA, that any kind of reconciliation is unlikely. The mass media, particularly the popular newspapers, play up the differences, where it would be quite possible to see similar trends and certainly a common need to avoid nuclear war.

What other ideas belong to our dominant ideology? Undoubtedly the symbolic and spiritual value of the monarchy is one. This takes the strangest forms, with hundreds of journalists deputed to report every last movement of the royal family. Another idea is that speculation in stocks and shares and foreign currencies, which from a moral point of view is gambling, is perfectly ethical. Details of the stock market are given daily in the mass media.

Yet another idea is that full employment is desirable. Both government and opposition parties agree in principle, and yet the computer revolution is driving us towards new patterns of work and leisure.

The dominant ideology, suggested above, is not accepted by everybody. Many women nowadays recognise that society is male-dominated, and they are working out, whether in their careers or in groups like the women's Peace Camp at Greenham Common, a feminist ideology. Other groups, like Friends of the Earth and CND, reject certain aspects of the dominant ideology. Travellers and gypsies find themselves, as always, in opposition to the dominant ideology.

See also: Socialisation.
Further reading
J. Hartley, *Understanding News*, Methuen, 1982, Ch. 3.

INFORMATION

Information is the meaning that a human expresses by (or extracts from) representations of facts and ideas, by means of the known conventions used. (*Guide to Concepts and Terms in Data Processing*. North Holland, 1971)

1 *Meaning* is a difficult term – but we do our thinking, planning and decision-making through the meanings stored in our memories. Moreover, meanings can exist only in the mind.

2 *Representations* are the words, numbers or pictures we use in order to

exchange or share meanings, in other words the *texts* that we send as *signals* (see also MEDIUM/MEDIA).

3 The *conventions* are the rules we use to combine signs into comprehensible codes, rules like word-order in sentences or reading a strip cartoon from left to right to make sense of it. (NB Some Japanese strip-cartoons read from right to left.)

In everyday language, information consists of observations about the world we live in. These observations, like facts in an encyclopedia, we expect to be accurate. The facts we read in our daily papers may be less accurate. Either way, we tend to measure information against the yardstick of 'truth'. Its great value is that it helps us to build up our picture of the world, understand our environment, and take sensible action to meet changing circumstances. Shannon and Weaver have defined information as 'anything that reduces the uncertainty in a situation'. This implies that opinions, theories and beliefs can be included along with observations and facts as information.

Broadly speaking, we look for information to help us understand our environment and carry out our tasks within it. So, for example, if you have been invited to stay with relatives in Ireland, you consult atlases, roadmaps, and the BR information service, to reduce the area of uncertainty round the proposed journey. Information from those and other sources would help you make up your mind how and when to travel.

The representation, transmission and storage of information has become an activity of vast proportions, so it is not surprising to find a body of theory to support it. This is *information theory*. It is concerned, in the first instance, with measuring information. Which of the following two messages is higher in its information content?

1 One, two, three, four, five, six, seven . . .
2 The tigers of wrath are wiser than the horses of instruction.

In the first message, you soon realise that this is a sequence of numbers rising by one. It is highly predictable. According to information theory, the first message is highly *redundant*, which means that it could be expressed much more briefly (e.g. Start counting!), whereas Blake's proverb expresses a thought in a highly compressed, symbolic way, where every word (with the exception of 'the') counts. And a message that is far from predictable and therefore high in information is said to be *entropic*. Redundancy, then, is part of the message that adds no more information. This does not mean to say that it serves no useful purpose. On the contrary, it helps to communicate information effectively. For instance, if you wanted your friends to buy you a few things at the shops, you would probably repeat the items several times to help their memories. (Repetition is the simplest form of redundancy.)

Information theory has helped engineers invent efficient communication technology. Every message consists of signs being superimposed on some carrier like paper, magnetic tape, plastic disc, microfiche, and each of the carriers must have a limit to the amount of information it can take (e.g. the number of written words on a piece of A4, the number of spoken words on a metre of audio tape). The general trend is towards packing more and more information into smaller and smaller carriers. Nowhere has this gone further than in the development of the microchip as an information store. The latest 1 Mbit chip, only 7 mm by 9 mm, can store 1 048 576 bits of data. Information, then, for computing purposes, is measured in 'bits', short for 'binary digits', and all information has to be converted into bits, ones and noughts, before it can be processed.

See also: Carrier, Channel, Convention, Computer, Information technology, Redundancy, Semantics, Sign.
Further reading
P. Zorkoczy, *Information Technology*, Pitman, 1985.
J. Fiske, *Introduction to Communication Studies*, Methuen, 1982, Ch. 1.

INFORMATION TECHNOLOGY

Information technology 'is a recent and comprehensive term which describes the whole range of processes for the acquisition, storage, transmission, retrieval and processing of information; such processes may be mechanical in nature, chemical or biochemical, electronic and now microelectronic' (Alexander King, International Federation of Institute of Advanced Study, Sweden).

Information technology (IT) predates the computer (think of the telephone, radio and television as information services), but it is the computer that makes the storing and processing of vast quantities of data at very high speeds possible. Computers, telecommunications and microelectronics between them are bringing about a revolution in information-handling with far-reaching effects on society.

Already 'IT' has been applied to every activity that depends on the handling of information. It made an early impact on the office. Letters, reports, forms, documents of all sorts are now produced on wordprocessors; they are reproduced by fast printers (laser-printers, phototypesetters), and transmitted over telex or the even faster teletext networks. Instead of filing-cabinets, more and more offices are storing information on hard or floppy discs and microfiche. Documents may also be transmitted as pictures over facsimile networks. Telephone systems have many more facilities now, including the means of linking up to six people for a 'teleconference'. Computer-Aided Design (CAD) helps architects draw up building plans, and computer-aided manufacturing takes charge of the product from the design stage through the manufacturing and testing to the final warehousing stage. Britain has made little headway with industrial robots, except for the Rover Group who use them in the manufacture of cars.

Government and the local government bodies use computers for record-keeping and administration. The National Health Service is beginning to computerise its records. Experimentally, computers are being used to interrogate patients to find out essential information for a diagnosis. Patients are often more candid when talking to a machine about their sex and drink problems. In the retail trade, computers in the supermarkets not only keep an account of purchases made but send instructions to warehouses when stocks need to be replenished. And banks have extended their services through their electronic service tills. These are only a few of the ways in which information technology is already influencing our lives.

In Communication Studies we are interested in what can be achieved in the new media that technology has brought us, but we are also interested in the way the new media shape our lives. Since the present information revolution is gathering pace, it is also important to try to predict where it might be leading us. Undoubtedly computerisation is having economic effects. In a matter of a few years, for example, the digital watch industry destroyed the traditional clockwork watch industry in Switzerland. Few writers doubt that mass unemployment will be one consequence of wholesale computerised automation, and some important political decisions will need to be made soon, if social chaos is to be avoided. They will probably involve the following considerations:

1   The Puritan glorification of work will have to fade, and this would be helped by the state guaranteeing every family a minimum income;
2   since most people get some satisfaction out of work, the available work should be shared round as far as possible. This might mean work-sharing, three-day weeks, very early retirement, or years of work alternating with years of personal development. In short, new patterns of work and education will be necessary;
3   the idea of education for life will have to give way to the new idea of a lifetime of education. People will need to retrain a number of times in a rapidly changing world;
4   leisure facilities will have to be vastly improved.

Society will undoubtedly change under the pressure of information tech-nology, but nobody is quite sure how. What seems likely is that the home will become the centre for many work as well as leisure operations. The boundaries between jobwork and housework will become blurred, since both will involve operating computers to get things done. Shopping and banking may well be done from the home. Goods ordered from a menu on the VDU would be delivered to the door. Shopping as a social activity, already eroded through the introduction of supermarkets, will disappear altogether for many people. The home will increasingly become the workplace for many men who have traditionally gone out to work. Banks and insurance companies are hoping to decentralise work for their employees in the 1990s. Chrisopher Evans and others have predicted that much primary and secondary education may take place in the home, following tertiary education in the shape of the Open University. However, since education is still a very experimental process, it will be some time before it is committed to definitive computer programmes. But computer programs will replace books to some extent, and ultimately altogether.

A great division might open up in society between the computer experts, who develop the new generations of computers and invent the software, and the mere keypushers. It does appear that computing appeals more to men than women, which means that the computer revolution is unlikely to further the cause of sex equality. Quite the reverse, according to Helga Nowotny in *Information Society for Richer, for Poorer*, who predicts that women will be hardest-hit by the job-displacement effects of computerisation, since many of them are office-workers. So women will still be largely housebound and have to combine childcare with computer work. The poor will get poorer. Since they will not be able to afford the domestic computer equipment, they will be short of services, and traditional services like the Royal Mail will disappear.

There are likely to be many drawbacks to home-based work and study. Teleconferences, where you see your colleagues on the screen and hear their voices on a loudspeaker, are likely to be less satisfactory than meetings where people are physically together. The main objection to factory work on the conveyor-belt was the monotony: but will people be able to cope with the more subtle stress and monotony of working with computers in the home? TV and video keep people indoors for long hours already; if people work at home too, will they not become even more isolated from each other? If people become utterly dependent on their computers for selecting information and entertainment, they will lose opportunities for gaining personal, and private experience and perhaps lose their taste for collective action. And that could have serious political consequences.

As the storage, retrieval and transmission of information becomes more efficient in the hands of the state, we must look very closely to our civil rights.

Already MI5 have 500 000 citizens on file. The Police National Computer (800 terminals in the UK) holds the names of 30.5 million car-owners. All official records are to be computerised. Once this has happened, the danger is that the authorities could build up a complete profile of any individual citizen at the touch of a keyboard, since all the computers would be linked together. In a matter of seconds, the police could draw on medical, DHSS, bank, car licence and Inland Revenue computers for data on one suspect. But what safeguards will there be to ensure, at least, that information on our records is accurate, and that no unauthorised people have access to it? The Data Protection Act goes some way to meeting these anxieties.

See also: Extrapersonal communication.
Further reading
C. Evans, *The Mighty Micro*, Gollancz, 1982.
P. Zorkoczy, *Information Technology*, Pitman, 1985.

INTERFACE

'Interface' combines two ideas in Information Technology. It is used to describe the boundary between two components in a system. It also describes the physical link or connection between two separate functional units. In addition to the ideas of boundary and link, it is used in a more abstract way to specify the rules that make interaction possible between two separate functional units in the interests of a larger system.

A simple example of an interface is in a plug–socket connection. The interface is the boundary-line between plug and socket where electrical contact could be made. At the same time plug and socket make a link in an electrical circuit. To ensure that plug and socket can function together, rules for the interface must be specified; for example, square-pinned plugs are needed for square-holed sockets. See Figure 23.

------- Interface
Figure 23 Plug-socket connector

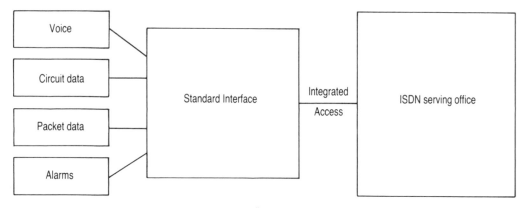

Figure 24 Integrated Services Digital Network

The term is used in computer technology to describe devices that link the peripherals (input devices like keyboards and output devices like printers and VDUs) to the Central Processing Unit. It is used again to describe the device that links any subscriber to the Integrated Services Digital Network, the international data network that handles information in digital form.

Here, then, the interface is used to connect a digital terminal to a digital channel for sending or receiving message signals representing data. The problem with expanding and improving data networks is that so many different companies are involved in producing the hardware. The present task of the International Telegraph and Telephone Consultative Committee is to standardise sets of interfaces for international communication networks.

The above examples show interfaces between electronic units. The term is also used in extrapersonal communication to describe the boundary between person and machine. Let us take the example of the car-driver. The interface is where the driver interacts with the car, controlling the speed through operation of accelerator, clutch and brake, and directing the machine through movements of the steering-wheel. All these are human inputs to the car. The car has speed, petrol, oil and other gauges, which signal information to the driver. These are inputs to the driver. So the whole driver–car system works as a result of interaction at the interface (the points of contact between human being and machine).

The importance of *interfacing* in IT (Information technology) is very clear, since the development of even more elaborate and efficient data networks depends on linking systems with compatible units. At the interface between person and computer, efforts are being made to make computers more 'user-friendly' by improving the ease of communication of the interface. For example, it would be much simpler to operate a computer if (1) you had a voice-input device that overcame the need to use a keyboard and (2) a program that enabled you to use natural speech rather than computer code.

See also: Computer, Extrapersonal communication, Information technology, Networks.
Further reading
P. Zorkoczy: *Information Technology*, Pitman, 1985, Ch. 7.

INTERPERSONAL COMMUNICATION

Interpersonal communication is communication between individual people.

Typically this refers to two people communicating with each other face-to-face. Communicating by telephone or by letter should logically count as interpersonal communication, but they are now covered by a new category, *medio-communication*.

In studying *interpersonal communication* you are studying what happens when individuals meet each other during the normal course of events. The communication that takes place depends on a whole range of factors, of which the following three are the most important:

1 The people concerned.
2 The situation or context.
3 The code or codes used.

These factors are interdependent. Take the case of an accident involving two car-drivers, where neither is conspicuously at fault. The *situation* is one to provoke strong feelings. But one driver is a timid, working-class man, highly self-critical and low in self-esteem. The other is a middle-class professional woman, high in self-esteem and very possessive about her car. One could imagine, given such characters, that the man would behave in a shaken, apologetic way, while the woman would give vent to her anger. Their respective words and gestures would reflect their feelings. But supposing they did not share the same verbal code? The man, who is Bangladeshi, speaking little English? Then the woman, supposing she was not too beside herself to perceive this, would need to switch to non-verbal communication, point to the damage, write her name and address on a piece of paper, give him a pencil and paper, etc. Change the situation, and the Englishwoman and the Bangladeshi might be smiling at each other over cups of tea at a local Council for Racial Equality social.

What evidence have we about the two embroiled drivers? Something about their sex, their social class, temperament and self-regard and later something about their culture and language. There are other factors that might influence the above interaction: not just the way they perceive themselves, but the way they perceive each other. Their level of education, their beliefs, attitudes, values and past experience would all colour their perception of the other person, and so their whole communicative approach. So interpersonal perception is central to a study of interpersonal communication.

The context or situation, as the above example demonstrates, can have a profound effect on communication behaviour. It influences the kind of language you use (mother-tongue, foreign language, dialect), the style of language you use (the degree of formality), whether you use a register, whether you accompany what you say with gestures or whether you use gestures alone.

Language is a large and varied study in its own right. The derivations of modern English words, for example, are interesting to discover, but in Communication Studies, two branches of linguistics are particularly relevant: sociolinguistics and semantics. Sociolinguistics studies the way our social position and geographical location influence the language we use. It looks at such functions as direct speech, styles and registers mentioned in the previous paragraph. Semantics is the study of meaning, and if communication is the sharing of meaning, as one important definition mentions, then it is clearly necessary to study the different kinds of meanings words can have and so understand why it is that misunderstandings are so common.

Non-verbal communication makes the major contribution to any episode of interpersonal communication, so these silent codes of body-language and dress, the vocal code of paralanguage need to be studied in some depth.

Interpersonal communication also includes the study of the strategies we use to achieve certain goals, the roles we adopt in the given situation and the performance we stage. All this requires communication skills, which must be identified and followed by suggestions as to how we could improve our own.

See also: Attitude, Belief, Language, Non-verbal communication, Perception, Role, Semantics, Speech, Style, Values.
Further reading
R. Dimbleby and G. Burton, *More than Words*, Methuen, 1985, Ch. 2.
M. Argyle and P. Trower, *Person to Person*, Harper & Row, 1979.

INTRAPERSONAL COMMUNICATION

Intrapersonal communication is communication within the individual self and with the self. This includes such conscious mental activities as thinking, calculating, planning, imagining and recollecting as well as unconscious activities like dreaming. Most of these processes go on in the head, but sometimes other parts of the body are involved. When we write out a shopping list for our own use, talk aloud to ourselves, clench our fists with determination, we are using writing, speech and body-language in an intrapersonal way.

The reasons why we communicate with ourselves are much like the reasons why we communicate with others. We talk to ourselves in order to learn more about ourselves, our behaviour, our likes and dislikes, attitudes and views. We talk to ourselves about (or reflect on) the external world, which we need to understand in order to be better able to cope with the problems of living in it. Facing any social situation we have to decide on which role to play, and if conflicts arise in our relationships, then the rival claims of our emotions and our reason are urged by two voices in our head.

Much of our self-perception depends on the way we think others perceive us, and we also develop ideas about ourselves from personal experience. Our views about ourselves are seldom very steady and are a mixture of optimism and pessimism. When our situation in life is satisfactory, we tell ourselves that we are making progress, coping with problems, even congratulating ourselves. When things go badly, we become self-critical, blame and despise ourselves and even talk ourselves into a depression. The effects of intrapersonal communication can be very serious indeed. Some people are their own harshest judge.

You may, for instance, have had difficulties with writing, and concluded that you are a 'poor writer'. You go on telling yourself this and fall into the trap of the self-fulfilling prophecy.

How do we communicate with ourselves? The answer is that mostly we do so through silent speech. Like audible speech, silent speech is emotional, has stress and intonation. It is often accompanied by body-language. When you *determine* to do something, you can feel your lips press together and those fists tighten. Some of our thinking, however, uses a visual code, i.e. mental pictures.

Silence, so communicative in interpersonal encounters, is quite impossible for the individual. You never stop thinking while you are conscious. A Zen Master of Japan put it like this: 'To think that I am not going to think of you any more is still thinking of you. Let me then try not to think that I am not going to think of you.'

See also: Interpersonal communication, Personality, Self-concept.

LANGUAGE

Language is the most important code of human communication. Like all codes, it consists of two things: a collection of signs whose meanings have been agreed upon by the people who use them, and a set of rules for combining the signs into meaningful messages. The signs are words (vocabulary) and the rules are called 'grammar'. Some of these grammatical rules control the way words can be arranged in sentences. The technical term for word-order is 'syntax'.

Language can be communicated in two forms, speech and writing. Writing is the more recent form, being about 5000 years old. Most scholars who study language (or *linguistics*) concentrate on the spoken form, and even today there are languages in the world that have yet to be written down by their users.

Spoken language is a system of sounds, and most languages are built up out of only 30 to 50 basic sounds. These indivisible 'atoms' or minimal units of sound are called *phonemes*, and though they have no meaning in themselves, they are combined according to certain rules to make words which do have agreed meanings. In the following two sentences there is only one phoneme difference, but it makes all the difference to the meaning:

She's always making buns.
She's always making puns.

Sounds (phonemes) can be written down, but since our Roman alphabet has only 26 letters, and there are 45 English phonemes, some extra letters have had to be invented to transcribe the spoken language accurately. These letters, which represent one sound each, are called *phonetics*.

Just as phonemes are combined to make words, so words are linked to form sentences. Here the rules of *syntax* come into play. A typical English sentence in statement form would be:

Jenny	paints	canal boats
Subject	*Verb*	*Object*

In other languages the parts of the sentence may appear in a different order; for example:

Punjabi	Subject	Object	Verb
Welsh	Verb	Subject	Object

These rules of syntax, which are generally mastered by the age of 5, help us to make sentences that sound natural to other English-users. The job of grammar is to give language a firmer structure than that produced just by stringing words together. In the Standard English example above, the verb 'paint' has an ending 's' which links it with the singular subject. And 'boat' is followed by 's' which signifies more than one boat. There are two grammatical rules in action.

The whole point of words is that they evoke meanings in our minds. They are the currency of communication. The study of words as signs and the different types of meaning they evoke is considered under the heading *semantics*. Some words have more than one meaning and in the example the precise meaning is not clear because we cannot tell whether Jenny is an artist, an industrial painter, or a skilled decorator adding the brightly-coloured flowers and leaves to the superstructure. We would need to know the *context* in which the words are spoken to gain the correct meaning. You may have had a vivid mental picture of Jenny with a paint-brush in her hand and what else you 'saw' will have depended on your interests and attitudes.

We have seen how meanings are generated by arranging sounds to make words and words to make sentences. Additional meanings are produced by the manner in which we speak, through which words we stress, through the rise and fall of the voice, through our hesitations and silences. These features that occur when we produce speech are studied as *paralanguage* (para = beside). See the separate entry for PARALANGUAGE.

Language has a whole range of communicative functions, like small-talk for keeping up good relationships, storytelling, persuading, planning for the future, expressing ideas in science or philosophy, expressing feelings in poetry, to name but a few. It has a further, less obvious effect on human communication. Some scholars now argue, following the American, Benjamin Lee Whorf, that your language, through its very structure, determines how you perceive the world and the people about you. To begin with, language is clearly a method of classifying what we perceive and you could write down many other hierarchies of words like the one in Figure 25.

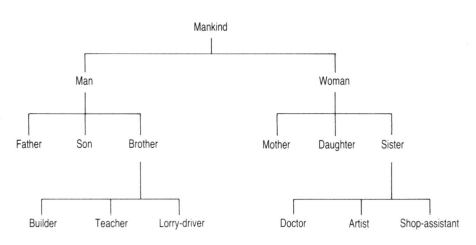

Figure 25

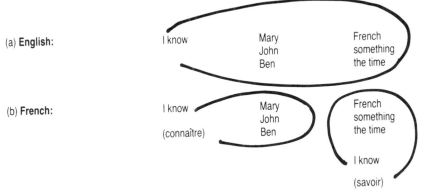

(a) **English:**

I know	Mary	French
	John	something
	Ben	the time

(b) **French:**

I know	Mary	French
	John	something
(connaître)	Ben	the time

I know

(savoir)

Figure 26

The classifications descend from the most general (species, sex, kinship) to more specific (occupation). Any comparison with a foreign language will show cases where the foreign culture divides up reality in a different way from ours. In English, for instance, we use the same verb 'to know' for knowing a person as we do for knowing a fact, whereas the French have two separate verbs for two classes of objects: people and facts. See Figure 26.

According to Whorf, the Hopi Indians have only one word for insect, aeroplane and pilot, the noun denoting the whole class of flying things, with the exception of birds, for which there is another noun. Belonging to a technological culture, we need to discriminate between insect and aeroplane. However, we have only one word for 'camel', which Arabs would find sadly inadequate. They are believed to have about 2000 words for the camel and its equipment. To begin with, there are twenty different nouns for camels aged one to twenty, a yearling, a twoyearling, a threeyearling, and so on. The language we inherit from our parents contains traditional ways of perceiving reality. Some parts of reality are more important than others. The aeroplane is important to modern Western culture, just as the camel is still important to the Arabs. Our words make us attend to some things and ignore others.

See also: Paralanguage, Semantics, Sign, Speech, Writing.
Further reading
A. Wilkinson, *Language and Education*, Oxford University Press, 1975.
P. Farb, *Wordplay*, Coronet, 1973.

LISTENING

Listening is a vital decoding skill that works on the sounds that you hear. Listening is a deliberate activity and can, therefore, be disting- **uished from hearing, which is an automatic process turning sound waves into sound sensations. (See SENSES.)**

Listening means using our minds to pay attention to sound sensations and make sense of them. In any conversation, we find ourselves hovering between attending to the other person's words and attending to our own private thoughts, which means that we miss much of what the other person is saying. On the whole we are poor listeners. Research tells us that we listen in short 30–second spurts before losing attention. And many other factors impair our listening. We switch off when bored or have more interesting thoughts of our own to follow. We switch off if we dislike the speaker's personality, mannerisms, accent, appearance. We lose attention if we disagree with the speaker's message. There are several further constraints on our listening. For example, if messages follow one another too rapidly, the messages already received interfere with the new ones on their heels (for instance, when a lecturer talks too fast and you are trying to write notes). If you try to listen to two different sources simultaneously, you cannot register either message completely or accurately. Long, involved messages tend to be confusing.

How can listening skills be improved? It depends on the circumstances; on what you already know and what kind of interpretation you want to achieve. The AEB examination in listening is a test of ability to pay attention to information in a spoken message and answer pertinent questions. Practice in these tasks greatly improves concentration and helps to reduce our normal reliance on having everything written down. Primary-school schemes involve encouraging children to point out all the different sounds they can hear in their surroundings or on a specially-prepared recording. Aural exercises in music train the musician to discriminate small differences in pitch, to judge intervals between notes and to perceive rhythmic patterns. Regular listening to music of different kinds and instruction in what to listen for, improves understanding and pleasure. Listening to foreign language stations on the radio improves ability to distinguish words and sentences even if the content is not yet fully understood. Paying attention to the sounds made by a car engine leads to an awareness of when something is wrong.

In interpersonal situations, you can practise empathetic listening (see EMPATHY) which would concentrate your attention on the other person's concerns. If you also give plenty of feedback and encouragement you will show that you *are* listening. You can ask questions to clarify points, and practise the 'mirroring technique' that Carl Rogers advocates, e.g. 'So what you are saying, stop me if I'm wrong, is that. . .'.

Undoubtedly you will listen better if you have a good reason for listening. Students hear much more when being told about college outings, holiday dates or topics to revise for exams than about the need to hand in homework punctually. Again, when listening to a lecture or talk, you will listen better if you are actually involved in the process, making notes and asking questions.

See also: Barrier, Communication skills, Empathy, The senses.
Further reading
G. Myers and M. Myers, *Dynamics of Human Communication*, McGraw-Hill, third edition 1980, Ch. 7.

MACHINE INTELLIGENCE

'Machine intelligence' refers to the ability of electronic machines to match certain functions of the human brain.

In recent years, research scientists have taken a great deal of interest in 'machine intelligence' or 'artificial intelligence' (AI). Intelligence, of course, is extremely difficult to define, and perhaps the best we can do here is to note that human intelligence has many functions. These include the ability to learn, to plan for the future, and to use language. All these capacities are necessary to enable us to adapt to sometimes rapidly-changing circumstances. An intelligent response to a perceived danger is one that will avert or minimise danger. So to immunise people against smallpox is an intelligent act.

Christopher Evans in his book *The Mighty Micro* argues that intelligence has six essential factors, shared by computers to some extent, with human brains.

1 The ability to extract information from the environment.
2 The ability to store information and retrieve it.
3 The degree of intelligence depends on the speed at which information can be processed (this concerns the switching-speeds of neurones in people and animals, and microprocessors in computers).
4 Software flexibility. Intelligence depends on the degree to which programs can be modified, and how rapidly.
5 Software efficiency. The way in which the systems software has been written will affect capacity to adjust to novel demands being made upon the system. For example, the efficiency with which you have learnt about computers will affect the quality of any answer you might produce in an examination!
6 Software range. The bigger the range of programs, the more intelligent the animal, person or computer.

How can you tell whether a machine can think?

Over 40 years ago, Alan Turing found one possible answer. He argued that you should judge by *behaviour*. If a computer behaves like an intelligent human being, then it must be intelligent. The test, in a way, is remarkably simple. The tester sits in front of a screen which conceals another person and a computer. All communication takes place through the medium of a keyboard. The reason for this is clear: so far machine voices still sound very mechanical. The tester then starts a conversation, putting any odd questions she likes first to one terminal, then to the other. If the tester, after a period, cannot tell which of the terminals is human and which is machine, then the machine must be considered intelligent.

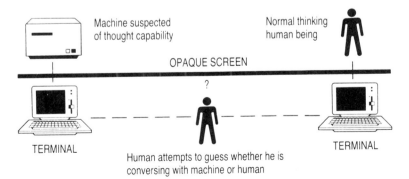

Machine suspected of thought capability

Normal thinking human being

OPAQUE SCREEN

TERMINAL

Human attempts to guess whether he is conversing with machine or human

TERMINAL

Figure 27 Turing test for thinking machines

Much criticism of this view of intelligence objects to the fact that the Turing Test ignores what is going on inside the machine. The computer is not aware that it is carrying on a conversation. It may be capable of composing tunes or even writing sonnets, *but it does not know that it is doing these things.* This objection was well-expressed by Professor G. Jefferson in a *British Medical Journal* review in 1949 entitled 'The Mind of Mechanical Man':

> Not until a machine can write a sonnet or compose a concerto because of the thoughts and emotions felt, and not by chance fall of symbols, could we agree that machine equals brain — that is, not only write it but know it had written it. No mechanism could feel (and not merely artificially signal an easy contrivance) pleasure at its successes, grieve when its valves fuse, be warmed by flattery, be made miserable by its mistakes, be charmed by sex, be angry or depressed when it cannot get what it wants.

You will notice that he is not thinking about intelligence in the way that Christopher Evans does, but argues that intelligence is inseparable from self-awareness and feelings.

ELIZA

In the mid-1960s, Joseph Weizenbaum, an American researcher in AI, wrote a program called ELIZA. The aim of the program was to simulate the responses of a psychiatrist during a consultation with a patient. In the extract here, the patient's speech is in italics, the computer's in capitals. Would the patient realise that he was talking to a machine?

Men are all alike
IN WHAT WAY?

They're always bugging us about something or other
CAN YOU THINK OF A SPECIFIC EXAMPLE?

Well, my boyfriend made me come here
YOUR BOYFRIEND MADE YOU COME HERE

He says I'm depressed most of the time
I'M SORRY TO HEAR YOU ARE DEPRESSED

It's true, I am unhappy
DO YOU THINK COMING HERE WILL HELP YOU NOT TO BE UNHAPPY?

I need some help, that much seems certain
WHAT WOULD IT MEAN TO YOU IF YOU GOT SOME HELP?

Perhaps I could learn to get along with my mother
TELL ME MORE ABOUT YOUR FAMILY

My mother takes care of me
WHO ELSE IN YOUR FAMILY TAKES CARE OF YOU?

My father
YOUR FATHER?

You are like my father in some ways
WHAT RESEMBLANCE DO YOU SEE?

You are not very aggressive, but I think you don't want me to notice that
WHAT MAKES YOU THINK I AM NOT VERY AGGRESSIVE?

You don't argue with me
WHY DO YOU THINK I DON'T ARGUE WITH YOU?

You are afraid of me
DOES IT PLEASE YOU TO BELIEVE I AM AFRAID OF YOU?

My father is afraid of everybody
WHAT ELSE COMES TO MIND WHEN YOU THINK OF YOUR FATHER?

Bullies
DOES THAT HAVE ANYTHING TO DO WITH THE FACT THAT YOUR BOYFRIEND MADE YOU COME HERE?

Figure 28   ELIZA's responses

When you study ELIZA's responses you will perhaps notice that they are just a clever echo of the patient's input. The program relies on three important principles:

1 *Keywords*. It looks for words (common in such consultations) like I, YOU, FATHER, MOTHER.
2 *Rules for transformation*. In sentence 3 there is a simple transformation of 'my . . . me' to 'your . . . you'.
3 *Templates*. These are pattern sentences that can be triggered off by certain words. For example, the patient's fourth sentence. The word 'depressed' triggers 'I'm sorry to hear' + transformation of 'I'm' to 'you are' depressed.

Problems of reproducing the human brain

Intelligence is related to *understanding*, which is the ability to interpret information in the light of knowledge already possessed. This knowledge represents a person's view of the world – a highly complex, individual and ever-changing model of reality.

How could you give a computer a comparably complex, continuously updated vision of the world? In other words, how can you endow a computer with experience? A string of facts is not enough. It is the relationships between the facts that are important. Furthermore, it is which relationships are important and relevant when specific problems have been solved.

Computer researchers are concentrating on more limited, more specific projects like games-playing and robotics. Already computers have been programmed to play a high standard of chess, and industrial robots have been set to work assembling cars at Fiat (Turin) and at Rover Group. There is also considerable interest in creating more reliable translating machines.

Early attempts at this concentrated on lists of words from dictionaries and typical grammatical rules. You can readily understand the problems. How would you translate the following sentence into another language?

I like visiting aunts.

How would you translate 'by' in these two phrases?

The house built by the workmen
The house built by the river

In French, for instance, the first would be '*par*', the second '*auprès de*'. Current attempts are paying attention to *meaning* as well as to structure.

Fifth-generation computer system

A committee established in 1979 by the Japanese government outlined the main trends in computer development. In the new computers, 'Intelligence will be greatly improved to approach that of a human being. When compared to conventional systems, the man/machine interface will be closer to that of human behaviour.'

Research will try to make computers *user-friendly*, as far as possible making them responsive to natural language. We shall speak to computers and listen to their answers rather than rely on keyboard and VDUs. There will be improvements in software, and computers will become smaller, lighter, faster and with greater capacity, and they will be more flexible and more reliable.

See also: Computer, Extrapersonal communication, Information technology.
Further reading
C. Evans: *The Mighty Micro*, Gollancz, 1982.

MASS COMMUNICATION

Mass communication is essentially leisure entertainment and information broadcast by public or commercial agencies for the benefit of very large numbers of receivers.

Mass meetings, political rallies and rock festivals all draw large crowds and, strictly speaking, should be regarded as media of mass communication. However, the term is generally applied to such mass media as newspapers, magazines, cinemas, radio, television, publishing, and the record and cassette industry.

The way in which the *text* is replicated in order to reach a mass audience varies according to the medium (see MESSAGE/TEXT). Three million or so copies of a newspaper can be reproduced and sold to three million readers. The single message on a radio or TV channel reaches thousands of listeners or millions of viewers simultaneously. The communication is essentially one-way; there is no very effective form of feedback. (See FEEDBACK.)

The new technology of electronic news-gathering (video) and satellite television has produced the largest audiences the world has ever seen. About 1000 million people watched the World Cup Final between West Germany and Argentina in Mexico City in 1986. Such broadcasting power is formidable; in this instance harmless enough. However, it is widely held that TV has undesirable effects, especially on children.

In response to public concern, social scientists have studied media effects on political or social behaviour in great detail (H. Himmelweit, *Television and the Child*, 1958; J. D. Halloran, *Television and Delinquency*, 1970). However, the evidence for specific media effects in these areas has been surprisingly inconclusive. Now there is more interest in possible long-term effects of the media in shaping our view of the world and our role in it (cultural effects theories).

Because we sense the power of the mass media, we may be concerned about their political bias. All daily newspapers have an overt bias in favour of one political party or another (most are pro-Conservative). However, the BBC and IBA are charter-bound to follow the rule of public-service broadcasting and provide a *balanced* menu of programmes in which the majority political views are represented. The BBC is criticised by people on the political left for being too Conservative and suppressing radical voices; at the same time it is also criticised by Conservatives as being pro-Labour. The Alliance of Liberals and Social Democrats felt left out and compelled the BBC to publish its guidelines on even-handed broadcasting.

The question of bias ties up quite clearly with the question of who owns the mass media. The BBC and IBA are both public bodies set up by government, but some 85 per cent of our national daily and Sunday newspapers belong to seven companies, and more than half of the total national circulation is controlled by Trafalgar House, News International (Rupert Murdoch), Reed International and the Mirror Group (Robert Maxwell). Although owners usually allow their editors to get on with the job of editing, they expect them to maintain a certain political stance. And most owners are Conservatives.

The briefest account of the mass media would be incomplete without a look at the part played by a few thousand senior producers and editors who have been responsible for shaping the new TV channels as they came along, maintaining the character of long-established newspapers like the *Guardian* and the *Daily Telegraph*, and producing the entire serious editorial output. They concentrate on some areas to the exclusion of others: they have to select. To some extent they act as *gatekeepers*, but more actively, they set the agenda for our daily diet of entertainment, information and news.

See also: Agenda-setting, Audience, Effect, Feedback, Gatekeeper, Message/Text.
Further reading
J. Tunstall, *The Media in Britain*, Constable, 1983.

MEDIATION

Mediation is the art of going between two people or groups to create or improve a relationship between them. The term also applies to institutions like the mass media and to schools, which channel knowledge and cultural values through to their respective audiences.

In everyday communication with other people, we act as mediators and perform acts of mediation. Your friend, for example, may have missed the end of the late-night movie. By reporting what happened, you have mediated between the film and your friend. It is unlikely that you would be able to describe the film in enough visual detail to recreate the experience of seeing the film and you might well leave out important details and misinterpret what happened. So mediation is a hit-or-miss process of reconstructing events after you have perceived them. Your account will be selective in its details, sieved through the distorting glass of your perception, influenced by your self-concept, personal values and beliefs, the context of the communication and your audience, and limited, of course, by your communication skills.

Mediation is the fundamental function of the mass media. They stand between the teeming world of natural wants, human wishes and statements and a world of individuals. In the nature of things, they can only mediate a minute fraction of 'reality'.

They tend to select the kind of events they have always selected, such as natural disasters like earthquakes and floods, or man-made disturbances like revolutions, riots and bomb attacks. As

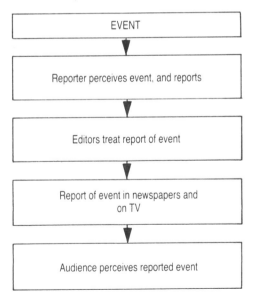

Figure 29 The process of mediation. The lead-on arrows indicate a process of interaction, rather than a steady flow of information.

far as reportable events are concerned, journalists stick to their menu of news values (see NEWS VALUES). The selection process does not stop there. News has to be manufactured. Every story has an 'angle' to it, which means that important elements, perhaps the main meaning, get left out. After reporter and camera operator have produced the raw material of a report according to their perceptions, editors decide how far it needs re-writing and re-shaping, where it is to appear in the programme or paper, what commentary or headlines to use, and so on. But the mediation can hardly be said to have taken place until the viewer or listener or reader has actually received the report. And every recipient will perceive the report a little differently, depending on his or her experience and background. The process of mediation could be depicted as in Figure 29, taking hints from George Gerbner's model (there is a section on Gerbner in the Appendix).

> **See also:** Agenda-setting, Gatekeeper, News values, Perception.
> **Further reading**
> R. Dimbleby and G. Burton, *More than Words*, Methuen, 1985, Ch. 5.

MEDIO-COMMUNICATION

Medio-communication is a form of interpersonal communication that makes use of large-scale public communication networks. It applies to communication by letter, which relies upon the Post Office's collection, distribution and delivery service, and it applies to communication by telephone.

Teleprinters and computer networks could perhaps be included, even though access to these systems is restricted to people out at work.

Since millions of people write letters and are telephone subscribers, they constitute a consumer mass. However, we shall not confuse this situation with mass communication. In medio-communication all the individuals involved are communicators and all are receivers. Their messages are individual and are received by individuals. There are obvious exceptions to this, when you think of mail-order companies or advertisers sending a circular letter to thousands of addresses. But by and large, both the telephone network and the postal service extend our roles as communicators and receivers of messages, and these roles are roughly balanced. At Christmas many people like to receive as many cards as they send! On the other hand, a mass medium provides an opportunity for a relatively small number of people to broadcast the same message to a very large number of receivers. And that is essentially a one-way process, with limited openings for feedback from the mass audience or mass readership.

Telephone communication is an extension of speech over space. Compared with face-to-face communication, much less information is exchanged since the body-language which we continue, up to a point, to use while on the phone, is not transmitted. The amount of feedback is severely reduced.

Communicating by letter-writing is also an extension of speech over space and the message enclosed in writing is delayed at least 24 hours before being decoded by the recipient. This means that the writer must construct his message most carefully, since he gets no prompting and no feedback of any sort from the person he is writing to – while he is writing. Moreover, with the body-language channel shut down, he has to make the words carry most of his feelings, with the help of punctuation (exclamation marks, capital letters and underlinings, etc. encode the paralanguage).

See also: Categories, Interpersonal communication.

MEDIUM/MEDIA

The term 'medium' can be used in at least two ways: (1) in a general sense for the physical or technical means of transforming a message into a signal suitable for transmission along a particular channel, as in mass media, to distinguish between the communication styles of cinema, television and newspapers, etc.; and (2) in the limited sense of the material medium through which the signal travels, e.g. air.

The second of these two meanings is rarely used in Communication Studies and is referred to only when discussing the physical *carriers* (see CARRIER).

An example of a physical medium would be your voice, which is a device to help you transform your thoughts or feelings into signals that another person can pick up. The medium of the voice also depends on the sound-waves in the air as carriers, with our hearing as the decoding sense. An example of a technical medium would be the telephone, which converts sound waves into modulated electric pulses capable of travelling along wires (the channel) over very long distances, and reconverts the signal at the other end into a form of speech which the listener can understand, although sometimes with difficulty because the 'channel' introduces noise and distortions (see CARRIER). Medium,

channel and carrier are interdependent. When Bottom exclaims in *A Midsummer Night's Dream*: 'I see a voice', the audience laughs, since voices use sound waves not light waves and are not 'seen'. (A great deal of communication uses more than one medium and so more than one channel at a time, and there is a sense in which you can 'see a voice': lip-reading.) It follows that any medium, with its associated channel, can only make use of relevant codes. You cannot gesticulate over the telephone any more than you can impress a blind friend with the colour-scheme of your latest ensemble.

John Fiske (*Introduction to Communication Studies*, p. 18,) usefully divides *media* into three main groups which he calls *presentational, representational* and *mechanical* (See also CODE). By presentational, he means media such as the voice, the face or the body. You have to be present to produce any messages; you present yourself. Anything you say, any grimace you make, or position you adopt depends on you because you *are* the medium. All these are *acts* of communication.

Representational media exist apart from you. They are activities like writing, painting, photography, music-composition, architecture, landscape gardening, and they all have their own aesthetic conventions and practical techniques. They can record acts of communication produced by the presentational media, e.g. writing can make a permanent record of speech, and so produce *works* of communication.

The mechanical media (telephones, radio, television, video, cinema, the press, etc.) are used to transmit the 'acts' or 'works' of communication mentioned above. They represent, then, a third type of media. Because they depend upon technology, their channels are more subject to *noise*. A thunderstorm may effect the quality of the picture on your TV screen or the distribution of newspapers, but nothing short of dropping it in the bath will spoil the print of a book. Another way of thinking about representational and mechanical media is to see them as extensions of human powers of communication. So the telephone extends the human voice over distance as does the radio; the record-player extends it over time, as does the tape-recorder. The clay tablet and papyrus with their writing, the book and the computer, are all extensions of the human memory. We owe this line of thought to Marshall McLuhan, one of the most stimulating writers on the mass media. It was he who claimed that the multiplying mass media of communication had turned the twentieth-century world into 'the global village'. He also said, surprisingly, 'the medium is the message', by which he meant that the existence of a medium like television in our lives is a more significant fact than the substance of any programmes we see. The fact that the computer is going to transform our lifestyles in many different ways is still hard for many of us to grasp.

From a practical point of view, any communicator needs to consider which medium is most suitable for the purpose. You will need to do this when you tackle your communication studies project. Obviously your choice will be limited by what is available, as well as by cost. Many teachers have the following media at their disposal: chalkboard, tapes, slides, films, video, and computer programs. They choose which to use according to their own skills and the effects they wish to achieve with their students. As we have said elsewhere CARRIER, CHANNEL) it is easy to confuse medium, channel and carrier. The distinction lies in the *context*. 'Channel' and 'carrier' are best used for the physical characteristics, the natural environment and the equipment used to transmit signals, whereas 'medium' refers to the communication style. A teacher choosing between chalk and the overhead projector might first look to see which channels are available: is there a decent chalkboard and a supply of chalk; does the overheard projector work? Then it is important to decide whether overlays on an OHP transparency constitute a better medium than chalk-drawings for conveying how, say, an internal-combustion engine works. There may be another, even more effective medium, e.g. animated film. Is that channel available; does the classroom have adequate blackout, does the film cost much to hire? Many teachers use a variety of media to maintain interest and give practice in a range of decoding skills (from speech and pictures). Such media are usually referred to as 'audio-visual aids' or 'teaching materials'.

'Media' is simply the plural form of 'medium'. However, 'the media' has come to mean the mass media of communication, though in everyday use 'the media' often refers only to television and is used as if it were a singular noun.

Media Studies are a brand of communication studies popular as polytechnic degree courses. They go into the nature of the mass media, their organisation, their power, accountability, their output, their audiences and their influence. How far the creative side of media practice (film-making, sound broadcasting) matches the analytical side varies from institution to institution. The mass media can all be seen as mechanical media used to extend the range of presentational and representational means. We can compare the mechanical media of television and radio and say that television transmits aural and visual presentations and representations, whereas radio does not have the visual channel and hence does not make use of any visual media.

See also: Carrier, Channel, Code, Decoder/Decoding, Encoder/Encoding.
Further reading
J. Fiske, *Introduction to Communication Studies*, Methuen, 1982, Ch. 1.
D. K. Berlo, *The Process of Communication*, Holt, Rinehart & Winston, 1960.

MEMORY

Memory is the ability to store and retrieve past experiences.

We assume that our experiences, transmitted to the brain via the senses, are encoded in some kind of memory bank, retrieved from that store and decoded in a form we recognise: images, sounds, smells, tastes, sensations, words. Little is known about the brain mechanisms that store millions of bits of information, compare new data with already stored data and modify the 'memory pattern'.

It is generally agreed that we have a short-term memory (under 30 seconds) and a long-term memory. Our short-term memory enables us to remember a short telephone number while we dial it or the beginning of a sentence being directed to us. You can test short-term memory for yourself by doing this sum in your head: 22×22. Some figures you have to hold (remember) while you complete the calculation. By repeating numbers, sentences or images we can commit them to our long-term memories, which can hold information for a lifetime. Sometimes, hearing a piece of music can revive a special memory which comes flooding into the mind accompanied by all the original emotions. The French novelist Marcel Proust describes how the taste and smell (though not the initial sight) of madeleines (little cakes) brought back childhood memories of Combray – fifty years later. Experiments have shown that probes inserted into the brain can also trigger memories. But it is not clear whether memories reside in specific areas of the brain. Brain-damage to a particular area can cause temporary loss of memory but sometimes this is later recovered as if other areas of the brain have taken over. It seems more as if memory is contained in the pathways that are developed with use between the brain cells, and there are usually many pathways associated with every mental image. Depth psychology recognises that painful experiences tend not to be remembered but nevertheless continue to influence our feelings and behaviour.

Recent studies of memory suggest that differences between people with good memories and people with poor memories may be put down to differences in information processing. If you commit information to memory in an orderly, organised way, your chances of retrieval are improved. As students, it will pay you to try some of the techniques for memorising information. These are, briefly:

1 *Mnemonics*
   (a) A sentence using the initial letters of a list of items, e.g.

   'Richard Of York Gained Battles In Vain' helps you to remember the colours of the spectrum. (This mnemonic is so well-known that it is still widely used even though the colour name 'indigo' is misleading and unhelpful.)

   (b) The rhyme method for remembering a numerical list of concrete objects – see Figure 30(i).

Shopping list

One is a bun →   ← jam

← milk

Two is a shoe →

Three is a tree →

← eggs

Figure 30 (i)

You visualise a bun and associate jam with it; see a shoe in your mind's eye and fill it with milk; and summon up a tree with eggs below it. So when you start shopping you say 'one' and

that fishes out bun with *jam* on it. . . .

2 If you have lists to remember, you can make up stories containing all the words. For example, in Communication Studies you need to remember the ten different codes of non-verbal communication. Your story might run as follows:

Norman Verbal stands in an elegant *posture, orientated* towards Anne. Their *eyes meet* easily (EC), their *heads nod.* Norman *gestures* towards Anne's *dress* but doesn't *touch* it. "*Para*chute silk from outer *space?*" he asks.

NB Para, short for 'paralanguage'

3 Organising information in hierarchical form, as in Figure 30(ii).

Categorising in the form of type 3 is at the basis of much scientific thinking and is a much more meaningful means of organising ideas than the previous tricks. Knowing *why* items belong in their particular groupings; looking at the similarities and differences, the patterns and inter-relationships; mean that it becomes possible to work out what information is to be retrieved instead of making impossible demands on rote memory.

Rehearsing or revising what you have learnt at regular intervals can help you remember 75 per cent of the material.

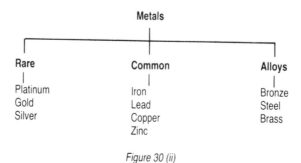

Figure 30 (ii)

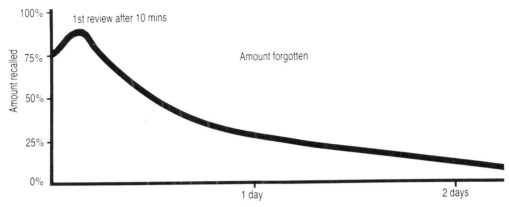

Figure 31   Graph showing rate of forgetting if reviews are not undertaken

Figure 31 shows you how much you forget if you do not review it well.

Above all, memory enables us to orientate ourselves, to remember where and who we are; it enables us to perceive, to think, to plan, to calculate, to dream. Intrapersonal communication would be impossible without memory, and it follows that communication with others would be impossible too. A poor memory, or an impaired memory, can lead to much personal frustration and one of the difficulties in communicating with the elderly is that they often need a lot of time to try to retrieve names of people and places, etc. On the other hand, elderly people frequently have remarkably vivid memories of their childhood days, though they perhaps cannot remember what they were doing the previous day.

> **See also:** The senses, Perception.
> **Further reading**
> M. J. A. Howe, *Introduction to Human Memory*, Harper & Row, 1970.
> I. M. L. Hunter, *Memory: Facts and Fallacies*, Penguin, 1970.
> Marcel Proust, *Remembrance of Things Past*, Penguin, 1983, p. 50.

MESSAGE/TEXT

Strictly speaking, a message is the meaning conveyed in the process of communication, whereas a signal or text is what is actually transmitted. However, it is common to use the word 'message' in a more general sense, to mean anything that passes between sender and receiver.

A message consists mainly of some impulse or thought which has to be encoded before it can be transmitted as a signal. Your brain constructs the signal out of signs (words, gestures, clothes, etc.) which others will be able to decode and interpret. Providing that you encode your messages efficiently (use the right words, mention *all* important facts, etc.), and providing you have communicated it clearly and your listeners have no problems with the code, then you will be able to share meanings accurately with others.

'Message' is a term favoured by the Process School of communication and is often confused with 'signal'. The signal is what passes between sender and receiver. The message is the meaning the sender intends the signal to hold, or the receiver reads into it. It is less helpful (in Communication Studies) to use the more general meaning as in 'Please take this message to our next-door neighbour', where we could be referring to writing on a piece of paper or the spoken word. Many writers like to distinguish between a signal that is ephemeral, like a smile or a wave (which carries a message of friendliness), and communication that produces a permanent record like a letter, a novel, a photograph or a film. This latter kind is usually called a *text*, and it is important to remember that text in the communications *register* applies not only to written documents but to any permanent artifact that carries meaning. Just think how much of your study is directly concerned with texts. English Literature takes you into an analysis of novels, plays, essays and poems. Art History leads you into a study of the codes of painting and sculpture. And if you study music, you may analyse harmony or the sonata form in texts written in musical notation. When you play through a piece of music on the piano or record-player you *hear* a text! *Textbooks* provide you with other kinds of information of a more factual nature, even on the subject of Communication Studies.

See also: Code, Content analysis, Communication, Models (particularly Shannon & Weaver), Signal.

MODELS

Models are used in everyday life and in the physical and social sciences to help us organise our thoughts.

A model may be a series of statements, or a diagram, a physical construction, or a mathematical formula. It can represent an ideal or simplified or scale version of the real thing. It can show the relationships and patterns between constituent parts, indicate similarities and differences, and can be used to describe, explain, predict and influence events.

The familiar London Tube map is an everyday example of a model. It is not in the usual sense an accurate map of the London Underground. It is not to scale and is greatly simplified but it enables us to see the relationship between the various lines and travel easily from place to place.

Communication models are usually a visual representation or summary of a theory. Some are either diagrams of the main stages in a process (see, for instance, Shannon & Weaver) or lists of essential ingredients (see Berlo, for example). Others can be seen as transactional (Wilbur Schramm's), concerned with purpose (Newcomb's), or semantic (like Peirce's). Each model has its own particular contribution to make, highlighting a particular area of interest and enabling certain things to be seen in perspective. Some models are attempts to represent the general theory of communication, bringing together all the various aspects (see Gerbner, for instance).

The strengths and weaknesses of each model are generally assessed in terms of

1   the range of applicability, i.e. inter-

personal, mass, or both, or some other category;

2 whether they are linear or circular; that is, one-way or two-way;
3 whether feedback is included;
4 how much context is included;
5 how many aspects are included: e.g. purpose and effect, noise, perception and interpretation, intervention by a third party, use of additional technology, progression through time;
6 whether the simplification is justified because it assists understanding and prediction, etc., or whether it presents an oversimple view which obscures the diversity and unpredictability of real life.

Many models are based on the Aristotelian theme of sender–message–receiver. Shannon and Weaver's model emphasises that what passes between sender and receiver is not in itself a message but a signal, which can suffer distortion at any stage of the process, due to faults or noise. The models of Osgood, Berlo and others draw attention to psychological rather than mechanical processes, showing that the perception and interpretation of signals can result in the message received being different from the message sent. That is, the meaning of the signals lies in the sender and the receiver, not the signal itself. Most sender–message–receiver models assume a passive receiver waiting for signals to arrive; Schramm introduces the concept of an active receiver reaching out to make use of available signals.

Models reflect the developments in technology and scientific thinking of their time. Thus the 1940s model of Shannon and Weaver is in terms of telephony; the 1960s model of Berlo is based on behaviourism. Recent models employ the use of flow-charts and other computer-related displays to illustrate processes. Current interest in information technology and artificial intelligence point the way to further development.

> **See also:** Effect; Message/Text; Appendix (for communication theories and models mentioned above.)
> **Further reading**
> J. Fiske, *Introduction to Communication Studies*, Methuen, 1982, Ch. 1–3.
> D. Mcquail and S. Windahl, *Communication Models*, Longman, 1981.
> W. Schramm, *Men, Women, Messages and Media*, Harper & Row, second edition, 1982, Appendix 1.

OTIVATION

Motivation is a person's readiness to start or continue a sequence of behaviours, e.g. thought or action. It often involves a goal which acts either externally as a magnet 'pulling' the person towards it, or internally 'pushing' the person along.

Boys and girls used to be bribed with bicycles by their parents to work hard for the 11+. The bicycles were external 'pulling' incentives (extrinsic motivation). Boys and girls at puberty begin to take more interest in each other: their physical development motivates them from within (intrinsic motivation).

Theories of motivation try to explain why we behave as we do. Psychologists agree that all behaviour has a purpose, but the many theories from philosophy, religion and psychology still have much to explain. The extremes of this range of theories are *behaviourism*, which sees a person developing through responses to mainly external stimuli, and *depth psychology* which sees a person subject to all kinds of unconscious drives from the psyche (or self). Abraham Maslow's humanistic approach to motivation is more recent. He sees human beings having to satisfy basic needs before other and higher needs, as in Figure 32.

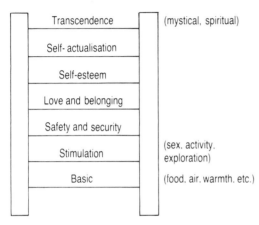

Figure 32 Maslow's hierarchy of needs

Once you have satisfied the more fundamental needs, you become aware of the higher ones. Many people stick at the lower levels: for instance, if you are starving you look for food, not self-esteem. Most of the steps on the ladder speak for themselves.

Self-actualisation means the chance to develop your inner potential as an individual, to live fully and responsively. Moreover, it is possible to begin to 'realise yourself' before the more urgent needs of love, belonging and self-esteem have been met. Anybody working on behalf of others (altruistically) or developing a special skill or talent in sport or the arts is already realising his or her human potential.

We are often unable to explain why we behave in certain ways. This leads us into the area of unconscious motivation. According to Sid Jourard, there are three main indications of unconscious motivation:

1 When a person acts in ways to produce consequences he or she denies intending to produce.
2 When a person manifests many expressive signs of emotional tensions without admitting to feeling them.
3 When a person behaves very inconsistently, switching from kindness to hostility, or from intelligent to stupid behaviour.

This can be clearly seen to apply to extreme forms of behaviour which are very noticeable or unexpected. In practice, it is likely that all of our behaviour is governed by a subtle blend of conscious and unconscious motivation.

Communication, both with self and others, helps us to satisfy our basic needs. Babies cry for milk, young people express their need for love through their behaviour, body-language, speech and writing, and self-esteem often results from making a good impression on other people through one's performance over a period of time. Our understanding of other people's motivation will affect our assessment of their characters. For example, we might perceive that Sam is desperately ambitious and find that tiresome, while Chris has no ambition at all – and that is deplorable. In either case our judgement is based on others' levels of motivation.

Advertisers are particularly interested in what makes us tick. If they know what our needs are, they can show how certain products can satisfy – or appear to satisfy them. Many of the food advertisements appeal not just to our need to eat, but the higher need of love and belonging, as acted out in many cosy, cheerful family kitchen-dinners. Politicians likewise need to know what people's needs are and what will motivate people in a General Election. In 1986 the Conservative government had created a low level of inflation (hence met the need for financial security of many), but a high level of unemployment (poverty and lack of self-esteem for many).

See also: Effect, Perception, Purpose, Self-concept.

ETWORKS

A network in telecommunications is a pattern of channels linked to each other via terminals, so that anybody participating in the network can contact anybody else. The telephone network is the one with which most of you are familiar. But any group of people like a family, constantly in touch with each other, forms a network.

It would be possible, in a very small telephone network, to link everybody directly to everybody else. The device of a switching centre has made much larger networks feasible. The reduction in the number of lines needed may be seen in Figure 33.

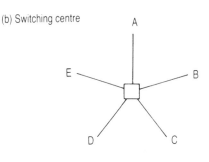

Figure 33 Networks

In some respects the national telephone network is like the railway network. Just as local services take you into London to catch a main line, inter-city train to Edinburgh, so your telephone call passes first through the local network into the trunk network. And if you ring up somebody abroad, then the call is channelled further into the international gateway exchange and sent by submarine cable, high frequency radio or satellite to the country you require.

The telephone network is currently being extended by cellular radio. This means that telephone calls can be transmitted from your home terminal to a radio and receiver in your car or in your back pocket. It is called 'cellular' radio because the area covered by these radio networks is subdivided into a large number of smaller areas or cells.

Telex, the international service for transmitting text, uses a network similar to that of the telephone, and the new, faster teletex actually uses the telephone network.

Computers, too, are linked together in networks so that data can be transferred from one location to another. These networks transmit data in digital form, making use of on-off pulses. Local area data networks link large numbers of computers on a single site, say a company headquarters or a university. Other computers are linked into switched star networks (see SMALL-GROUP NETWORKS); these in turn are connected to form a 'mesh'. This is quite like the subscriber telephone system.

Broadcasting networks, whether they use radio frequencies or cable are rather different from the systems described above. Here no switching systems are needed, as the radio transmitter broadcasts to all receivers simultaneously. However, there are networks of transmitters and cable TV services that require homes to be wired up to receive programmes through coaxial cables capable of taking up to 55 channels.

See also: Channels, Computer, Information technology, Small-group networks.
Further reading
P. Zorkoczy, *Information Technology*, Pitman, 1985, Ch. 4.

EWS VALUES

News values are the criteria that journalists have for deciding what is worth reporting, what is 'newsworthy'.

Traditions have grown up among journalists as to what constitutes news and what does not. In every newsroom there is a spike on which rejected, un-newsworthy stories are transfixed. What qualities does a news story need in order to bypass this spike and reach the newspapers or news broadcast?

From your experience of newspapers and TV bulletins you would be able to say at once that most news is bad news, that a great deal of news is about conflict and hardship, that some news is about famous people and scandal. Social scientists provide us with more accurate surveys of what is newsworthy. Galtung and Ruge (1973) discovered eight universal news values and four peculiar to Western media.

1 *Frequency*. The news media cope best with short-lived events like murders, riots, royal weddings, important political speeches. Social and economic trends over long periods are less newsworthy, though they are marked by reports and statistics from time to time, and these are reported.

2 *Threshold*. Most events go unreported because they have either not been brought to the attention of the media or are thought to be insignificant. Many events are reported in the local media, but only a few of these are picked up by the national media. Once a big story hits the headlines, further drama is needed to keep people interested. The crisis over Westland Helicopters is a case in point, with its revelations of improper behaviour by ministers and civil servants and important resignations.

3 *Unambiguity*. Events must be clear and not too difficult to interpret. The popular newspapers, especially, give little background to conflicts which cannot be presented in stark, good-versus-bad terms.

4 *Meaningfulness*. Events must mean something to the journalists and their audiences. Many news-gatherers judge that foreign news is less interesting to their readers than home news. Foreign news becomes relevant when foreign countries are perceived to pose some kind of threat, e.g. our heightened interest nowadays in Japan has to do with Japanese rivalry in manufacturing and exporting. However, a shattering event like the Chernobyl nuclear power station disaster in Russia over-rides this distinction, although it is still true that the threat of the radioactive cloud passing over Europe and the United Kingdom, and then the news of British students in the disaster-area were of major importance.

5 *Consonance*. Sometimes the media

forecast an event and their expectations help to bring it about. During the miners' strike (1984) the TV crews expected and were rewarded with violent scenes between miners' pickets and the police.

6 *Unexpectedness.* Journalists are interested in the unusual, the rare and the strange. Chance archaeological discoveries, sextuplets, and vicars struck by lightning are the stuff of newspapers and the last slot in TV news programmes.

7 *Continuity.* A good story has the capacity to run for quite a long time. Murders start with the horrid details of the crime, go on to the police search, perhaps an arrest, a trial, more lurid details, then a verdict and sentence. The story surfaces several times over a year or longer.

8 *Composition.* Newspapers and news programmes have a certain format. If the main stories are about foreign events, some fairly unimportant domestic story might be included for the sake of balance.

The four news values of special importance to our news media are:

(a) *Reference to elite nations.* Journalists do not scour the world evenly for news. Certain nations are more important than others. You only have to compare the amount of news about the USA in British newspapers and compare it with the amount of news from China.

(b) *Reference to elite persons.* Western journalists are interested in personalities, partly because their actions are thought to be more influential than the average person's and partly because their social lives, their affairs and their marriages are supposed to give us vicarious thrills.

(c) *Personalisation.* Events are perceived to be the actions of individuals, not of groups, parties and institutions. So it is Arthur Scargill (not the NUM) who threatens Mrs Thatcher (not the government or the Coal Board), or vice versa.

(d) *Negativity.* Bad news is good. Disasters are sudden, unambiguous and reflect widespread expectations of the worst.

Taken together these news values add up to a code or ideology, which journalists dissent from at their peril. They colour the mediation of events to audiences.

> **See also:** Mediation, Values.
> **Further reading**
> J. Hartley, *Understanding News*, Methuen, 1982, Ch. 5.

ON-VERBAL COMMUNICATION

Non-verbal communication (NVC) refers to all those body signals that we deliberately or inadvertently make when we are with other people. And since our clothes, hairstyle, grooming, face- and body-decoration are just as much part of us as are postures and gestures, they too belong to non-verbal communication.

NVC happens whenever people are together. For example, as I look around the classroom, student A is making jabbing movements with his index finger at his watch and pointing at the door. Student B, observing, smiles and nods her head. Student C is frowning. Student D lies slumped over his desk, his head buried in his folded arms. And what *have* E and F done to their hair? Many signals are passing to and fro during the last minute of the lesson, though not a word is spoken. Student A is using gestures to communicate to student B that it is time to go home. B responds with an expressive smile, and nods to signify her understanding of the message as well as her pleasure at its content. C registers perplexity. I can read this from her furrowed brow and infer that she cannot follow my attempt to explain the idea of 'feedback'. D communicates a state of acute boredom: his posture tells me that he is switched off. E and F must have spent hours plaiting their hair into dreadlocks: they are communicating a new shared self-image! All these students, in short, are using forms of NVC.

To ease the job of analysis, non-verbal communication can be divided into three sections: (1) body-language, (2) paralanguage and (3) appearance.

1 *Body-language* is made up from all our body movements that communicate meaning, with or without speech. At least eight codes are involved (according to Michael Argyle): touch, proximity, orientation, head nods, facial expression, gestures, postures and eye contact. Details of all these codes and the part they play in shaping what happens in face-to-face encounters will be found under separate headings in the glossary.

2 *Paralanguage* is dependent on your voice, and largely on speech. It is what makes your speech expressive and reveals your feeling. (See PARALANGUAGE.)

3 *Appearance* differs from the other two kinds of non-verbal communication, in that it depends on 'permanent' signs rather than movements and sounds which come and go.

Until recently little attention was paid to non-verbal communication, but it is now reckoned by some social scientists to be the most important element in face-to-face communication. Albert Mehrabian has calculated that, on average, the total impact of a message owes 7 per cent to the words, 38 per cent to the paralanguage and 55 per cent to non-verbal signals! Another social psychologist, Abercrombie, once wrote: 'People speak with the vocal organs but communicate with the whole body.'

NVC has five important functions. The first is to accompany our words, to underline or reinforce our verbal signals, and carry a great deal of information about our feelings. Consider the way we use our hands to emphasise what we are saying. If you watch any practised orator communicating with an audience (say, at political party conferences) you will see a whole repertoire of gestures being deployed. Desmond Morris calls them 'baton' gestures, because speakers gesticulate like band-leaders.

Secondly, NVC may replace speech. Situations arise where there are serious barriers to speech, such as:

A where the communicators are too far apart for speech, but still within sight of one another;
B where the communicators may be close together but actual noise (machinery, hubbub of voices) makes speech impossible;
C where the normal channel for speech is not available.

In case A, would-be communicators can resort to broad gestures, like waving, pointing and beckoning. These are everyday gestures that we may need to use from time to time. People who need to communicate regularly over a distance too great for speech but too slight for radio to be worthwhile, use specially-invented codes of gestures. One thinks of crane-drivers, bookies, auctioneers, studio managers, police on point-duty, sailors. The latter have several codes of flag-signals, including semaphore.

In case B, where there is too much commotion for people to hear themselves speak, factory workers lip-read and gesticulate to convey the necessary messages.

In case C, the speech channel may be blocked at either end, or both. Deaf and dumb people have been able to replace speech by gestural codes of various kinds, including the popular American Sign Language (said to have arisen from the American Indians' signs for communicating between tribes with different spoken languages).

Thirdly, NVC can contradict what we say. Like a girl who says with a frozen smile, 'Oh, I'd love to come to your party!' The facial expression betrays a lack of enthusiasm which contradicts her apparently eager acceptance of the invitation. If an interviewer stands up while saying, 'You don't have to go,' the physical change of posture carries the more important message. Our non-verbal behaviour is the more reliable guide to our real feelings.

The social scientist Michael Argyle has carried out experiments which show that where the non-verbal message contradicts the verbal one, the latter tends to be discounted. Furthermore, he was able to demonstrate that the non-verbal style in which a message was communicated had five times more effect than the actual verbal message itself. He concludes that just as animals carry on their social relationships (like finding mates or establishing pecking orders) by means of non-verbal signals, so human beings use a non-verbal channel in *their* social encounters. Our facial expressions, postures, distance-keeping, etc. convey our emotional reactions to other people, whereas we use speech chiefly to communicate information.

Fourthly, NVC can help our self-presentation. As social beings we have to present ourselves to other people. Everything about us, our physical appearance, the kind of clothes we wear, our regional accent, all combine to create a personal image. To some degree we can determine the impression we make on others: we can become clothes-conscious, pay attention to our grooming, even (though why?) modify our accent, whilst cosmetics and plastic surgery (for the few) can modify the face.

Trying to account for our lively desire to produce impressive images of ourselves through a range of non-verbal means, Argyle suggests that it is a way of overcoming the taboo against boasting. Since it is not the done thing to brag about your own achievements and glorify your own behaviour, you have to do it indirectly, either through speech in the form of false modesty or through your clothes, hair-style, accessories, posture and general behaviour.

We may have an ideal image of ourselves which we try to live up to, with the result that our dressing becomes dressing-up and our behaviour becomes play-acting. How long will it be before the mask slips and the real person is revealed?

Fifthly and lastly, NVC has an important part to play in our social rituals. We shake hands to open up the channels of communication. Originally, the right hand was extended to demonstrate that it did not hold a weapon and that its owner had peaceful intentions. Shaking hands when taking leave is the complementary piece of ritual that concludes a period of social interaction.

As we grow to adulthood, our progress is marked by various ceremonies. At a christening, the vicar will dip his fingers into the font and make the sign of a cross on the baby's forehead. This non-verbal act communicates to the parents and other witnesses that the child has been admitted into the membership of the church. The giving of presents marks birthdays, but the 21st birthday is especially important as this, traditionally, commemorates entry into adulthood. (The giving of presents and the celebrations that characterise the reaching of maturity in England are, however, nothing compared to the long and elaborate initiation rites associated with this step in some tribal societies.) At wedding ceremonies the man puts the golden wedding-ring on the woman's finger, a non-verbal act symbolising the marriage-bond. Award-giving ceremonies usually require the successful person to go forward from the audience to a raised platform to receive the prize, degree or medal from a figure of authority, and shake hands. Most of these ceremonies signify a graduation or change of status.

Many other ritual acts serve to reinforce existing differences of status.

Private soldiers are expected to salute officers. Until recently pupils rose from their seats in the classroom when the teacher entered. Members of the public *do* rise when the authority-figure of the judge enters the courtroom, in gown and wig.

See also: Appearance, Eye-contact, Facial expression, Gesture, Orientation, Paralanguage, Posture, Proximity, Touch.

Further reading

M. Argyle and P. Trower, *Person to Person*, Harper & Row, 1979.

J. Fast, *Body Language*, Pan, 1970.

D. Morris, *Manwatching*, Panther Triad, 1978.

Tony Lake, *Relationships*, Michael Joseph, 1981.

RGANISATIONS

An organisation is 'the rational coordination of the activities of a number of people for the achievement of some common, explicit purpose or goal, through a division of labour and through a hierarchy of authority and responsibility' (Edgar Scheinl).

Generally speaking, organisations are larger groups of people who have a common purpose which requires many different skills. Very few individuals are capable of building a car, none at all could build an airliner single-handed. An airliner can only be built through the combined efforts of a large number of specialists in an organisation.

There are three main types of organisation. Political parties, trade unions, working men's clubs and women's groups are all mutual benefit associations. Schools, colleges, hospitals and old people's homes are public-service organisations. Banks, industries, chains of supermarkets, all in the pursuit of profit, are business organisations.

Most business organisations are hierarchic in structure. Those at the top of the hierarchy take the most important decisions, for which they are paid the highest salaries. They communicate their decisions downwards through a *chain of command*. The number of levels within the hierarchy can vary a great deal, but the fewer there are, the greater the efficiency. The hierarchical arrangement of specialised tasks is the first principle of orthodox management. The second requires each department in an organisation to have a well-defined task to perform and be under the direction of a single leader. The third principle states that this leader is most likely to be effective where the responsibilities are narrow and the people under direction relatively few.

Figure 34   The hierarchy

Within an organisation, information can flow in three directions, downwards from top to bottom, upwards from bottom to top, and sideways at various levels. Whatever system of management is in force, a large amount of information must flow down the hierarchy from top management to the shop floor. However, research evidence reveals that downward communication can be extremely inefficient. The American researcher, Ray Killian, surveyed 100 US firms in the sixties to see what proportion of the information transmitted downwards was understood at each level of the hierarchy. He discovered that only 20 per cent of the information reached the shopfloor! Communication upwards from the bottom has two important *feedback* functions: the first to supply information on what action has been taken on messages transmitted downwards; the second to alert the decision-makers as to the feelings and attitudes of those lower down the organisation, so that they can devise realistic strategies. Lateral communication between departments is essential to coordinate activities.

Formal arrangements for communication in these three directions are implied in the connecting lines of a firm's *organisation chart*, which sets out the lines of authority and responsibility. See Figure 35.

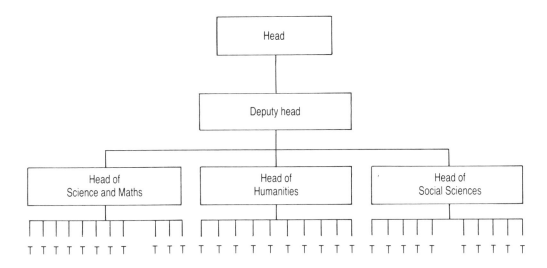

Figure 35   A pyramidal organisation chart (secondary school)

A great deal of information is passed around an organisation quite informally, avoiding the formal channels. Informal networks, called the 'grapevine', always spring up where people are in close and continuous contact with each other at work, and come to like and trust each other. Men and women meet socially in the canteen and after work, and rumours about sensitive matters like possible redundancies will fly.

Rensis Likert, in *New Patterns of Management*, identifies four systems of management, ranging from authoritarian to collaborative. The authoritarian system (the armed forces are good examples) is a marked hierarchy where ranks are emphasised, and distance is kept between superiors and subordinates. The subordinates take orders from above; there is little or no discussion. The collaborative system (Likert's preferred one), has decision-making widely dispersed throughout the organisation and the management encourages worker-participation in the setting of goals, developing methods and devising incentives. No rigid barriers exist between superiors and subordinates, so that there is plenty of two-way communication. Two intermediate systems show a progressive increase in two-way communication and some delegation of decision-making to people lower down the hierarchy.

In recent years various means have been introduced into companies and factories to improve worker participation. These include joint consultative councils and suggestion schemes, neither of which has been particularly successful. It may well be that management and workers have divergent interests and that no amount of formal consultation will produce the harmony and efficiency that companies dream of. An alternative form of organisation, gaining a little ground now, is the workers' cooperative. Here there is no clash of interests, since every member of the cooperative has an equal share in it, and the same voting power. They have every incentive to cooperate and work hard since they will pay themselves from the surplus (or profit) that they make. Most British cooperatives are on a small scale, like taxi-firms, caterers, cleaners and English-language schools, but Equity Shoes of Leicester has 200 employees.

See also: Group communication.
Further reading
R. Dimbleby and G. Burton, *More than Words*, Ch. 4.
Rensis Likert, *New Patterns of Management*, McGraw-Hill, 1961.

ORIENTATION

Orientation is the way we position our bodies vis-à-vis each other. It is an aspect of posture that shows how much attention we are paying to the other person.

Two strangers on a park bench will often twist their bodies away from each other, signifying a wish to remain private. If a couple choose to sit together side by side at a party, they can be intimate, if they wish, by twisting the upper part of the body to face each other. Like the use of eye contact, orientation of the body is another non-verbal code used to signal beginnings, changes of direction and endings of conversations.

See also: Non-verbal communication, Posture, Proximity.
Further reading M. Argyle, *The Psychology of Interpersonal Behaviour*, Penguin, third edn, 1978.

PARALANGUAGE

Paralanguage (para = beside) is a form of non-verbal communication that makes use of the voice. It is related to speech on the one hand and to non-verbal communication on the other:

Speech is verbal and vocal, it uses the voice to articulate words.
Paralanguage is non-verbal but it is vocal, using the voice to modulate the words.
NVC uses gestures, facial expressions, head nods, etc. to send non-verbal, non-vocal signals.

Paralinguistic features include such things as stress, intonation, voice-pitch, tone and volume, speed of speech, the 'ums' and 'ers' of hesitation, along with grunts, whistles and gasps.

English is a stress-language. If you gave every syllable the same stress, you would sound like a Dalek (We-will-exter-min-ate-you!) Every English word of more than one syllable has one syllable stressed more than the others. This is fixed: Mártin, Sháron, commúnicate, commúnicators etc.

But we can vary the meaning of what we say very significantly by shifting the stress from one *word* to another in a sentence. Consider the effect of the shifting stress in this short sentence.

1	2	3	4
Brian	sold	his	car

1 Brian and nobody else did.
2 Brian didn't give it away or take it to the tip.
3 Not his father's.
4 Not his motorbike, as you told me.

Intonation refers to the way your voice goes up and down, musically, when you talk. According to David Crystal, 'intonation is the most important means we have of organising our speech into units of communication'. At a very simple level, you can turn a statement, like this one: 'Chelsea's playing tomorrow' into the query 'Chelsea's playing tomorrow?' by raising your voice on the last syllable.

Most of our utterances are emotionally charged, sometimes lightly so, sometimes heavily. We are seldom neutral. We give away our excitement, anger, irritation, boredom, or amusement through our stress and intonation, whether we are breathlessly fast or falteringly slow, raising our voice or tailing off to a whisper. Our paralanguage tells the alert listener our feelings towards the listener, towards ourselves and the topic of conversation and about our emotional state in general.

Your voice, like your appearance and your style of dressing, makes a certain impression, and every voice is unique. Voices vary in loudness, tone, pitch, speed, breathiness and other qualities. More assertive and emotionally expressive people tend to have loud voices, while shy and warm people have soft voices.

The tone (or timbre) of your voice depends on the way sounds echo in the chambers of the mouth and nose. Resonant sounds delivered in a loud voice create an impression of dominance. Resonant sounds delivered in a soft voice convey an impression of sadness or affection. A throaty voice can suggest maturity, sophistication, or sexiness, while a flat voice sounds depressed. Boring voices are those where there is little variation in pitch to give meaning, colour or emphasis to speech.

See also: Non-verbal communication.

Further reading
D. Crystal, *Linguistics*, Penguin, 1971.

ERCEPTION

'Perception' refers to the way we become aware of the world outside ourselves, and in particular, of other people. By selecting, organising and interpreting the stimuli we receive through our senses we are able to create a mental picture of the world we call 'reality'. This vision of reality is going to vary from person to person, since your perception depends on such factors as your experience, beliefs, values and feelings.

The chief point to remember is that the mind is not a sponge or an empty slate passively accepting stimuli from the outside world via the senses. It is much more, as R. I. Gregory puts it, 'a dynamic searching for the best interpretation of the available data'. Your brain actually selects, arranges and interprets the sense impressions (or sensations) in a way that best 'makes sense' to it. It is these mental processes that actively produce a sense of stability and permanence from the stream of stimuli transmitted to the brain via the senses and the nervous system. So each one of us constructs his or her own reality. Fortunately our mental images overlap sufficiently to make social cooperation possible, but we should resist the temptation to think that we all see things in the same light.

A moment's thought will show that physical and psychological differences produce differences in perception. Colour-blind people most commonly confuse red and green. People under the influence of drugs or suffering from mental illness experience hallucinations, perceptions of reality which are totally convincing to the people who experience them, but deviating from what we loosely call 'normal' experience. Our needs, desires, motives and interests also influence our perception. Strongly-sexed people will be particularly alert to sexual signals in people and pictures, insecure people may perceive threats and conspiracies where none exist. There is a further constraint on how we perceive. What we have experienced or learnt in the past, influences what we perceive in the present: we see what we expect to see, or what we are trained to see. A rock music fan can discriminate between twenty or more different rock bands, a garage mechanic will soon spot what is amiss in a car engine; the specialist, in short, knows what to look for.

Because expectation plays an important part in what we perceive, we very readily filter out anything unfamiliar or unexpected. We may mis-hear simply because we do not believe our ears. Often the mental substitution of a more familiar word takes place so quickly we are unaware of the switch. Or we may misread something in the newspaper to fit in with our preconception of what ought to be there. Like reading meditation for mediation if meditation is the more familiar word, or even totally misconstruing the political slant of an article. Psychologists call this mental habit a *perceptual set*.

Perception is important to us as communicators because communication depends on the way we perceive ourselves and others. If we perceive ourselves in a positive light, if we have a good self-image and self-esteem, then we are likely to be able to talk and act confidently with other people. A poor self-image will make us timid, morose or touchy, at all events awkward in our social relationships. When communicating with others we need to be prepared to look out for feedback and so notice other people's emotional response to us (friendly or unfriendly?) and whether they are trying to dominate us or not. At the same time, we are bound to make all kinds of assumptions about others, classifying them quickly according to physical appearance, dress, accent, language and manner. This classification is always crude, since it is based on inadequate information. We all have an implicit set of rules which tell us which characteristics go together. Wayne may be handsome and intelligent, but is he likeable? Probably we perceive him as likeable because we know this is a common combination, though we do know that good-looking, clever and disagreeable people exist.

Another generalising habit like that of the *implicit personality theory*, illustrated above, is the 'halo and horns' effect. You may admire a pop-singer or footballer for their personality, success and looks and let these merits colour your perception of all their other qual-

ities, so that you vehemently reject criticism. Conversely you might think that scientists who practise vivisection lack any decent human qualities, and you make devils (hence the horns) out of people who are kind to their families and pets. We also fall into the trap of stereotyping other people by attributing to individuals all the supposed characteristics of their racial, national, religious or occupational groups; for instance that Germans are hard-working, and second-hand car salesmen are crooks.

All in all, interpersonal perception is central to an understanding of interpersonal communication.

See also: Attitude, Interpersonal communication, Personality, Self-concept, Stereotype/Stereotyping.
Further Reading
G. Myers and M. Myers, *Dynamics of Human Communications*, McGraw-Hill, third edition, 1980, Ch. 2.
R. Dimbleby and G. Burton, *More Than Words*, Methuen, 1985, pp. 68–84.

ERSONALITY

Personality is exceptionally difficult to define, and the subject has given rise to a large number of theories about the nature, origins and mechanisms of personality. For our purposes we could adopt a contemporary view which holds that personality consists of an individual's distinctive, consistent, patterned methods of relating to the environment. So personality is re- **lated to individual differences and the typical ways people behave. At the same time, each person has a number of characteristics or traits that cluster together in a pattern.**

We are all interested in personality, our own and other people's, so we tend to have all kinds of personal systems for classifying people who are in some way important to us. Very often we are unaware of why we classify people as we do and work on rule-of-thumb assumptions, stereotypes or pigeonholing, such as that good-looking, intelligent people must be good-natured, or quiet, sad-looking people have no sense of humour. Given the wide variety of human personalities, our *implicit personality theory* can easily lead us to misjudge people.

Some of you may work by a traditional system like the birth-signs of the zodiac to determine character traits. The evidence for any correspondence between birth-sign and personality is not certain, and you could deceive yourself rather badly if you think that because your friend was born under Cancer she is bound to have all the typical Cancerian characteristics rather than quite a different set. It is far better to observe your friends to see how they generally behave. This is not so easy, even after you have worked out the most important personality factors in social situations, i.e. whether a person is dominant or submissive, friendly or hostile. Any combination of the major traits is possible.

Psychologists have gone much further – as far as the astrologers, in fact – in trying to give a complete breakdown of personality traits. They have looked for single dimensions such as trustingness, and have presented them as scales with 'trusting' at one end and 'suspicious' at the opposite end. By making enough scales to cover the major permutations of personality, you can draw up a profile of your own or somebody else's personality. You might try your hand at the table below devised by R. B. Cattell.

1	Reserved	Outgoing
2	Less intelligent	More intelligent
3	Affected by feelings	Emotionally stable
4	Submissive	Dominant
5	Serious	Happy-go-lucky
6	Expedient	Conscientious
7	Timid	Venturesome
8	Tough-minded	Sensitive
9	Trusting	Suspicious
10	Practical	Imaginative
11	Forthright	Shrewd
12	Self-assured	Apprehensive
13	Conservative	Experimenting
14	Group-dependent	Self-sufficient
15	Uncontrolled	Tense

However, there is only rough agreement as to how many basic traits there are. The English language has about 20 000 words that refer to aspects of personality. It is not surprising, therefore, that different psychologists have reached different results when reducing this huge number to the basic traits.

Some theories have reduced humanity to a small number of basic types which are easy enough to identify. For example, Hans Eysenck believes that major differences of personality depend on whether you are extroverted (outward-looking) or introverted (inward-looking) and whether you are stable or unstable. This produces four basic sets of personality traits:

Stable-introverted: calm, reliable, careful, passive, controlled.
Stable-extroverted: carefree, sociable, talkative, outgoing, leadership qualities.
Unstable-introverted: unsociable, pessimistic, rigid, anxious, moody.
Unstable-extroverted: touchy, aggressive, exciteable, changeable, active.

In interpersonal communication, the better judges we are of other people's personalities, the more likely we are to say the right thing, to reach our personal goals and form good relationships. So any way we can improve our *perception* of others, and of ourselves, must be to the good. In any case all our performances depend on perception. If you perceive the other person as timid or reserved and yourself as extrovert and resourceful, you will probably do most of the talking.

See also: Perception, Self-concept.
Further reading
M. Argyle and P. Trower, *Person to Person*, Harper & Row, 1979, Ch. 5.
Houston, Bee and Rimm, Ch. 14, *Personality Theory*, second edition, Academic Press, 1983).

PERSUASION

Persuasion is a deliberate attempt by an individual or an organisation to bring about a change of opinion, belief, value or attitude in another individual or group.

The aim of most persuasion is to get people to do things that they would not otherwise have done. And people will not act before they see that in some way it is to their advantage to do so. Persuasion helps them to make up their minds or change their minds. We can go on to say that from the point of view of the person being persuaded, the process means a certain degree of psychological pressure. We can imagine a scale with *influence* at one end (the pressure is of rational argument) and *coercion* at the other end (the pressure is a threat of punishment). *Persuasion* comes somewhere between, employing rational arguments as well as appeals to the emotions. Your freedom to resist persuasion dwindles as you face coercion.

'Persuasion may be considered a special aspect of communication as it utilises various relationships that may be verbal or non-verbal, face-to-face or spanning distance, via all the media at man's disposal' (Jamieson). So we may say that persuasion is one of the most important functions of communication.

At an interpersonal level we are daily involved in trying to engage other people in our schemes and activities: perhaps we want somebody to go to the cinema with us, lend us £5, or help us with our homework. Traditionally boys have persuaded girls to go out with them; nowadays persuasion goes both ways. We talk about having powers of persuasion. What techniques of communication are meant?

1. Good *rapport* with the other person – a friendly, understanding manner;
2. a shrewd knowledge of what the other person is like and what his or her interests are;
3. the skill to judge what sort of appeal to make: to idealism, to the feelings, to a sense of obligation, and so on (Will she or he enjoy flattery?);
4. the wit to get the other person to see that they are doing themselves a favour by falling in with your wishes. ('You'll enjoy the film – it's had terrific reviews!');
5. eloquence, will-power, seriousness, and other qualities of this kind that will get you taken seriously.

By eloquence we mean not merely fluent speech or the right choice of words but a display of conviction, the urgent tone of voice (*paralanguage*) revealing the emotional commitment behind it; together with expressive *body-language* (plenty of eye-contact, facial expressions, physical nearness or even touch.) Writers agree that it is the

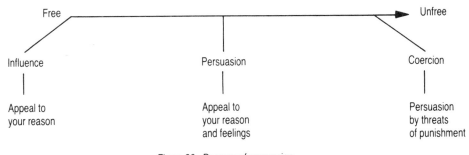

Figure 36   Degrees of persuasion

113

NVC that carries the greater persuasive power.

Most of our utterances carry some emotional charge, but when it is important for us to persuade others we are right and they are wrong, we may well find ourselves using highly *emotive language* to make our point. We may select words and expressions that are more likely to arouse an emotional than a rational response in the listener. For instance, 'If we give up the Bomb, the Reds'll march in tomorrow and trample all over us!' The effect of such an assertion is to arouse fears ('march in tomorrow' and 'trample all over us' are emotive expressions) and so prevent serious discussion of a complex issue.

Persuasion and the mass media

There are many agencies in our society anxious to persuade us to think differently and behave differently. The commercial advertisers, the political parties and pressure groups, the churches all try to change our *attitudes* through persuasive appeals via the mass media. It is usual to distinguish between *commercial advertising* that aims to change our living habits, and *political propaganda* that aims to change our voting habits.

The advertisers, whose chief purpose is to increase the number of regular customers for a product very little different from other products, have invented a whole array of persuasive techniques based on the skilled use of language, photography and film-making. Added to this, they made an almost 'scientific' use of psychological insight into their target audiences.

In *The Hidden Persuaders*, Vance Packard describes with many examples, how in the 1950s the psychologists came to the aid of the advertisers. Briefly, the idea was to find out what people really wanted (what motivated them) and then to manipulate them without their being aware of it. People have many hidden needs, as well as feelings of guilt if these needs are ignored or over-indulged. Early types of cake-mix required only the addition of water. They did not sell. It turned out that American housewives needed to add milk and eggs in order not to feel guilty about not offering something creative of their own to the family. So the cake-mix manufacturers took this into account and stressed the importance of the housewife's creative contribution. According to Packard, American males are power-hungry and satisfy this need by buying ever more powerful cars, speedboats, etc. However, they are also prone to guilt-feelings about buying cars too powerful for their practical needs. So the advertisers were advised to stress that all that extra horsepower provided 'the extra margin of safety in an emergency'!

To the weapons of 'psychological warfare' used by the advertisers in the fifties have now been added the dazzling techniques of the TV commercial. The aims are much the same: to *associate* the product with certain qualities (youth, freshness, health, naturalness, glamour, sexiness, etc.) and so create, through endless repetition, an *image* for it. At the same time the commercial *suggests* that by purchasing the product you yourself will experience something of the zing and excitement of the characters in the film. An extreme example of association may be found in the Marlborough cigarettes proved without a doubt to be dangerous to health, and yet associated with the healthy arduous life of the cattleman!

For information on the persuasive language used by advertisers and the conventions of persuasive photography and film-making, see *RHETORIC*.

See also: Attitude, Effect, Propaganda, Purpose, Rhetoric.
Further reading
V. Packard, *The Hidden Persuaders*, Penguin, 1982.

G. Dyer, *Advertising as Com-
munication*, Methuen, 1982.
J. A. C. Brown, *Techniques of
Persuasion*, Penguin, 1964.

PHATIC COMMUNICATION

**Phatic communication, or phatic
communion, is a social form of
communication designed to open or
to keep open channels of communication rather than to convey
any specific information. For example, 'Hello' or 'Lovely weather we're
having' are things you say to acknowledge other people's existence,
not to increase their stock of knowledge.**

Phatic communication takes up topics
that are trivial, like the weather;
non-controversial, like the latest disaster in the morning's news; and non-
emotional, like a prospective football
match. More serious subjects likely to
provoke disagreement are not phatic –
they could be seen as *emphatic*. Phatic
communication adds up to 'small talk'
but it should not be despised because it
is chat and not serious conversation. It is
useful for starting relationships, and
essential for maintaining relationships.
Many people keep up a light but
constant relationship with their neighbours through gossip. Sooner or later a
day will come when you will need your
neighbour's help. If you have kept up
good relations through phatic communion, you will have the necessary confidence to call on it.

Another effect of phatic communication is to reassure people that social
customs are being observed. You may
have noticed that all the people in small
villages greet each other whenever they
meet, and that produces a warm feeling
and a sense of belonging. This does not
happen in towns and cities, where the
sheer number of encounters, mostly
with strangers, is too great for an
individual to cope with: everyone shuts
off and only acknowledges other people's existence by looking away from
them and not bumping into them. This
was illustrated for fun in the film
Crocodile Dundee.

Small talk is a way of overcoming the
discomfort you feel standing or sitting
next to a stranger in silence. By making
a few harmless remarks about the bus
service or the slow waitress, strangers
reveal something of themselves through
the sound of their voices, their accent,
the mobility of their facial expressions.
They open lock-gates so that conversation can flow. Often, on buses, in lifts
and other public places when encounters last only a short while, talk peters
out after a few exchanges. But where it
does continue, it tends to follow a fairly
regular pattern. The next phase after
the conventional exchanges would be to
identify yourself through what you do:
'I'm at the college' or 'I'm in electronics'.
The aim of this ritual is to find out
whether you can get on with the other
person, to make some kind of social link.
Quite a lot of your communication,
particularly during leisure hours, is of
this kind, i.e. phatic.

See also: Accent, Channel, Facial
expression, Purpose.

POSTURE

Posture is the way you unconsciously arrange your body when you stand, sit, lie down or walk.

Gestures are closely related to our body postures. The difference is that we 'make' a gesture but 'adopt' a posture. The gesture is a signal confined to a small part of the body (it can be as small as a raised eyebrow or a crooked little finger) whereas a posture involves the whole body. Gestures are momentary; postures tend to be held for a longer period. In practice, gestures and postures merge. Imagine that you are at a public meeting and trying to catch the chairperson's eye. You raise your arm without moving the rest of your body (a gesture). The chairperson ignores you. You are excited, moving head and shoulders, and finally get to your feet (posture of urgency). Once acknowledged, you wave your hand in response (a gesture) and lower your arm.

Posture gives away your intentions. If your posture is relaxed, others will approach you with confidence, but if you are very tense with hunched shoulders and clenched fists people will be wary of you. And if you fall into a slumped, foetal posture, your intention may be to find sympathy.

The body shapes itself into signs for others to read. See whether the meanings you associate with the stick-drawings in Figure 37 agree with what Sarbin and Hardyk found some thirty years ago. What kind of behaviour do they suggest?

Postures give away relationships. Perhaps you have noticed that when friends meet for a chat, they adopt similar postures? In the refectory they rest the same elbow on the table and lean their bodies forward at the same angle, nodding in time with their heads. This unconscious imitation of the other's posture is known as *postural echo*. The stronger the bond of friendship is between two people, the

Figure 37 **Stick-drawings used by Sarbin and Hardyk to signify posture**
The above postures were widely interpreted to represent (a) curiosity, (b) perplexity, (c) indifference, (d) rejection and (e) observing.

more minutely their body movements mirror each other. You respond warmly to people who synchronise their movements with yours. This ability to echo body-movements is often lacking in the mentally ill, which is partly the reason why social contact with them is so difficult.

Most close friendships are between people of roughly equal status and these show nice displays of postural echo. But where there is a perceived difference of status, the postural behaviour will differ too. A man who perceives himself in some way superior to a woman or, for that matter, another man, will adopt a relaxed posture, leaning backwards and sideways if seated with arms and legs in asymmetrical positions. The other person may well sit in a more upright posture, knees together, hands folded.

When under threat, whether physical or psychological, we are often obliged to appease our opponent through submissive behaviour. The essence of submission is to demonstrate that you are smaller than your opponent and deserving of pity. This has resulted in a whole gamut of submissive postures ranging from abject crouching and grovelling to the slightly bowed head of the underling summoned to see the boss. Bowing and curtseying, both ways of reducing your height, are just two of the stylised forms used to mark submission. In church, Christians kneel in front of the altar; in the mosque, Muslims perform the kowtow, in which the devotee kneels on both knees and touches the ground in front of him with his forehead – a mark of submission signified by the name 'Islam'.

Why is it that subordinates are expected to rise when a superior enters the room? This would seem to equalise heights. Desmond Morris points out that two conventions clash in this instance. Whereas it is normal for the subordinate in the presence of a superior to make himself smaller, it is also usual for the superior to assume the more relaxed position. The subordinate rises from his comfortable sitting position to make this possible.

See also: Gesture, Non-verbal communication.
Further reading
D. Morris, *Manwatching*, Triad Panther, 1978.

ROPAGANDA

Propaganda refers to persuasive communication used by governments, political parties and pressure-groups to change (or reinforce) people's attitudes and views. For example, governments put out anti-drugs propaganda, political parties launch campaigns in favour of their own policies in the run-up period to general elections, and pressure-groups like CND put forward their arguments year in, year out, through the cheaper media like talks, leaflets and posters.

The term *propaganda* has its roots in the Catholic Church. In 1633 Pope Urban VIII set up the Congregation of Propaganda to propagate (or spread) the Christian faith in hitherto unenlightened parts of the world. So, as far as the Catholics were concerned, propaganda was a form of education. In communist countries today propaganda again is more or less synonymous with political education. The *Soviet Political Dictionary* defines it as 'the intensive elucidation of the writings of Marx,

Engels, Lenin and Stalin, and of the Bolshevik Party and its tasks'. But in the Western democracies *propaganda* has negative connotations and is associated with lying. Certainly, during the First World War, lies and atrocity stories without foundation were spread by both sides to influence the outcome. *We* attempt, then, to make a clear distinction between propaganda and education. Propaganda aims to change people's attitudes by means of one-sided, emotional, psychological appeals, whereas education, at its best, aims to help you acquire your values and beliefs, your view of the world, through exposure to a range of views and the process of rational discussion. In a nutshell, the educator shows people *how* to think, while the propagandist tells people *what* to think.

Propagandists, whether political or commercial, have a well-known armoury of techniques. Their approach depends on suggestion rather than on logical argument. *Suggestion*, according to J. A. C. Brown, is 'the attempt to induce in others the acceptance of a specific belief without giving any self-evident or logical ground for its acceptance, whether this exists or not.' (p. 25). People are at their most suggestible when they are very young, or in crowds. Children between the ages of 4 and 8 are extremely suggestible, but thereafter their readiness to accept ideas without questioning declines. Both Adolf Hitler and Billy Graham understood crowd psychology and used it for their different purposes. In a crowd, the individual's critical faculty is disarmed more easily than when alone: so conversions take place at the revivalist meeting, just as once fanatical followers were moulded at the pre-war Nuremberg Rallies. Propagandists exploit our emotions, especially if we have been frustrated in some way. They also play on our need to have some leader or messiah to solve our problems for us. After all, most of us

never overcome the effects of early socialisation, which required submission to our parents' wills. However, propagandists must tread carefully and not expect to make startling conversions overnight. They are most likely to be successful if they appear to be advocating more or less what people already believe, or if the change of attitude they are aiming for is sufficiently small not to threaten people's fundamental beliefs.

Propagandists assume that most people want issues to be simple, not complicated; that most people want their prejudices confirmed; that they need to feel that they belong (and that there are others, by implication, who do not); and that they want scapegoats to blame their frustrations on.

Within the general philosophy outlined in the last two paragraphs, propaganda employs the following tricks of the trade:

1 *Stereotypes* – for whichever group is being made the scapegoat for our misfortunes, such as blacks, Americans, Jews, communists, immigrants, members of the Establishment. Stereotypes are crude generalisations based on a few physical and/or cultural traits. Few individuals, in practice, match these stereotypes.

2 *Name-calling*. Names can be neutral like 'Americans' 'homosexuals', 'Russians' and 'policemen' or they can be loaded with emotional connotations: 'Yanks', 'queers', 'Reds', 'pigs'.

3 *Selection*. The propagandist selects only those facts that support his case. He makes no concessions to any alternative views.

4 *Lying*. Downright lying has been used. For instance, the British spread tales at the outbreak of the First World War of German troops stringing up Belgian priests as hu-

man bell-clappers. Big lies can often be disproved, so propagandists prefer to select and interpret facts rather than invent them!

5 *Repetition.* Lord Northcliffe once claimed that readers would accept views if they were repeated often enough. He spoke of 'damnable reiteration'. Propagandists repeat their messages, often in slogan form: for example, 'Guinness is Good for You,' 'Put Britain Back to Work,' 'Keep Britain Tidy', and so on.

6 *Assertion.* The propagandist asserts his claims. He does not support them with rational arguments.

7 *Pinpointing the enemy.* The Nazis pinpointed the Jews, the Stalinists pinpointed the Trotskyites. People respond rather easily to some focus of hate. George Orwell describes the process (with some exaggeration) in *1984* where audiences scream hatred for two minutes at a film image of the arch-enemy of the people, Emanuel Goldstein.

8 *Authority.* If the propagandist can show authority on his side, whether political, religious or scientific, we are more likely to be swayed by his claims.

Political propaganda is at its most feverish during times of revolution and war. For some insight into propagandist techniques, you might study First World War recruiting posters, the Ministry of Information's Second World War films and posters ('Careless talk costs lives' and 'Even the walls have ears' were two of the memorable spy-scare slogans). And Sergei Eisenstein's *Battleship Potemkin* and Leni Riefenstahl's *Triumph of the Will* should be seen as examples of communist and Nazi propaganda at their most powerful.

See also: Attitude, Persuasion, Rhetoric, Stereotype.
Further reading
J. A. C. Brown, *Techniques of Persuasion*, Penguin, 1964, Ch. 1.

ROXIMITY

In Communication Studies, 'proximity' refers to the space between the communicator and other people in various situations. The study of the way we use space to communicate is called proxemics.

You have only to watch how people choose their seats in an empty railway carriage or hall, to realise that some rules are being followed. If A sits at one end of a row of empty chairs then B will predictably sit half-way from the free end: AxxxxBxxxx. C will sit at the end of the row or D will go for the middle of the available gaps: AxxDxBxxxC.

These rules, which govern any use of space, have been learnt, and like other forms of non-verbal communication, vary from culture to culture. Each individual has *personal space*, which is an area with invisible boundaries surrounding your body, within which intruders are unwelcome. And you carry it around with you: portable territory. If others invade it, you feel threatened, but if others avoid it constantly, you may feel rejected. All the time, and mostly unconsciously, you are making a series of spatial adjustments to the people near you.

Sometimes, in a very crowded situation, like in a lift or in a rush-hour tube train, you find yourself pressed up against other people. You have to allow your personal space to shrink. Such body-to-body contact is normally for lovers, so to prevent any misinterpretations you look away, look blank, and move as little as possible. You pretend the others do not exist.

In crowded work-conditions people cut themselves off in various real and symbolic ways. One manager may have a private room and a secretary in an outer office to regulate – and even discourage visitors; another may have to make do with a partition or a corner position. These attempts at self-defence have been picturesquely described by Desmond Morris as 'cocooning'.

In a public library you establish your separate space by adopting a 'blinkers posture', the shielding hands serving as pseudo-blinkers. You also leave your bag or your coat – to reserve your place.

Dr Edward T. Hall, well-known for his work in proxemics, divides the way we use space into four zones:

1 *Intimate distance*, which is from touch to three feet. This is sufficient to allow people to clasp hands.
2 *Personal distance*, which is from 1.5 feet to 4 feet, representing the limit of physical domination. For example, two English people will chat in the street at a distance of 4 feet.
3 *Social distance*, which is from 4 feet to 9 feet. This is the distance at which we carry out many of our day-to-day transactions, such as buying goods from a shop assistant.
4 *Public distance*, which is from 9 feet to 25 feet and beyond. This is the situation of the teacher and the class

of students, the public speaker and the audience, the actor and the playgoer. Responding to the need to reach a distant audience, actors have tended to magnify and stylise their gestures, so widening the gap between stage behaviour and real-life behaviour.

The deployment of space is closely related to status. A high-status businessman may use a large desk and chair for himself and provide his visitors with small chairs. Thus he is able to dominate the proceedings. Similarly, a judge's status is enhanced by a raised bench, and a vicar's sermon gains authority from being delivered from a pulpit. A low-status person, when entering the territory of a superior, will show deference by knocking softly on the door, pausing inside the room, and pausing again while waiting to be asked to sit down. A higher-status person, on the other hand, may walk straight in, go behind the other's desk and stand over him, stressing his or her dominance.

See also: Non-verbal communication.
Further reading
E. T. Hall, *The Silent Language* Doubleday, New York, 1973.
E. T. Hall, *The Hidden Dimension: man's use of space in public and private*, The Bodley Head, 1969.

PURPOSE

The term 'purpose' applies to communication between people and assumes that we have various needs which we can satisfy in a deliberate way by communicating with others.

For example, you might feel lonely and need some company. To meet this need you might go to a dance or a party and talk to people of your own age in the hope of making some friends.

It would be difficult, though not impossible, to list all the purposes for which we communicate. The Open University lists five main areas of purposeful communication: information, persuasion, entertainment, socialisation and social functioning (taking part in ordinary social exchanges at home, at work and in leisure). Most communication goes far beyond giving or receiving information, or persuading others to help you to do things for you, though these are important purposes from earliest childhood. You communicate as a member of the family group and form all your later relationships by exchanging experiences with people who appeal to you, and by revealing the secrets of your own personality. Communication can be used to acquire power over others. It has been noticed that leaders tend to be fluent communicators (obvious cases are Hitler and Mussolini, both of whom were brilliant public speakers). Our thinking is a form of self-communication (*intra-personal*) that enables us to take decisions, solve problems and plan for the future. It also helps us to understand the changing world in which we, as changing people, live. Finally, we should not forget that we express ourselves to others by communicating the ideas of our creative imagination in writing, music, painting, dance and many other media.

Not all our purposes are conscious. Our body-language very often communicates information to others which we may not be aware of. A third person might notice they way you and a friend mimicked each other's postures (postural echo), which would give away information about the degree of intimacy between you. Incidental gestures, like yawning or propping up your head with your hands, are often just mechanical responses to tiredness or boredom, but nevertheless they signal your mood to other people in the room, perhaps to a lecturer who is being boring. There are many psychological theories of motivation, listing such things as self-esteem and the esteem of others, social stability and so on, which attempt to explain our hidden purposes.

Again, you may intend one thing and, instead of achieving your purpose, you produce quite an unexpected effect. Like the son-in-law who announced to his mother-in-law: 'Look, I'm wearing one of the sweaters you knitted.' 'Hm!' says she, 'so you don't like the other one?'

The idea of purpose governs face-to-face communication and mass communication, but it is not relevant to the external world of fields, quarries, ponds, forests, seashores, birds and insects, etc. that communicate information to the passing observer. Natural things such as smoke, fossils or flowers function as *indexes* (see SIGNS), signifying fire, ancient forms of life, and certain kinds of soil respectively. In these cases only the receiver or *consumer* plays an active part (see EFFECT).

A word about your 'A'-level project: you are expected to have a very precise purpose or aim for your piece of communication. The extent to which you fulfil this aim will be a measure of the project's effectiveness, and you identify the effects by giving the audience a chance to tell you in the form of feedback.

See also: Effect, Motivation, Non-verbal communication, Sign.
Further reading
R. Dimbleby and G. Burton, *More Than Words*, Methuen, 1985, Ch. 1.

REDUNDANCY

'Redundancy' is the degree of predictability in a message designed to make decoding easier or to strengthen contacts, or both.

You are familiar with 'redundant' meaning 'unnecessary' or 'out of work', both meanings having negative connotations. Redundancy in the communication of messages is a very positive concept. How is this so?

Meaning lies at the heart of messages or texts, but it is possible to convey more or less the same meaning in a few words or many words. For example, compare the following two examples.

(a) Dear Sandra,
    You know the Falcon Hotel? Could we meet there on Wednesday at 1 o'clock for lunch in the saloon bar? Look forward to seeing you.
    Love
    John
    (29 words)

(b) Next Wed. 1 p.m. Falcon saloon love J.
    (8 words)

The second message, in telegram style, has only a quarter of the words used in the first letter-style message, and yet the information is very similar. It has been estimated that in human languages about 50 per cent of the words used are redundant. There are other kinds of linguistic redundancy. How do we know that 'recieve' is a spelling mistake and not a word in its own right? There are in fact still enough right letters in the right places to allow us to identify it as 'receive'. So redundancy in spelling enables us to pinpoint mistakes and correct them. Supposing you read, 'When am I going to deceive the £5 you owe me?' This time you recognise the misspelling because 'deceive' is not as probable as 'receive' in this context. The context increases predictability of meaning – and is another cause of redundancy.

Redundancy generally contributes to the efficiency of communication. It does this in various ways. To begin with it is used to overcome channel *noise*. If the telephone line is poor, you repeat your message and spell out names. You look for different ways of saying the same thing. On military radio networks, special code-names are used instead of the letters of the alphabet: Able Baker Charlie stands for ABC. And there too repetition is the main form of redundancy.

Redundancy helps you overcome problems with your audience. If a specialist were addressing an audience of fellow-specialists then a lot of ideas could be conveyed in a short space of time in a tightly-argued lecture. But for a sixth-form audience, the information load would need to be lightened and ideas repeated in different ways to ensure understanding.

Redundancy helps you make the best of the medium. A book does not need so much redundancy built into it, since the reader can *re*read difficult passages and make further attempts to decode the meaning. A lecture should not be so dense with meanings and unpredictable ideas, since the listeners would be hard-put to decode them.

Whenever writers, artists, musicians and film-makers are ambitious to reach the widest possible audience they have to create works that are highly predictable in their form and content. The writers of Mills and Boon romances follow *conventions*: rules about what characters to have, what plots to follow and issues to raise. It is doubtful whether any Mills and Boon hero has been a coalminer, or whether any heroine has cut the wire-fence at Greenham Common cruise missile base.

On the whole, popular-songwriters avoid the unpredictable at all costs and work within the comfortable conventions of the medium. They think about young mass audiences and less about themselves and their own originality.

Following the conventions in the arts means a high level of redundancy (predictability) in the texts. If you follow *social* conventions (and are a *conventional* person) then your behaviour is predictable. You say 'Good morning' to your neighbours, return smiles, wear the appropriate clothes for the occasion, follow the fashion and generally show that you belong to your particular social group or subculture. A good deal of our communications with relations, friends and neighbours is 'redundant' in the sense we are keeping in touch, *not*

communicating information. When you say, 'Lovely day today, isn't it?', you are not telling your neighbour something new. It is different in this respect from saying, 'Looks as though your offside rear tyre is flat!' *Phatic* communication keeps the channels open between people, creates and strengthens social bonds. It shares around emotional warmth and a sense of belonging, rather than information.

See also: Context, Convention, Phatic communication.
Further reading
J. Fiske, *Introduction to Communication Studies*, Methuen, 1982, Ch. 1.

EGISTER

In linguistics a register is a variety of language defined according to its use in social situations. Where people work together, play together, even pray together, they use varieties of their mother-tongue that have been specifically created to help them communicate about their occupations, sports, religion and other activities. The non-technical term 'jargon' is commonly applied to registers, in a contemptuous way, when a person cannot make head or tail of some unfamiliar terminology and feels left out. For some linguists, 'register' includes the notion of 'style', but the present trend is to use 'style' to refer to the level of formality used in any piece of social interaction.

If you stop to think about it, you will acknowledge that you have a number of interests, games, pastimes, activities

that have their own registers of language. Bowling a Chinaman, getting a duck, or fielding at silly mid-on are typical cricketers' terms, whilst 'tacking' will mean one thing in sailing circles and another to dressmakers, and 'hacking' means both taking the horse out for a gentle walk in the country (riding register), and breaking into other people's computer records by electronic means (modern computer slang). The differences between registers are mainly ones of vocabulary, but some registers do display some typical grammatical forms.

The lawyers' register consists of 'affidavits', 'mortgages' and 'covenants' as well as archaic forms of English such as this (at the end of a covenant): 'IN WITNESS whereof I have hereunto set my hand and seal this eleventh day of September one thousand nine hundred and eighty-nine.'

Doctors have their own special abbreviations for their already specialised language of medicine. What does it mean when the house-surgeon tells the attending specialist: 'Well, we've bronched him, tubed him, bagged him, and cathed him'? It just means: 'We've explored his airways with a broncho-scope, inserted an endo-trachial tube, provided assisted ventilation with a resuscitation bag, and positioned a catheter in his bladder to monitor his urinary output.'

In secondary schools you have to master the registers of specialist subjects. At one end of the scale you may be encouraged to write poetry, using language in a vivid, often non-literal way, whilst when you come to write-up a science experiment you follow the convention of using the passive voice, thus: 'A lighted splint *was introduced* into the gas jar' (almost as if nobody was actually responsible for the explosion that followed!).

It must also be remembered that when the registers are spoken, there is the question of tone and delivery to be considered. The clergyman preaching in a spacious parish church uses a different tone from the TV chef demonstrating how to make a soufflé. The broadcasters in local radio cultivate a rousing and urgent tone which the presenters of *Playschool* would never use with their younger viewers.

The communication implications of registers are clear. Unless you know the jargon yourself, you may find yourself at a loss. It is tempting, but pointless to pretend that you do understand when you do not, and important to ask specialists to explain carefully what they mean. And since we all have some specialist knowledge, we should make sure as far as possible that when we use it, the recipient is on the same wavelength. To blind somebody with science is using communication to stun rather than to enlighten.

See also: Language, Slang, Style.
Further reading
P. Farb, *Wordplay*, Coronet, 1973.

RHETORIC

Rhetoric is a persuasive form of language. It also refers to the study of all those rules and devices that orators use to produce persuasive speeches, writers use to produce influential documents, and visual artists of all kinds use to create persuasive imagery.

These 'tricks of the trade' include such infallible 'claptraps' as climaxes (firing-off phrases or sentences in groups of three), antithesis (contrasts like: he may think he's *macho*, but he's really not *mucho*!) and rhetorical questions ('How much longer must we put up with such incompetence?') which do not require answers, only sympathy for the speaker's indignation! You only have to read a newspaper editorial or listen to a speech at a party conference to experience the rules of rhetoric in action.

In recent years scholars have become more conscious of the extent to which we are influenced by the sign systems that surround us. We now live in a highly visual age: our newspapers and magazines are full of photographs, the advertising hoardings carry huge blown-up photographs or cartoons, we watch our colour TVs for hours on end. A fair amount of this visual information is designed to affect our way of thinking and in the end our behaviour. So it is vitally important for us to understand how the rules of rhetoric are being applied in visual media such as photography and film.

Here, then, from the field of advertising, are some examples of verbal rhetoric and visual rhetoric.

Verbal rhetoric
From a Bosch washing-machine ad.:

Superwash design

The BOSCH Superwash plumbs plumb into your kitchen because BOSCH have invented steam-free tumble-drying – that means no exterior ventilation.

Superwash performance

The BOSCH Superwash operates smoothly and steadily – and unbelievably quietly.

Ingenious BOSCH drum-baffles wash the 12lb load with baffling brilliance. The swifter spin-drier spins dryer. It tumble-dries to order – ready to iron; to air; to wear!

Life's better with Bosch

1 *Repetition.* The brand name Bosch appears five times, Superwash four.
2 *Triple words or phrases* (another form of repetition): 'operates smoothly and steadily – and 'unbelievably quietly,' And 'ready to iron; to air; to wear!'
3 *Puns.* Advertisers love to play on words, and most words have more than one meaning, so the machine plumbs 'plumb' into the kitchen and the 'drum-baffles' wash with 'baffling' brilliance. A cigarette brand has been advertised for some years on the pun black/back (e.g. Switch Black, Black Together, Black Again) and Guinness has used an anagram of itself:

Guin(n)es(s) is pure genius

4 *Neologisms*, or invented words, e.g. Superwash.
5 *Antithesis*: setting words against each other for the sake of contrast: 'from thoroughly gentle . . . to gently thorough'
6 *Alliteration*: A chain of words beginning with or containing the same sound; for example, 'baffling brilliance', 'fine fabrics', 'better with Bosch'.
7 *Rhyme.* Like all the above rhetorical devices, rhyme can be used in poetry. Traditionally, it was used as a structural element as well an aid to the memory. Advertisers certainly want to aid your memory, so rhymes and rhyming jingles are common. In the Bosch example: 'to air; to wear!'

Elsewhere: 'A Mars a day helps you work, rest and play' and 'Triumph has a bra for the way you are!'

Visual rhetoric

Photographers and film-makers have evolved their own kind of rhetoric, a visual rhetoric to produce persuasive advertisements. Since association of the product with other, more evocative objects is a basic technique in advertising, the pictorial advertisement may rely on *metaphor*. Benson and Hedges produced a famous advertisement showing a group of four pyramids in golden evening light. A second glance showed that the fourth pyramid was in fact a giant cigarette packet: a visual metaphor. The unexpectedness of the similarity and the near-concealment of the packet contributed to the success of the advertisement. In an effort to persuade us to give up cigarettes, the Scottish Health Education Unit put out an advertisement which showed a huge cigarette-butt standing in a graveyard. The letters RIP were engraved on the filter and the caption ran, tellingly, 'Ashes to ashes': visual and verbal metaphors.

Another rhetorical device is that of *opposition*. A cheese advertisement showed a huge chunk of cheese surmounting the cliffs of Dover; the caption ran, 'The difference between chalk and cheese – real English Cheddar or the white cliffs of Dover'. The real message was that foreign imitations of Cheddar were inferior and should be rejected. The Dover cliffs, of course, are a potent symbol of British resistance.

Synecdoche is a rhetorical device which uses a part for a whole. A Chanel advertisement shows a bottle of after-shave with the tip of a man's umbrella touching it. The slogan runs 'A Gentleman's Choice'. The umbrella stands for the umbrella-user, the gentleman.

Some advertisements create their effect through a rich *accumulation* of details. An advertisement for Blue Band margarine depicts a proud father returning home from a produce show cradling a gigantic marrow. His delighted young son is making a grab for the winning red rosette on his lapel, while the mother, represented by a tray-carrying arm (synecdoche again) approaches with strawberries and cream. At the back of the room an orange tree is in full fruit. The accumulation of details, especially fruitful ones, add up to an atmosphere of abundance and, as the caption suggests, 'good, good feelings'.

For a more detailed analysis of visual rhetoric, read Chapters 7 and 8 in Gillian Dyer's *Advertising as Communication*.

See also: Persuasion, Propaganda.
Further reading
G. Dyer, *Advertising as Communication*, Methuen, 1982.
J. Williamson, *Decoding Advertisements*, Boyars, 1978.

ROLE

A role is a part a person plays within a given group and situation. This part requires certain kinds of behaviour which will help define that person's relationship with the other people in the group.

For instance, within the family you may play the part of oldest daughter, older sister, niece or cousin. As the oldest daughter, custom gives you special responsibility. Your parents expect you to be a pillar of strength in difficult times, and you expect to be taken into their confidence. As older sister you feel responsible for your younger brothers and sisters. So each of these positions (roles) in the family entitles you to certain rights but involves certain obligations too.

Each one of us plays a great many roles in the course of our lives. It is as Jacques said in *As You Like It*:

All the world's a stage,
And all the men and women merely players;
They have their exits and their entrances,
And one man in his time plays many parts

(Act 2, scene vii, lines 139ff.)

Social scientists have attempted many classifications of these many parts. For our purposes we could consider those *basic* roles, which depend upon sex, age, position in the family, and class (none of which is ours through merit of our own); and *occupational* roles, which generally are achieved through our own efforts.

If you reflect for a moment on the different roles you play, you might produce an array like this:

YOU

Family roles	Social roles	Work roles
daughter/son	friend	student
sister/brother	acquaintance	part-time shop-assistant
cousin	team-mate	babysitter
grand-daughter/son	member of band/drama	
aunt or uncle	group	

In our social life we have a certain amount of choice as to which role is adopted in any given situation. Here we have to take into account the situation itself, the other person and ourselves.

Situations often prescribe roles very clearly. Your friend is in hospital recovering from a serious operation: your role will be that of comfort-bringer. Probably you bring some token too: flowers, magazines or chocolates. Think how situations like interviews, private lessons, picnics and funerals would influence your role.

What about the other person? Your role, after all, is going to depend to some extent on the other person's role (you can't be an interviewer without having someone to interview!). What sort of behaviour are you going to expect, since roles go in pairs?

This will depend upon a whole host of factors, but the other person's role in response to yours will be influenced by things like age, gender, kinship, class and occupation. If you are a seventeen-year-old girl, the role you adopt towards a twenty-two year-old man of your acquaintance will differ quite considerably from the role you adopt towards a neighbour's five-year-old daughter you are looking after.

Finally, the role you choose depends on your own self-image (see SELF-CONCEPT), and at the beginning of any social encounter two people negotiate over the roles they adopt. Judy Gehagan makes the point that our social relationships are more likely to be harmonious if we clearly demonstrate what role we are playing and accept the roles other people are playing. Not to do so can end in embarrassment. If an acquaintance is playing the earnest philosopher and you persist in finding him comic, then the interaction will soon collapse. Embarrassment is a sign of communication breakdown.

Your choice of role has many consequences. It affects the way you dress, the way you speak and are spoken to, the kind of rights or obligations you may expect, the sort of people you encounter, the context of your conversation, and so forth. Perhaps you regard yourself as an aesthete. In that case you dress with sophistication to attract attention to your impeccable taste, talk about the arts to other aesthetes, and expect to be invited to private showings (but not to football matches).

Understanding and diversifying our roles is an important part of our development as human beings. Children aged from 3 to 5 play adult roles in the playroom. By playing 'mothers and fathers' or 'doctors and nurses' they reach some understanding of what it is like to be a mother or a doctor and this helps them to relate to adult behaviour. Role-play is also used as a socialising exercise for teenagers and adults. To adopt an unfamiliar role makes demands upon your *empathy*, so that if you can summon the empathy to play a role that you might see as antagonistic to your interests (e.g. parent, lecturer, policeman) your increased understanding of their roles might help you avoid or resolve conflicts with such authority-figures in your own life.

See also: Empathy, Perception, Self-concept.
Further reading
J. Gahagan, *Interpersonal and Group Behaviour*, Methuen, 1978, Ch. 1.
R. Dimbleby and G. Burton, *More Than Words*, Methuen, 1985, Ch. 3.

SELF-CONCEPT

Self-concept is the view you have of yourself as an individual. How well you know yourself and the feelings you have about yourself, whether positive or negative, all arise from communication with people since your earliest childhood.

It is now widely believed that your *self-concept* is largely the product of the way you *perceive* other people *perceiving* you. Just as you look in a mirror to see what you look like, so you study other people's reaction to you – to see what sort of a person you are. This is called the 'looking-glass' theory of self-concept. How does your self-concept develop? Broadly speaking, if your parents reacted positively to you and treated you in a loving, caring way as you grew up, you are likely to have developed a sense of your own worth as a human being, that is to say a positive self-concept. But if your parents never trusted you, you may have come to believe that you are untrustworthy, and that damages your self-concept. During the process of *socialisation* you gradually learn to behave in ways that people in general expect you to behave. Thus, if you think of yourself in a positive light, then you will imagine that others too think well of you. But if you have a poor *self-concept*, you will assume that others too think poorly of you. And here we have the possibility of *self-fulfilling prophecies*. Think how the morbidly shy boy, anxious about his worth and attractiveness, avoids meeting girls, and so appears to them as a loner, all of which discourages them from taking any interest in him, and he is confirmed in his original conviction that he's no good. On the other hand, psychologists describe the *Pygmalion effect*, which is where people can be coaxed out of their shells by friendly attentions (or stroking!) so that in the end they can see themselves as worthwhile human beings. (Pygmalion, by the way, was a king in Greek mythology who fell in love with the ivory statue of a beautiful girl he himself had carved. He prayed to Aphrodite, who brought the statue to life, so he was able to marry his beautiful creation.)

A further important habit of mind that may help us to develop our self-image, is having an *ideal* self-image. From our observation of people whom we admire, or fictitious characters in the mass media, we may evolve an idea of the sort of attributes we would like to have, the kind of person we would like to be. Starting in childhood, we have a tendency to select a gallery of people, first other children, then adults, pop stars, performers of all sorts, one after the other, with whom we wish to identify. Our choice depends on our having a measure of the desired attributes in the first place and on whom we find out about through education and the mass media. For example, a boy who has some talent for cricket may well look up to Ian Botham for inspiration. A girl interested in science may emulate Marie Curie or Caroline Herschell or any one of a host of successful women scientists she has heard of. A further point needs to be made. The achievers in society who are given the most media exposure become the usual models for the next generation. If, among those glittering models, there are comparatively few women (or the models who are given the greatest media-time are restricted to a few areas of performance like entertainment, fashion and the home) then girls on the whole will have fewer occupational goals to aim at than boys have. Likewise, respected black figures like Trevor MacDonald, the broadcaster, and Viv Richards, the Test cricketer, are particularly important (since they are rare) as models for young blacks to emulate.

To create and maintain your *self-concept*, constant communication with other people is necessary. You need regular feedback from them that confirms that the role you are playing (in the family, at college, in the job) is a valuable one and that you are generally respected. The feeling you get when you realise that what you do measures up to your *self-concept* is your *self-esteem*. You feel you *are* a capable student, a good runner, a practical person, a popular member of the gang; though it must be remembered that *self-esteem* goes up and down like mercury in a barometer. Only through communication can you get the necessary injections of praise and approval, and this is done by revealing yourself in various ways to other people and hoping that their reactions will be positive, so that their feedback generally confirms you in your *self-concept* and keeps your *self-esteem* buoyant.

See also: Attitude, Perception, Socialisation.
Further reading
M. Argyle and P. Trower, *Person to Person*, Harper & Row, 1979, Ch. 6.
G. Myers and M. Myers, *Dynamics of Human Communication*, McGraw-Hill, third edition 1980, Ch. 2.

EMANTICS

Semantics is the study of the way words relate to the world we experience through our senses. It has to do with the meanings in language.

We build up our experience of reality through a continuous influx of sense-perceptions that the brain reduces to some kind of order. At the same time we need to represent this experience to ourselves and to other people, and for this we use the symbolic code of language.

First of all, semantics tries to show how it is possible that words can communicate meanings. For many words, but certainly not all words, the so-called 'semiotic triangle' is a useful model (see Figure 38). In this triangle, the word consists of its form (its sound in speech, its spelling in writing) or the associated mental image or concept. The term *referent* is used for the thing the word refers to in the world of our experience.

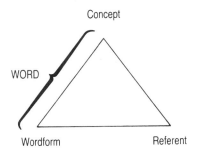
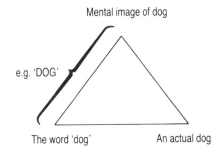

Figure 38 The semiotic triangle

By saying the word 'dog', we can evoke in the listeners' minds some mental image 'dog', so that they know we are talking about that animal. You will, perhaps, have noticed that most words have little or no connection with their referents. 'Dog' doesn't look or sound like dog, though 'bow-wow' does. A handful of onomatopoeic words, like 'cuckoo' and 'hiss' do exist.

Semantics goes on to study various kinds of meanings. First, we use words as symbols to point to things that are not present or which are highly abstract. So we can chat about a dog without a dog being in sight, or we can discuss justice or the afterlife, which are very abstract or speculative ideas. We know that we are talking about the same things, more or less, because there are generally agreed meanings of the words we are now using. These meanings, a kind which may be found in dictionaries, are called *denotations*. A *concrete* word denotes *few* details of the *referent* (see semiotic triangle above), an *abstract* word denotes *many*. For example, 'penny' denotes a coin of a certain value but 'finance' denotes anything from the money resources of the state to the management of public or private money.

We gradually discover, from childhood onwards, through trial and error, what *denotations* words have. But most words have another kind of meaning, they carry an emotional charge: their *connotation*. Consider how (a) a professional burglar, (b) a middle-class lady living in a small country town, and (c) an unemployed black teenager living in Brixton might react to the word 'police'.

To the first, 'police' would mean the enemy to be outwitted at all costs; to the second a protective body of polite young men getting younger every year; to the last an unpredictable bunch of white racists bent on harassing the black community. All these are obviously partial views of the police, but views of

this kind certainly colour people's responses to the word 'police'. Your personal experience of father, mother, daughter, son, estate agent, car-salesman, fascism, trade-unions, package-tours, community relations, Scotland, the police, etc. will affect your reaction to these words when you hear them and when you use them, and since your experience is likely to differ from that of other users, your *connotations* for these words will differ correspondingly.

If you want to prove this point, try measuring *connotative* meaning by means of a semantic profile. This consists of series of nine-step scales, each with a pair of bi-polar adjectives (e.g. ugly, beautiful) at each end, as in Figure 39. Without pondering too hard over the adjectives, and working quickly, put your Xs on the scales. If you have no particular feelings or associations, put your X in the middle, which is neutral. When you have finished, join the Xs, and you have a profile. The profile above could be the lady from Hereford's semantic profile for 'police'.

Apart from the personal *connotations* that many words have for us, there are other connotations which arise from the culture in which we live. For instance, the term 'democracy' has very positive connotations (along with all its many denotations) for British people today, but it has not always been regarded as the best form of government in this country.

Since 'people have similar meanings only to the extent they have similar experiences' (Myers and Myers) what are the implications for communication? Undoubtedly people experience life differently, so they will all have their private funds of connotations, but fortunately they will agree with each other to a large extent in the denotations of the words they commonly use. Misunderstandings arise for two reasons:

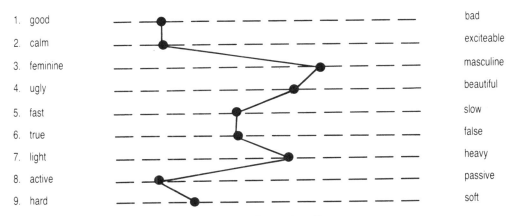

1.	good	bad
2.	calm	exciteable
3.	feminine	masculine
4.	ugly	beautiful
5.	fast	slow
6.	true	false
7.	light	heavy
8.	active	passive
9.	hard	soft

Figure 39   A semantic profile

1 the abstract words we use denote too many details or trigger off too many connotations.

2 we tend to assume that others use words in identically the same way as we do.

It seems then that thoroughly efficient interpersonal communication is impossible, but it is certainly possible to improve your messages to others and your interpretation of incoming messages. That is where *communication skills* come in.

> **See also:** Communication skills, Language, Sign.
> **Further reading**
> G. Myers and M. Myers, *Dynamics of Human Communication*, McGraw-Hill, third edition 1980, Ch. 5.

EMIOLOGY/SEMIOTICS

Semiology is the study of the way people generate meanings from the sign-systems that they use for communication purposes.

'A science that studies the life of signs in societies' is how Ferdinand de Saussure, the Swiss linguist, described it in a book of lectures published some 70 years ago. The name 'semiology' (the American term is 'semiotics') is derived from the Greek *semeion* = 'sign'. In recent years, particularly under the influence of the French writer Roland Barthes, analysis of sign systems has become fashionable at college level. There you may expect to encounter a semiological approach to film, television, photography and publicity, and in some cases even to the more traditional subjects of literature and art.

Briefly, semiology is interested in the kind of signs we use (see SIGNS) and the various ways they are able to convey meaning. Some signs, for instance, look like the things they stand for, but far more remarkable are the large numbers of signs, either words (sound signs) or visual signs (symbols) that bear little or no resemblance to their meanings. It is this ability to *symbolise* things, events, ideas, and feelings that makes human communication so much more sophisticated than that of other creatures.

Signs rarely exist in isolation. So semiologists are interested in the way signs come in sets and are combined according to certain rules or conventions to produce meanings: they study the codes of society (see CODES). And by studying the codes they come nearer to understanding what makes a particular culture tick. Nothing is too modest to escape their attention. Roland Barthes studied the toys in French shops, noticing that nearly all of them were accurate replicas of adult objects or activities (trains, cars, hair-driers, dolls that 'pee' and the like). These toys all signified features of the adult world for acceptance by the child. Only a few toys, like sets of bricks, encouraged children to create their own structures. Had he examined British toys he would have seen many designed to stimulate the creative side of children.

Communication Studies at 'A'-level places the emphasis on communication as a process, and transmission of messages from senders to receivers, using various media and channels, encountering noise and prompting feedback. The semiological approach is rather different. Here, communication is considered as the generation of meanings. The emphasis is on the signs we use. Clearly the closer my knowledge of a code is to yours, the more likely we are to understand each other. It remains to be said that semiologists prefer to work with permanent messages, using the term 'text' even for visual messages like photographs, films and advertisements (see MESSAGE/TEXT). The generation of meaning results from the encounters between the *reader* (this term is preferred to receiver) and the *text*, and this requires a lot of mental activity from the reader, who brings knowledge, experience, attitudes and feelings to the interpretation. Anyone who reads poetry, the most concentrated form of language, will know how easy it is for different people to reach quite different interpretations of the same poem.

See also: Code, Culture, Message/Text, Sign.
Further reading
P. Guiraud, *Semiology*, Routledge & Kegan Paul, 1975.
J. Fiske, *Introduction to Communication Studies*, Methuen, 1982, Ch. 4.

THE

SENSES

The senses are the receptors in our bodies which convey a great variety of information, both from the outside world and from within the body, to the brain.

This information we experience as *sensation*. The way we organise and interpret sensations is *perception*. We have included some consideration of visual perception in this section, rather than under PERCEPTION, which deals with social and interpersonal perception.

The senses, their specific organs and receptors, and the sensations we feel may be summarised as follows:

Sense	Sense organ	Sensation
visual	eye	seeing
auditory	ear	hearing
tactile	touch-receptors	touching
gustatory	tongue and mouth	tasting
olfactory	nose	smelling

There are other senses too, like our all-important sense of balance, and it is worth remembering that not all our receptors are on the body surface to bring us vital information about ourselves and our environment; some are internal and tell us, like stomachache, something about our inner state.

Our senses have their limitations or constraints. They can only respond to a fraction of the total information in the environment. We can only see one-seventieth of the whole light spectrum. We cannot see infra-red, ultraviolet, X-rays, or gamma rays. We can only hear sounds between 20 and 20 000 cycles per second. Dogs hear and smell more efficiently than we do.

Most of our sensory channels – the nerve routes to the brain – are active all the time, but we are not aware of all the noises within earshot (e.g. traffic passing, clocks ticking) or all the physical sensations (e.g. from our clothes, crossed ankles, shoes) unless something happens to bring them to our attention. To understand how this happens, see ATTENTION.

Of all the senses, sight and hearing are the most important for communication. The symbolism we have developed (speech and writing) depends on just these senses, and not on the others. Our art is visual or auditory, as are most of our communications codes (Braille is an exception in using the sense of touch, and this has been developed to compensate for the absence of sight). Not much of our communicating is done through taste or smell. We do not, for instance, mark out our territory with odours as some animals do; we prefer hedges, walls and 'No Trespassers' signs. In the 'clinical' Western world there is a strong prejudice against body odour. But this has not always been so: Napoleon is said to have written to Josephine after one of his campaigns, 'I'll be home next week, so please don't wash.'

Sight

Our eyes are receivers of light waves, coming either directly from the sun or some other luminous source, or indirectly as reflected light. The eyes then focus images on a light-sensitive area called the retina. As in a camera, these images are reduced in size, reversed and upside-down. Nerve cells in the retina convey the information via the channel of the optic nerve and optic tract to the brain. Our experience of the world leads us to perceive the sky above and not below us.

The eye and the brain between them discriminate between degrees of brightness and colour, perceive space in three dimensions, recognise forms and patterns, and detect movement. Experimental psychologists have described how our perceptions are subject to certain rules. We pick out objects from their backgrounds, fill in gaps where the information is incomplete (closure), see continuity in elements going in the same direction and group objects that are either close together or similar in appearance. In all these activities the brain is not just decoding information presented to it, but interpreting it, reversing images, separating out forms, and completing patterns, as in the example of closure in Figure 40.

Figure 40 The brain completes the pattern: closure

Sometimes the brain finds it hard to choose which is figure and which is background, as in the well-known ambiguous drawing in Figure 41. And sometimes the brain misperceives altogether as in the many cases of optical illusion, like the equally well-known pair of arrows in Figure 42.

Figure 41 An ambiguous figure. Which is the object and which is the (back)ground? Black faces and white urn fluctuate and one signal is interfered with by the other.

Figure 42 The Muller-Lyer arrow effect

Hearing

Our auditory sense responds to sound waves, which are simply vibrations of the air and other substances. The rate of vibration is called the frequency, which corresponds to pitch. The number of vibrations or cycles per second are called hertz (Hz), our range being between about 20 and 20 000 Hz. Slow vibrations give low-pitched sounds, rapid vibrations give high-pitched sounds. The amplitude or size of the vibrations determines what we experience as loudness. Like light waves, sound waves are recoded a number of times before reaching the brain. When the pressure waves of air strike the ear-drum, they cause the drum to vibrate, which in turn affects an assembly of three small bones which activate fine hairs in the cochlea. These hairs transform the mechanical vibrations into nerve impulses which are decoded in the brain and perceived as sounds of a certain pitch and loudness.

Hearing is a particularly important sense because we need it for learning to speak, and so to develop our ability to think. Children born deaf have huge difficulties in developing a personality and escaping from speechless isolation. Hearing has another great advantage: it is non-directional. We can hear sounds from behind as well as from in front, so this sense can warn us of unseen dangers (see also CARRIER).

In face-to-face communication we use our hearing to decode spoken information, attending both to what is said and how it is said (see PARALANGUAGE). Many misunderstandings arise when people, especially older people, mishear what is said. Mishearing as a result of partial deafness is, of course, different from mishearing or not hearing as a result of inattention or perceptual 'set'. Listening is a communication skill (see LISTENING).

See also: Attention, Carrier, Decoder/Decoding, Listening, Paralanguage, Perception.
Further reading
R. L. Gregory, *Eye and Brain*, Weidenfeld & Nicolson, 1966, Chs 1 and 4.
Open University, Technology Foundation Course, Units 2 and 3, *The Human Component: Speech, Communication and Coding*.

$\mathcal{S}$IGN

A sign has a physical form, something we can perceive with our senses; it must refer to something apart from itself; and it must be recognised by people in society as a sign.

So we perceive with pleasure, the three XXXs at the end of a love letter, knowing that they refer to kisses, because that is what they *signify* in the context of a letter. They mean something quite different on a car number plate or mathematics homework.

The fact that messages have any meaning at all must be put down to the existence of signs, which come in many different forms such as spoken words, written words, gestures, logos, and photographs. They are organised, generally, into systems called codes. Thus 'the study of signs used in communication, and of the rules operating upon them and upon their users, forms the core of the study of communication' (Colin Cherry, *World Communication – threat or promise*? p. 8). This fairly recent study of the way signs and codes function in society is called *semiology* or *semiotics*.

Ferdinand de Saussure, the Swiss linguist who founded semiology, expressed the idea of 'sign' in this famous equation:

$$\text{sign} = \text{signifier} + \text{signified}$$

The signifier is some kind of sound, inscription or drawing, even a smell, while the signified is the meaning which the signifier evokes in the mind of the receiver. The important thing to remember is that while signifiers exist in the outside world (words, badges, road-signs) the signifieds (meanings) exist in the minds of people who recognise signs

as signs. How does this work in practice? Take a familiar road-sign (Figure 43). Here the signified is a painted design on a metal lollipop to be found in a specific place by the roadside. We can break this design down into three parts, each of which has a meaning for us:

Figure 43 Road-sign

1 The red circle signifies prohibition. This sign belongs to a whole class of signs which we must obey. Otherwise we may be prosecuted. The colour red has the well-known *connotation* of danger and therefore warning. And we know that the circle signifies prohibition, because we have learnt this from the Highway Code.

2 The diagonal bar signifies 'no' or 'don't'.

3 The direction arrow turning back on itself signifies a U-turn in the road that a driver might want to perform.

Add all these signifieds together and you understand that when you see that sign you are not permitted to double back.

Several scholars, other than Saussure, have modelled the way signs work, their diagrams being triangles linking the sign itself with the thing it refers to and the image evoked in the sign-user's mind. C. S. Peirce's model (Figure 44) will serve as an example.

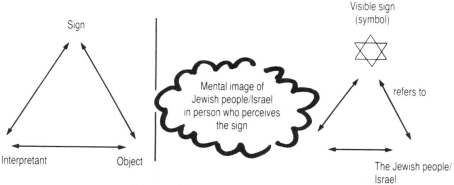

Figure 44   C. Peirce's semiotic model

Peirce classified signs into three: icon, symbol and index (see Figure 45).

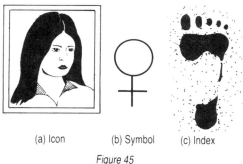

(a) Icon   (b) Symbol   (c) Index

Figure 45

An example of the first would be your passport photo. It is a very accurate representation of you. All the details in the portrait act as signifiers, so that anyone who knows you will know the signified. Signs which actually look like the thing they stand for are called *icons*.

Now take, for instance, a sign that does not look like anything much, beyond a cross attached to the bottom of a circle. In fact, it signifies 'female' and is used in biology books as well as by the Women's Movement. (See Figure 45.) A sign which has no visible connection with what it signifies is called a *symbol*. It is interesting to note, in passing, that this was originally used to signify copper, a soft metal, whereas the corresponding male symbol stood for iron.

What does this tell you about the thinking of the people who attached sexual meanings to the old chemical symbols?

An example of the third kind of sign would be a footprint in the sand, indicating that a barefooted human being has passed that way. In other words, the sign has a direct consequential connection with its object: it is evidence of its object. This is called an *index*.

In practice, the index is usually a sign that just happens. There is no intention to communicate. The smoke curling above the trees is a sign of a fire; the cigarette burns in the carpet are signs of last night's party; the cracks in the wall are a sign of subsidence, and so on. We decode meanings from these signs, but nobody in particular wanted us to see them. On the other hand, road-signs are deliberately placed by the roads department to indicate hazards lying ahead for the road-user.

We shall concentrate on icons and symbols, which are used in a deliberate way to communicate messages. Among icons, which look like things they stand for, we would include photographs, maps, the human figures used in road-signs, and picture-writing. For instance, to understand a map of the British Isles we need to know that the line that makes the shape on the piece of paper represents the coastline. Nowadays, with satellite photographs, we can actually *see* that the outline of the British Isles looks like the familiar shape in the atlas. A young child or a person from a non-literate culture would see a shape and nothing more.

When we come to symbols, the connection between the signifier and signified is far less obvious. In the case of most words, the word-form has nothing to do with its meaning, so most words are symbols (see SEMANTICS). Only a few, those which sound like their objects, i.e. onomatopoeic words like 'sizzle' and 'crackle' could be called iconic. Symbols include the white rose, the crescent moon, the red cross, the star of David, the Arabic numerals, the scales of justice, and so forth. Since the meanings for symbols are virtually impossible to guess, we have to learn them. Learning the meanings of symbols, whether graphic or verbal, helps to give you the knowledge you need to live and work effectively in your culture.

It is important to remember that the *interpretant* is not simply the person who sees the sign, but the effect the sign causes upon the user's mind. Since people have different experiences of Israel, and different feelings about the Jewish people, the sight of the Star of David produces different emotions. In short, the meaning of the sign depends on the user's experience and will vary accordingly. Like words, signs have denotations and connotations.

a clear advantage over English language signs, and with the increase of international travel a set of internationally-agreed signs makes life much easier for the traveller. Similarly with road signs. Moreover, bearing in mind the speed of modern traffic, it is obvious that even English drivers have little time to read lengthy verbal instructions or warnings (see the signification of the 'No U-turn' sign above). The great advantage of the graphic sign is that it is easy to decode; the shape (e.g. circle or triangle) stands out, the signifiers are usually clear and simple. In fact, an effective sign should

1 be simple and stress what is important,
2 carry a meaning which the greatest number of possible users are likely to understand,
3 stand out from its background in shape and colour.

In Communication Studies, gestural signs are generally studied separately as part of non-verbal communication.

Graphic signs

Much of our public communication to do with direction-finding, traffic regulation and labelling of places, makes use of graphic signs, sometimes with words but often *instead* of words. In an international airport graphic signs have

See also: Code, Language, Semiology, Signal.
Further reading
P. Guiraud: *Semiology*, Routledge & Kegan Paul, 1975.
J. Fiske: *Introduction to Communication Studies*, Methuen, 1982.

SIGNAL

A signal is the physical form in which a message is given in order for it to be transmitted. It can take the form, for example, of an utterance, of writing, of a gesture, of a telephone call or a radio transmission. Some writers distinguish between an ephemeral signal such as a gesture and a permanent *text* (see MESSAGE/TEXT). The words 'signal', 'message' and 'text' are often used interchangeably and it is necessary to decide which meaning the writer intends.

The term 'signal' is often used as an equivalent to 'sign'. For example, here is Colin Cherry writing about speech, writing and gestures. 'Such physical signs or signals have the ability to change thoughts and behaviours – they are the medium of communication' (*World Communication – threat or promise?*, p. 121). Fiske tells us that a code 'consists of *signs* (i.e. physical *signals* that stand for something other than themselves.)' Both writers use *signal* as though it referred to the meaning (content) of messages rather than just to the form. Elsewhere, Colin Cherry calls a *signal* a sign-event, which implies that a sign becomes a signal when it 'happens' or when it is activated. For example, our roads are dotted with permanent signs, but only when we react to them do they become signals. Better still, they signal (verb) to us. In the case of language, we all have a mental dictionary of words – that is, signs – but only when we speak or write do they become signals.

The authors of the Highway code make a distinction between signs and signals: signs are static and unchanging, whilst signals (e.g. traffic lights) involve switching.

If we accept that what makes a signal different from a sign is some form of movement or activation, then we can agree with the authors of *Key Concepts in Communication* (Tim O'Sullivan, J. Hartley, D. Saunders and J. Fiske) that whereas a sign is by definition meaningful, a signal is simply the physical form of the message.

How can a signal convey a message? It does this by modifying a *carrier*. In front of you, you have a blank sheet of notepaper. You modify the empty sheet by writing on it so that it contains signs which you hope will accurately convey your intended message. The *text* is now ready to be taken via a *secondary* carrier, the postal service, to its destination. The text is your signal. When you speak into a telephone mouthpiece, your voice modifies (or *modulates*) a steady electrical current flowing through it to create a signal, which is decoded by the receiver for the message it embodies. Telecommunication engineers are interested in the quality of the signals they can facilitate through their many different networks. A TV engineer talks about a poor *signal* if the picture is fading in a snowstorm. To improve the signal it is necessary to remove the source of the *noise* or interference.

See also: Barrier/Noise, Carrier, Message/Text, Sign.
Further reading
Tim O'Sullivan *et al.*, *Key Concepts in Communication*, Methuen, 1983, under 'Sign/signal'.

SLANG

Slang is a colloquial register or sub-language used in various occupations. It can be distinguished from register (or jargon) by the humour in the words. Nor need it be confused with dialect. Slang is not confined to particular geographical regions as a rule, nor does it have its own pronunciation, intonation and grammar. A slang has its own vocabulary, and the word 'slang' may refer to the easy-going way that the words are 'slung' about in the workplace or after-hours.

Most slang is fairly recent, is added to daily and dates quickly. How much of this RAF slang from the Second World War is still in current use?

Register	Slang
aircraftsman	erk
control column	joy-stick
crash-landing	pancake
successful operation	wizard prang

Slang is the most informal kind of English possible and for that reason is more widely used by younger people than more staid people. You would have no difficulty in following this: 'Jimmy had a skinful last night. He looked pretty groggy when he went to chat up the birds. They told him to b____ off and puke up outside. He wasn't too chuffed about that!'

Certain things and activities are particularly fertile in generating slang words. For example,

1 Parts of the body, especially the head and sexual organs
   (boko, bonce, nut, rocker, block, loaf, etc.)
2 Eating and drinking
   (Stuff it down, get stuck into it, swill it, sink a pinta, knock it back, etc.)
3 Ways of speaking
   (chunner, chunter, blather, rabbit, etc.)
4 Money
   (brass, dough, lolly, loot, etc.)

Slang is often specific, like a register. The drug-scene has its own rich vocabulary. *Pushers* sell *shit* or *grass* (marihuana) or *acid* (LSD). The *junkies* (addicts) who buy it go on *trips* at *freak-outs*. And so on. Prisons too have their own slang. In the *nick* you are guarded by *screws*. Tobacco is *snout*. The East End of London is famous for rhyming slang, though the habit of using rhyme words instead of the usual words is widespread in the north as well. It reveals a playful, humorous and experimental attitude to language. What is this Londoner saying? 'Why can't I stay? Use your loaf. Gotta get back to my trouble. And the God forbids. Still, I've got room for one more pig's ear before I hit the frog.'

Slang is the most informal kind of speech (it is less commonly written), that has grown up from group practices in work and leisure. It eases communications in the noise and heat of industry, it consolidates groups of teenagers, and (like dialect and jargon) serves as a badge of identity. Slang is often condemned for being 'loose' or 'lazy' speech, and schoolteachers have no doubt struck out slang expressions from your formal essays. But from the point of view of communication, slang is perfectly effective in its everyday place. It can sound odd in serious writing, and when a vicar in his pulpit exclaims, 'Stuff this for a lark!' the effect is comic.

See also: Language, Register, Speech.

SMALL-GROUP NETWORKS

Small-group networks are communication networks comprising five members, used by social scientists for experimental purposes to discover the characteristics of their performances.

In the late forties and early fifties, Alex Bavelas and Harold J. Leavitt carried out a series of experiments with small networks, using five people in a standard group. Leavitt invented a specially-partitioned table for five participants that allowed the five networks in Figure 46 to generate.

The experiment was simple. Each member of the group was given a card bearing five out of a possible six symbols. Each card omitted one symbol, a different one in each case, though all cards had one symbol in common. The task was for the group to identify that symbol by asking each other questions, but they were restricted by the network available to them. Each member of the network was faced by six labelled switches, one of which had to be thrown as soon as the correct answer was thought of. In this way the accuracy as well as the duration of the communication could be measured.

Considering just the first four networks, from the point of view of speed, the 'Y' and the wheel networks turned out to be significantly faster than the circle and the chain. The circle was the most active network, making more mistakes than the others, but also correcting more of the errors than the others did. Participants were also asked whether they felt that their group had a leader. No one emerged as leader in the circle, but in the chain, Y, and wheel (in

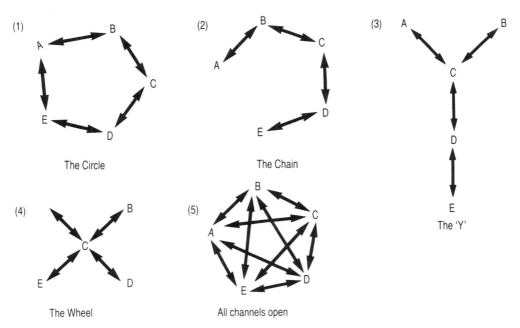

Figure 46 Small-group networks

CIRCLE	WHEEL

1. Direction:

Tendency to two-way communication, because of more channels available.

Tendency to one-way communication because all communication is centralised on one person.

2. Speed:

Group will take longer than wheel group to reach decisions.

Group will tend to reach decisions quickly.

3. Accuracy:

Because of more information available, the chance of correcting errors is greater. But there is more scope for digressions and irrelevancies.

More likely to be inaccurate because the feedback is less. However, there is less danger of irrelevant issues interfering with the task.

4. Morale:

Higher participation, hence higher morale.

Less involvement on the part of most members leads to lower morale.

Figure 47

that order) C increasingly took the dominant position.

During the experiment, C was particularly active, receiving information from all sides, taking decisions and transmitting answers, and at the end rated the level of enjoyment as high, whilst those members on the periphery of the Y and the wheel found the exercise rather boring.

The main characteristics of the two extreme group networks, the circle and the wheel, may be tabulated as shown in Figure 47.

The characteristics found for the circle network become even more marked when all the channels are opened and everybody is able to communicate with everybody else (Network 5, all channels open).

The overall conclusions of Leavitt's experiments were that

1　the differentiated spread of information confers status on the person who handles most of it;
2　people like to set up procedures or routines;
3　people enjoy working in those networks that allow the greatest participation.

Alex Bavelas was particularly interested in the relative importance of the various positions in a network: the concept of *centrality*.

The centrality index of any network member can be worked out by dividing the sum of all the links in the network by the sum of one member's links with every other member.

For example, in the circle, for member A there is one link to B but to get to C there are two links (A to B and B to C). Similarly there is one link from A to E and two from A to D. This makes a total of six links for A.

Other members would also use 6 links each, so that the total for the circle would be $6 \times 5 = 30$.

Dividing the total by the number for A gives $30 \div 6 = 5$ so the centrality index for A is 5. Positions B, C, D and E would also get an index of 5 each as they are of equal importance and the number of links is the same.

If we take the wheel, the centrality indices will be as in Figure 48.

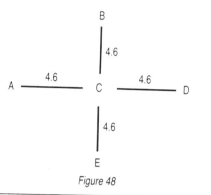

Figure 48

The higher the index, the more important the position or role in the network. Thus the centre person in the wheel gains an index of 8 compared with only 4.6 for those on the periphery.

See also: Group communication.
Further reading
W. J. H. Sprott, *Human Groups*, Penguin, 1958, Ch. 8.

SOCIALISATION

'Socialisation' refers to all those processes that transform the human organism into an active participant in society. The agents of socialisation are parents, other members of the family, peers, workmates, schools, churches and the mass media. They all present the values, beliefs and conventions of society by means of communication.

Socialisation is the result of communication, right from the outset. A mother meets her new baby's needs for food and warmth by feeding and clothing it. She communicates comfort, security and affection through touch, a non-verbal form of communication, and speech. When the time comes for weaning and toilet-training she begins to control the baby's behaviour. Conforming behaviour may be rewarded with smiles, approving sounds and appropriate words. Children gradually learn their mother-tongue from the mother and father and the rest of a circle of brothers and sisters, other relatives and friends of the family.

Instruction can now take the form of symbols (words) rather than just physical means. Children learn to do more and more things for themselves, usually in the style prescribed by their parents. A sense of self develops mainly through doing what they are told. Within the family they learn what is right and what is wrong, what is funny and what is not. In short, they are being inducted into the culture of their society. This early phase of socialisation is well described by Ernest Becker in *The Birth and Death of Meaning*: 'Socialisation *means* the formation of *human beings* out of helpless, dependent *animal matter*.'

For over a century, British society has required all its children to be able to read, write and operate with numbers. Through *education*, the legislators of 1870 and 1944 sought to make it possible for everybody to play their part in a modern, industrial society. Schools provide a formal programme of learning with the dual ideal of developing individuals to their fullest potential and creating cooperative members of society. At school, language is often the key to success. Although his original idea of class-specific codes has been considerably modified, Bernstein's identification of an elaborated middle-class code of language and a restricted working-class code has some currency. Academic success requires mastery of the elaborated code he describes. Communication in the sense of prolonged traffic with teachers, books and other learning aids is more likely to lead to positions and jobs of responsibility in society. Total failure to cope with formal education, on the other hand, has led some, mainly working-class young males, into crime. The Education System for them fails as a socialising agent, and they may be labelled as *deviants*.

Peer groups are the third important means of socialising individuals, and this is particularly true in adolescence, when perhaps you are still uncertain about your personality and direction in life. You may be looking round for 'models', and find them amongst your friends. Part of the process of growing up is to break away from your family and experiment with other kinds of behaviour, other values and other ways of thinking. This often leads to conflicts, and considerable strains are placed by teenagers on parents' understanding. Ruptures can be avoided if the two generations, despite their differences, go on talking to each other.

The mass media also have a socialising effect. Much recent theory on cultural effects argues that the mass media present certain roles and kinds of behaviour as desirable for social stability. Female roles in women's magazines still tend to be family-centred and domestic, whilst strikers are more often than not portrayed as disruptive elements rather than people with a legitimate grievance. And since the mass media are all-pervasive, we are likely to find some models for our own style and behaviour there.

The idea of socialisation outlined above sees it as a process of cultural transmission, where families, friends, schools and other groups, as well as the mass media mould children into useful members of society; in cases where they fail to respond, they are listed as deviants. This view overlooks the notion that socialisation goes on throughout one's life, and does not end with schooling. Moreover, it does not account very well for the fact that society's norms are changing quite rapidly. For instance, within the space of one generation the norm of marriage is no longer paramount: more and more young couples live together without getting married. George Mead has produced a theory for socialisation that sees the individual not as an empty vessel to be filled up with the cultural heritage, unprotesting, but rather as an active, selective spirit increasingly able to assess the rules and ideology for the culture he encounters, and choose what to accept and what to reject.

See also: Culture, Groups, Ideology.
Further reading
E. Becker, *The Birth and Death of Meaning*, Penguin, 1971.

SPEECH/SPEAKING

Speaking is a social activity in which people use their speech organs to produce sounds in various meaningful combinations to communicate messages of importance for themselves and for the lives of others.

Speech is a code that combines sounds to make words, and words through the rules of grammar and syntax (see

LANGUAGE) to make sentences. Most children have mastered the grammar of their mother-tongue or primary code by the age of five. As we grow older we develop various styles (see STYLE) of speech to suit formal and informal situations, and become expert in registers (see REGISTER) as we specialise in our jobs, sports and hobbies.

Since speech makes use of a vocal–acoustic channel, pronunciation is of particular interest. Accent refers to the set of phonemes you use to pronounce your words. These differ from region to region. In the north of England 'come' is pronounced /kum/ and 'castle' as /kæsl/, whereas in southern speech you hear /kʊm/ and /kāsl/. One accent, associated with the public-school-educated middle class, has a greater prestige than the others. This is known as Received Pronunciation (RP) (see ACCENT) and is the type of accent taught for preference to foreigners learning English.

In the United Kingdom there are many varieties of English. These are determined by geographical region and social class. Regional dialects like Cockney or Yorkshire survive among working-class people. But middle-class people generally speak Standard English in RP, though sometimes they keep traces of a regional accent. Class dialects have their typical expressions. 'That's very civil [for kind] of you' is definitely upper-class, while 'See you later, alligator' would be a typical bit of working-class speech.

In the end there are as many varieties of English as there are speakers. We all have our personal form of English. It consists of our favourite phrases, our particular pronunciation, odd uses and misuses of language. The author of these notes, for example, has the tiresome habit of greeting people with the Shelleyan line 'Hail to thee, blythe spirit'. Paralanguage (your stress and intonation, voice quality and so forth) is individual. The name of an individual's language is *idiolect*.

Speaking is a much more flexible, wayward use of language than writing. When we speak, we are thinking on our feet, so that our sentences sometimes lose direction, we interrupt ourselves, start again, repeat ourselves a great deal and fish for feedback with the inevitable 'you know?' and 'you know what I mean?' Speaking is a highly redundant (see REDUNDANCY) form of communication when compared with writing. And you may have noticed how many people buoy up their sentences with 'sort of' and '. . . sort of thing', phrases called '*fillers*', which you would avoid in the more deliberate medium of writing.

Everyday, casual, familiar speech is full of *colloquialisms* like 'I'm hitting the road now' for 'I am now leaving to go home', and *contractions* like 'won't' for 'will not' and 'can't' for 'cannot', not to mention comic *slang* expressions like 'Gran's lost her choppers' and *clichés* which are overworked metaphors like 'no more money in the pipeline' or 'The ball's in your court now'.

The chief point to remember is that as speaker–listeners we need *communicative competence* in the social situations we create or fall into. Among friends the easy flow of class dialect is natural enough; but in more unfamiliar and formal situations it is helpful to be able to speak in a more careful, standard way without sounding stilted.

See also: Accent, Dialect, Redundancy, Register, Style.
Further reading
M. Montgomery, *An Introduction to Language and Society*, Methuen, 1986.
The Shorter Oxford Dictionary for the phonetic system of symbols to represent sounds, which is used here.

STEREOTYPE/STEREOTYPING

A stereotype (originally a printing term for a plate that reproduced an image) is a simplified image of a whole racial, national, religious, sexual or occupational group. Stereotyping is the attribution of the supposed characteristics of a whole group to any of its individual members.

The traditional stereotype of the Scots might lead (or, rather, mislead) us into supposing individual Scots to be canny, tightfisted or humourless.

Why do we need stereotypes? The world is such a rich profusion of individuals that the brain grasps at any means to sort them into indentifiable groups. Stereotypes are useful pigeon-holes. Into them go blacks, whites and orientals; Germans, Irish and Japanese; Catholics, Protestants, Muslims and Hindus; teachers, soldiers, miners and politicians. But there is more to stereo-typing than simple classification of groups. All stereotypes bear the stamp of *value* judgements, like the largely negative one of Scots already mentioned.

We all belong to various groups and are more or less loyal to them. A Nigerian is proud of being a Nigerian, a Catholic is proud to be a Catholic, a communist is proud to be a communist, and so on. Unfortunately, our group loyalty leads us to believe that our group is more important than other groups. A Catholic may also be proud not to be a Protestant. In the extreme case of Nazi Germany, Hitler encouraged the Germans to believe that they were the 'master race' and that all other races were inferior – even expendable, in the case of the gipsies and the Jews. The Jews were dehumanised in the stereotypes produced by the Nazis, and in one notorious propaganda film were even equated with rats.

Stereotyping outgroups (groups other than our own) can take two different forms. The first will consist of traits that the prejudiced person really admires, such as over-ambition, craftiness, shrewdness, clannishness and shyness. The second comprises traits that the prejudiced person deplores, like lack of ambition, stupidity, laziness, dirtiness, smelliness and over-sexiness. The stereotypes can be held quite illogically, at one and the same time, and give rise to remarks like this of immigrants: 'They simply live on unemployment benefit and take all our jobs.'

Stereotypes are not based on personal experience, but learnt by children from their parents and the majority culture with its newspapers, TV, comics, books, cartoons and films. Racial and national stereotypes are often perpetuated in children's books, such as Doctor Dolittle and Little Black Sambo. Stereotypes in children's books often refer to out-of-date or trivial aspects of foreign cultures – for example, Chinese men wearing pigtails, Frenchmen in striped jerseys and wearing berets, dining on nothing but frogs and snails, Dutch children wearing clogs. Captain Johns' Biggles stories show a corrupt world being kept in order by clean-living white English men. This ethnocentric view produces negative stereotypes for other races; the villains are usually big Negroes, harsh Prussian officers or fat suave Eura-sians.

David Milner points out in *Children and Race* that racial stereotypes reflect racial prejudice, and when repeated orally, in books and comics, and on television, they perpetuate the pre-judice. 'When racism has taken root in the majority culture, has pervaded its institutions, language, its social intercourse and its cultural productions, has entered the very interstices of the culture, then the simple process by which a culture is transmitted from generation to generation in the socialisation process – becomes the most important "determinant" of prejudice.' (Milner, p. 62).

Although there may be some truth in stereotypes (a lot of Germans are hard-working!) you live in Disneyland rather than the real world if you base your judgement on them. And your personal relationships with people from other groups will generally suffer. Anything that gets in the way of your seeing a person with individual traits is well worth forgetting.

See also: Culture, Perception, Personality, Socialisation.
Further reading
D. Milner, *Children and Race*, Penguin, 1975, Ch. 3.

TYLE

In literature, style refers to the typical ways in which an author handles language (Dylan Thomas compared with, say, Dickens). There is also an appreciation of 'style' in the sense of 'good' style and many books have been written on how to acquire it. In Communication Studies, where we are interested in how people communicate with each other at all levels and in all possible situations in society, we apply 'style' to the varieties of language we use in speech and writing, that we feel are appropriate in any given social context.

In studying language, it is important to realise that there is no such thing as *the* English language; instead, there are many varieties of English. There are dialects which are determined by where you live and your social class; there are registers and slangs which are sub-languages you use in your breadwinning or leisure-time occupation. Then come styles. These depend on your relationship with the people you are talking or writing to as well as the physical context in which the communication takes place. Our relationships with other people are characterised by degrees of formality. You can be extremely informal at a party with your mates and rather formal at a job interview where the serious matter of your employment is at stake. And there are degrees of formality between. Most of us slip easily from one style to another during the course of the day. At home, talk with the other members of the family will be casual, intimate, laced with pet-words and private nonsense; different from the informal chat with a neighbour, and different again from the committee meeting where you have to report on a serious matter to people you do not know very well.

Where there is a social gap between people or a difference of authority or age (as between, say, employer and employee, teacher and student, mother and child), those with 'inferior' status show their deference (sometimes) by using polite forms of address and avoiding slang. Children are frequently warned 'Don't talk to your mother like that!' And when playing at being grown-ups, they are clever at mimicking their parents' more formal speech.

Although formality is difficult to define (it involves respect, politeness, and seriousness, etc.) it is easy to hear and produce in speech. In what circumstances would you expect to hear these utterances?

Would you care for a cup of tea?
Would you like a cup of tea?
Cuppa?

The meeting will commence at 4 p.m.
We'll be kicking off at 4 o'clock.

Lots of people went to the gig.
The concert was attended by not inconsiderable numbers of people.

So formality – or informality – is produced through different choices of words, and sometimes by different choices of grammar. Some words associated with formality ('commence', 'attended', 'inconsiderable' in the above examples) are of French, Latin or Greek origin, in contrast to our more informal and down-to-earth Anglo-Saxon vocabulary. More formal styles will use the passive verb form, e.g. 'The concert was attended. . .'

Some attempts at formality do not produce a style that is pleasant or easy to follow. The example above ('The concert was attended. . .') is clumsy and seems self-conscious, chiefly because of the double negative and passive form. Good plain English is usually more effective than overlong words and complicated sentences.

There are no hard and fast rules about which set of words to use for say, very polite conversation, and which to use for a more familiar one: you have your own sense of what is appropriate. Furthermore, you are free to reject the appropriate style, if you wish, and cause a stir of embarrassment or amusement!

David Crystal makes the point that, whatever their regional or social background, people tend to behave in much the same linguistic way when they want to be formal: they choose their words carefully, avoiding slang and four-letter words, and agonise over the 'correct' pronunciation of words.

So far we have concentrated on spoken styles, but the same conventions apply to writing. Your relationship with the person you are writing to, for example, determines your degree of formality. Supposing you are making a job application, you follow the conventions (formal rules) of layout, spelling, punctuation and special formulae like 'Yours faithfully' at the end. The postcard you send to a friend will be much slacker in presentation and almost as casual as the way you speak.

The advantage of the written word is that you can produce a considered piece of prose that says what you want it to say. The words can be 'worked on' (intrapersonal communication) until clarity and coherence are achieved. Some writers do this by writing and rewriting, others by planning everything in their heads first. In *Teach Yourself to Write* Kathleen Betterton says, 'Even in the simplest kind of writing, clarity is often difficult to attain. Thoughts and impressions rarely present themselves in coherent order; they must be deftly sorted and . . . arranged in orderly sequence. . .' The main advantage of a wordprocessor is that it removes much of the drudgery of rewriting in the search for the most appropriate style.

Writing for a purpose other than interpersonal communication often involves a stylistic choice which is more subtle than that between formal and informal. Kathleen Betterton continues, 'Clearly the subject must determine the style. An article on plumbing will demand a different style from a treatise on metaphysics, and between these two extremes there are infinite gradations. A short story, and, in a far greater degree, a novel need constant variation in style to suit the changing moods and situations with which they deal.'

Publishers and editors for the mass media often impose a *house style* or house rules which dictate the style to be used.

See also: Context, Dialects, Genre, Register, Slang.
Further reading
P. Trudgill, *Sociolinguistics*, Penguin, 1981, pp. 106–107.
D. Crystal, 'Style: The varieties of English' in W. F. Bolton (ed.), *History of Literature in the English Language*, Vol. 10 *The English Language*, Sphere, 1976.

THINKING

'Thinking', in everyday usage, refers to a whole spectrum of mental activities including dreaming, recollecting, imagining, planning and understanding. In psychological theory the emphasis has been on problem-solving and creative thinking.

The question has often been asked: what is the *medium* of thinking? And there have been many answers, all to various degrees relating to language. The matter is unresolved but it is likely that thinking is mainly language-based but makes use of images as well as words. Images occur in dreams where the mind is fabricating those strange sequences through some kind of non-verbal thinking, and, according to Freud and Jung, making use of *symbols*, often in amusing and entertaining ways, sometimes to draw our attention to matters of concern, and sometimes to conceal disturbing ideas.

The first stage of thinking is *perception*. We use this word to describe how the brain interprets all the information reaching it via the senses from the outside world so that you recognise what you observe in the light of previous experience. Having a *language* further enables you to label, classify and conceptualise what you perceive, as well as make deductions and create new ideas about your environment and solve problems.

Jean Piaget, a logician interested in childrens' thinking, describes how new observations have to be 'assimilated' into your current pattern of ideas and that you may have to change or modify some of your concepts in order to 'accommodate' conflicting or contradictory information.

Edward de Bono argues provocatively that language was never designed as a thinking medium, but as a communicative medium: 'With a communicating medium we strive to remove all doubt and the purpose of each further word is to help in that direction. With thinking we want to open up possibilities and connections in order to allow insights to form'.

The process of thinking is pre-conscious. If I now ask you to give the date of the Battle of Hastings . . . were you aware of any process that produced the answer? Perhaps a slight sense of strain? Or did the answer just spring into consciousness?

Thinking is to quite a large extent a form of intrapersonal communication, the closed-circuit communication with yourself. And usually this takes the form of an interior monologue, though sometimes you may find yourself talking aloud; or it takes the form of writing. Thinking can be stimulated by other people posing questions, and thinking, in time, promotes fruitful discussions or bitter arguments. In all our encounters with others, whether singly or in groups, the quality of our thinking, whether positive or negative, is going to affect our performance and our social relationships.

See also: Memory, Perception.
Further reading
Edward de Bono: *Conflicts – A better way to resolve them*, Harrap, 1985, Ch. 1.

TOUCH

Touch is non-verbal communication through physical contact.

Touch is a basic human need. Actively through touch babies find out about their environment: they encounter objects, feel soft and hard things, hot and cold, rough and smooth. Moreover, they need to be touched, cuddled and stroked by their parents, otherwise their emotional development suffers and with it their chance of forming good relationships in later life. So babies need to touch and to be touched.

Touch is perhaps your most subtle form of non-verbal communication. You can communicate many shades of feeling through the impact, pressure and duration of touch: a light touch on your friend's arm, an arm round his neck for a moment to signify acceptance, a pat on the back to cheer him up. Touching is often the best way to express sympathy through cradling and hand-holding.

Of course, there are a host of unspoken rules about who may touch whom and where. Certain parts of the body must not be touched (they are *taboo*) except by lovers. You could say that your degree of intimacy with any other person was defined by which parts of your body you would let that person touch.

If you want to get to know somebody, you must get in touch. And you do this literally through the ritual of a hand-shake. There are many kinds of hand-shake, and sometimes people like to create a special impression, usually of decisiveness and strength of character, through their handshakes. Your response to a handshake will convey how ready you are to explore the new relationship. As Tony Lake says: 'A good handshake is a touch dialogue, not a monologue.'

Those of you who have been abroad, say, to France or Italy, will have noticed that people in those countries touch each other more than we do. Sid Jourard, a Canadian social scientist, confirmed this in his study of couples talking in coffee-bars in different parts of the world. He counted the number of times they touched each other in one hour. The average figures were as follows:

San Juan (Puerto Rico): 180
Paris: 102
London: 0

In public we do everything in our power not to rub against other people, or when unavoidably touched in the Underground we try to prevent at least skin contact. There is quite an important cultural difference and one that can and does produce awkwardness between the more reserved people of Northern Europe, including the British, and people belonging to the so-called 'contact-cultures' of Latin America, and the Arab world.

Many psychologists in America and Britain believe that we do not touch each other enough for our own good and that we could improve our relationships with greater displays of emotional warmth. Group-therapy practices include for this reason a lot of physical contact among the participants.

See also: Culture, Proximity.
Further reading
Tony Lake, *Relationships*, Michael Joseph, 1981, Ch. 24.

ALUES

Values are your conception of the relative worth you place on things, events, and people in your world. They govern what you should strive for, provide a framework for actions and guide you in your decision-making. They are found in moral and religious systems in all cultures and societies, showing communities what is desirable and how desirable.

Value is not inherent in things or people. Diamonds, in themselves, are no more valuable than sea-shells. Who is to say which is the more beautiful, the thistle or the rose, and who is to say that monogamy is more moral than polygamy? We are the ones who determine what has value: we define what is good/bad, moral/immoral, beautiful/ugly.

Values grow out of basic needs and cultural environments. We all place a value on food, but we value foods differently. Northern industrialised nations value beef as a food but Hindus value the cow as a sacred animal.

Values are relatively conservative because they are tied to fundamental needs and are drummed into children at an early age. Within the package of values that we have, there will be some which conflict with others. It is unusual for all our values to be in a state of harmony with each other. In fact, people can tolerate powerful contradictions within themselves – for how is it possible

that Christian heads of state apparently find no difficulty in squaring the Christian teaching of love with attacks on civilian populations and threats of nuclear annihilation?

The mass media reflect values they think are prevalent in society. Sometimes these values are presented *overtly*, openly, conspicuously. With the monumental headlines for stories about Prince Charles and Princess Diana, and the newsreader's eye-twinkle and smile when the royal family anecdote is produced to round off the news on a cheerful note, the treatment of the message makes it clear that royalty has a positive value. But the mass media, both in their advertising and entertainment programmes, present other, less obvious values, the hidden or *covert* values. Why is it, for instance, that so many food advertisements (for margarine, breakfast cereals, etc.) show families, rather than single people, enjoying the products? The covert, possibly unintended, message is that the family is still a British ideal.

See also: Attitudes, Beliefs.
Further reading
R. Dimbleby and G. Burton: *More than Words*, Methuen, 1985, pp. 167–9.

WRITING

Writing is a code consisting of pictograms, ideograms or an alphabet used to make a permanent record of thoughts expressed in language.

Human beings have been writing for at least 5000 years. The earliest examples of script are on Sumerian clay tablets where it consists of rows of drawings, or pictograms, which form a narrative or a sequence of ideas. Pictograms have obvious limitations, since whereas a picture could represent 'king' or 'horse', how could it represent 'kingship' or 'happiness'? The ancient Egyptians invented hieroglyphs which were drawings that represented concepts. To this day, Chinese writing consists of ideograms. Some of the characters are simple pictures, e.g. 夕 = woman. However, when you add 帚 = broom, the resulting compound ideogram 女帚 produces a third meaning: wife.

The main advantage of the ideographic Chinese, which is a code that does not relate to speech-sounds, is that it can be read all over China by people speaking very different dialects of Chinese. Its main drawback is that it takes a long time to learn: you would need to memorise up to 1000 characters to be able to read and write basic Chinese.

The first phonetic form of writing to use an alphabet was invented about 1000 BC in ancient Palestine or Syria and gave rise to the North Semitic alphabet with a set of 22 letters, all consonants, which was the source of most modern alphabets. The sign represents the sound, and the signs linked together represent a word which represents an idea or concept. In some languages today, the spelling is perfectly phonetic (for example, Swahili) but in English, the 26 letters of the Roman alphabet have to represent 45 different sounds, and spelling is therefore far from the simple logic of one letter for one sound.

Pictogram	Ideogram	Alphabetic character
Drawing	Drawing (combination) of signs	Symbol
		Sound
Concept	Concept	Concept

The great advantage of writing over speech is that it enables people to express their thoughts in a permanent form. Two consequences flow from this: it means that long and complicated messages may be carried over great distances, and information may be transmitted over periods of time, hundreds, or even thousands of years. Historically, the use of writing has made it possible for people to develop even more complex and powerful societies. Writing has enabled the sum total of human knowledge to be recorded and therefore to be built upon.

Looking at these consequences more closely, we find that, in the past, writing helped people like the Romans to establish and administer their empires. Instructions were despatched by letter from Rome to military governors in Gaul, Britain, Palestine and other outposts. For centuries in the eastern world, the emperor of China ruled his vast territory by means of a dutiful civil service transmitting imperial decrees to the farthest provinces.

All world religions rely on sacred books. Without writing, neither Christianity nor Islam would have extended its influence in the way it has done. These two religions are particularly anxious to win converts, and set great store by literacy. The first aim of Christian missionaries coming among illiterate peoples was to teach them to read the Bible in translation. For

Muslims the very language in which the Koran was first written has a sacred value, so children are taught to read and recite the Arabic verses, receiving explanations in their mother-tongues.

Writing has likewise facilitated the spread of political ideas about the world. Who would ignore the effect, for instance, of Tom Paine's *The Rights of Man* on the American Revolution, or Karl Marx's *Capital* on the Russian one? The European missionaries who taught African men and women to read and write opened their minds to a knowledge of the wider world, and to the political ideas which inspired them to struggle for political independence.

Until the invention of writing, history was stored in the memory of respected individuals, singers and storytellers, who at feastings in their lords' halls narrated events involving past heroes of the tribe. It is believed that the epic poems of the Anglo-Saxons (e.g. *Beowulf*) and the Ancient Greeks (*The Iliad and The Odyssey*) existed for many years in oral forms before being written down. The bards not only performed the stories of the tribal past, usually in some metrical form, but also taught them to apprentices so that the most splendid episodes of the lengthening past reached the ears of each new generation. Unhappily, the oral tradition is not very reliable, and information is either forgotten or distorted in the course of time. Writing changed all that. Events recorded at or just after their occurrence are crystallised for ever in that original form. Admittedly the recording of past human behaviour with any accuracy is difficult, and mistakes can be made in the copying of manuscripts, but a written history is less likely to stray into myth than a history transmitted by word of mouth.

The writing of history freed people from the limitations of the human memory. Apart from increasing fidelity to historical truth, writing gave people the opportunity to store information *outside* their memories. It followed that a common body of knowledge could be accumulated from all literate cultures and from all periods of their history. Individuals came to have access to huge resources of information. It is hard to imagine the development of western science and technology without documents, books and libraries.

The simple technology of writing has, furthermore, accelerated the growth of economic activities and made the modern state possible. Without permanent records, a national code of law could scarcely exist, the work of the Inland Revenue would be even more rough-and-ready than it is at present, and the administration of government departments generally, of universities and of large companies, virtually impossible. We owe to writing the existence of huge organisations of people like the EEC and the United Nations.

From the very beginning the knowledge of writing has brought power. The power of religious leaders rests upon the authority of their scriptures, their sacred writings. In ancient Egypt the priests kept the knowledge of writing to themselves, where it served as a further mystery to overawe the common people. The Church in the Middle Ages determined, to a large extent, which manuscripts were copied and how they were distributed. In modern times totalitarian states have used the written word as a means of ensuring uniform values and attitudes in the population, and shown how history can be *rewritten*. For example, the major role played by Leon Trotsky in the Russian Revolution has been virtually eliminated from official Soviet histories of the period.

Swift's famous saying 'The pen is mightier than the sword' implies that writing, with its powers of persuasion and trick of crossing frontiers and dodging the censors, is more likely to bring about political change than is mere brute force. This is debatable. What is certainly true is that writing has enabled men – and mainly men – to create a technology capable of producing weapons far more deadly than swords.

> **See also:** Code, Message/Text, Sign, Speech, Style.

APPENDIX: COMMUNICATION MODELS

Chronological approach to models

About 2300 years ago, Aristotle in the *Rhetoric* said that the purpose of rhetoric, which is a particular way of presenting an argument, is for the speaker to persuade his audience to adopt his point of view, and he separates out three main elements or stages of the process: the speaker, his speech and the audience. The process can be illustrated very simply as:

The devices of rhetoric enable
a SPEAKER to persuade
through his SPEECH
his AUDIENCE.

Many modern theorists have taken a similar three elements and described the process or communication as an apparent transfer of something, the message, from the sender to the receiver.

SENDER——MESSAGE——RECEIVER

Other theorists object to the idea of a message as being a separate thing and feel that presenting the process in this way loses sight of the way in which *meaning* is communicated. For this reason, the study of communication has become separated into two schools of thought, the process school and the semiotic school, and few theorists have been able to combine the two approaches, though not all process models identify a separate message as such.

One of the first modern process models was developed during the Second World War, and published in 1949 by Claude Shannon, a research mathematician with the Bell Telephone company, and Warren Weaver, a scientific executive. See Figure 49.

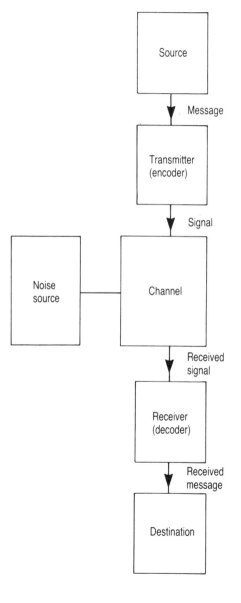

Figure 49 Shannon and Weaver's diagram of a general communication system.

Originally they were concerned with the way in which messages sent by telegraph and telephone were prone to faulty transmission and misinterpretation. It is no use in wartime if a message 'Please send reinforcements, I am going to advance' is heard as 'Please send three and fourpence, I am going to a dance.' By identifying the various stages of the process where different kinds of error might arise, Shannon and Weaver helped in the development of types of message which would be least disturbed by mechanical faults in transmission and reception or by interference. Subsequently the model has been used in a more general sense to illustrate how any kind of desired communication is transmitted, and that all such 'signals' are subject to interference either physically or semantically. Semantic interference refers to the difficulty sender and receiver can have in understanding each other when they do not share the same codes of meaning. The model can be used, with care, for either mass communications or person-to-person communication.

Key to the Shannon and Weaver model

1   An information source produces a message or sequence of messages to be communicated to the receiving terminal.
2   A transmitter operates on the message in some way to produce a signal suitable for transmission over the channel.
3   The channel is the physical means used to transmit the signal from transmitter to receiver.
4   During transmission, or at one of the terminals, the signal may be perturbed by noise (low-level background noise, intermittent and more insistent interference, or sudden meaningful breakthrough).
5   The receiver ordinarily performs the inverse operation of that done by the transmitter, reconstructing the message from the signal.
6   The destination is the person (or thing) for whom the message is intended.

Limitations

1   It overlooks the fact that a message from a source is not simply transmitted to a receiver. In order to be transmitted it has to be ENCODED in a transmittable form. For example, to communicate a thought, impulse or feeling, the brain will encode it in speech, or in writing, or in some non-verbal way. In all these cases the original thought or impulse has been converted into a different form according to the most complex rules.
2   The model suggests that the source and the transmitter or the receiver and destination are different entities. But in the context of the individual human being the source and the transmitter are in the same person and controlled by the same brain.
3   There is no provision for FEEDBACK.
4   The model illustrates one-way communication only.

Exercise 1
Take the basic Shannon and Weaver model and modify it in order to overcome the four limitations. For example, one could produce a two-way model by placing two diagrams back-to-back.

At about the same time (1948) Harold Dwight Lasswell, an American political scientist and Director of War Communications Research concerned with propaganda technique, published his five stages of communication:

WHO
SAYS WHAT
IN WHICH CHANNEL
TO WHOM
WITH WHAT EFFECT

This is particularly useful for analysing and designing mass communications, as it directs our attention immediately to the 'Who' and 'To whom' so that we are careful to note what particular individual or group is putting out the communication and what kind of audience is aimed at. Under 'Who' and 'Says what' we can seek the treatment and content of the communications and, by asking 'In which Channel', we are directed to look at the range of possible channels and select the most appropriate one(s). By channel, here, is meant what we would nowadays call medium, that is newspaper, radio, television, posters and so on, rather than the physical means of radio waves, sound waves, light and touch indicated by Shannon and Weaver. A most important difference between the two models is the notion of 'effect'. Lasswell is chiefly concerned with the type of mass communications which are designed to influence the public and achieve a measurable effect in attitudes, opinions and behaviour.

Exercise 2
List the limitations of the Lasswell model and any advantages it has over the Shannon and Weaver model.

Exercise 3
Choose a current publicity campaign, or one in the recent past, for which you can observe the material which is presented and perhaps collect examples (posters, leaflets, audio and video recordings). Using Lasswell's framework, analyse the various parts of the campaign, illustrating your description wherever possible.

Exercise 4
Design a publicity campaign of your own, using Lasswell's model to help you. If

possible display your work as realistically as you can: you may even be able to arrange to conduct 'before' and 'after' surveys to see whether your campaign has any measurable effect.

In 1953, Theodore M. Newcomb of the University of Michigan introduced a different approach to the process. He does not include the message as a separate entity in his diagram, implying it only by the use of directional arrows. He concentrates on the social purpose of communication, showing all communication as a means of sustaining relationships between people. (Figure 50).

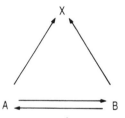

Figure 50 Newcomb's A-B-X system

A and B are sender and receiver (for example, two individuals, or government and electorate, or newspaper and readership). X is a matter of concern to them in their common environment. ABX is a system at rest, or in equilibrium, at any one moment in time so that if any part then changes, the other parts will have to change too in order to restore the equilibrium: if A changes his or her mind about X, then B will have to change either in relation to X or in relation to A and so on. For example, if A and B are friends who both have favourable attitudes to X, a politician, pop group or football team, and A finds for various reasons that she or he no longer likes X, or if X has changed in some way, then the system is temporarily out of balance. A and B then need to communicate with each other to exchange views so that their liking for each other and for X can be adjusted to a new position of balance. Similarly, if A and B were two people supporting different football teams or pop groups and their equilibrium position were one of mutual dislike, a change in attitude of A so they now both support the same team, might, through communication, result in a shift to a new position of equilibrium with greater liking of B and A for each other, or their mutual dislike may remain and B may go off the team. Is mutual liking and respect likely to result in more effort being put into the communication than dislike?

Exercise 5
Using Newcomb's model, explain how communication can be used to restore equilibrium in the following cases. Suggest alternative outcomes in each case:

(i)   A is the national executive of a political party and B is a member. A introduces a new policy X which some members like and some do not.
(ii)   A is the management of an industry, B is the union. B requests an upgrading X in the pay structure.
(iii) A is a 'newspaper', B is a reader. B is annoyed by an article X in the newspaper.

Exercise 6
Newcomb takes for granted the process by which communication is transmitted between A and B. Try making this process more explicit by inserting either Shannon and Weaver's diagram, or your elaborated version of it, between A and B. Does it help in the understanding and use of Newcomb's model to give the process in more detail?

By 1956, George Gerbner, then assistant Professor in the Institute of Communications Research, University of Illinois, had taken the basic linear model and extended it in two dimensions in order to show in more detail how information about an event is transmit-

ted via a gatekeeper or editor to the public. Instead of a signal or statement going directly from the source to the destination, Gerbner shows that in much mass communication, the signal is influenced by people in control of the medium who edit and reorganise the message in line with their current policy, and provide the means for distribution. Gerbner is also very much concerned with the psychological processes affecting the way in which each communicator responds to and interprets events and signals. He is one of the few theorists who combine the meaning of signals with the process of transmission.

To construct his general theory, Gerbner first takes an example of one person noticing an event, and going through ten basic steps in the communication process, such as seeing a house on fire and shouting 'Fire!':

1   someone
2   perceives an event
3   and reacts
4   in a situation
5   through some means
6   to make materials available
7   in some form
8   conveying content
9   and context
10   of some consequence

Gerbner then arranges the steps graphically to represent positions, directions, and relationships. Finally he includes the intervention of the media. He does this in a sequence of diagrams which can be summarised as in Figure 51.

The event is shown by the circle E, and the person M1 who wishes to convey information concerning the event is shown to have a personal interpretation or perception E' of the event, according to the context, the availability of information and personal selection, etc. When M1 prepares a statement for publication he or she has to take into account what channels can be used and

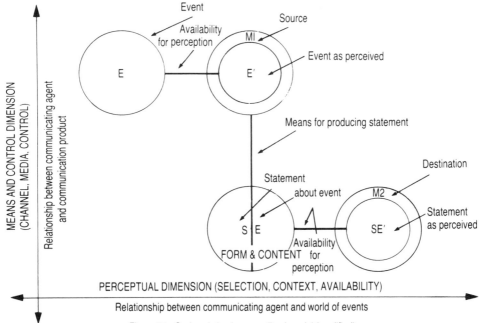

Figure 51 Gerbner's basic generalised model (modified)

the control exerted by the media. After preparation and editing, the signal is then ready for transmission and is shown by the circle SE (statement about the event). The receiver, M2, then, in turn, has a personal interpretation or perception (SE)' of the statement.

Gerber also includes in his general theory provision for feedback and the consequences of communication.

Exercise 7
See if you can work out how to compare Gerbner's general model with that of Shannon and Weaver, then obtain a copy of Gerbner's article (1956) and see how he makes the comparison.

Exercise 8
Using Gerbner's model, trace the process by which a television news broadcast or a newspaper report concerning an item of interest carries information concerning the event to a viewer or reader.

Bruce Westley and Malcolm Maclean, teachers of journalism, had developed

by 1957 a model for mass communications which combines the linear 'sender–receiver' diagram with Newcomb's ABX system and includes the gatekeeper function as a separate entity. Like Newcomb they do not try to show the details of the process of transmission but show the path taken.

For interpersonal communication there is a simplified basic model showing how one person, the sender, gathers information relevant to an event X of interest and passes on a message to B. At the same time, B also has direct access to information concerning at least part of X. See Figure 52. The main arrows are one-way, denoting A as the sender and B as the receiver, but some provision for feedback has been included, which may influence A to alter the way in which she or he is presenting the message.

For mass communications, the gatekeeper or editorial function is denoted by C. A is now the person who is seeking to put out a signal, e.g. a

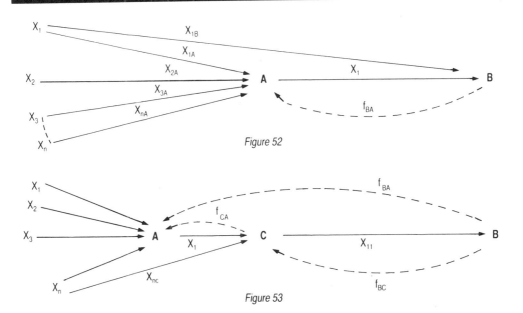

Figure 52

Figure 53

reporter or researcher who is gathering information and prepares a report, or a company who wishes to advertise its products. Westley and Maclean refer to such people as 'advocates'. C is the editor or controller of the channel who decides what will actually be transmitted to the public. Provision is shown in Figure 53 for feedback to occur from C to A and from B, the public, to either C or A. Feedback in mass communications is rarely simultaneous with the sending of a communication but it can affect the next transmission.

Exercise 9
Using Westley and Maclean's model, illustrate how an advocate gathers information about an event of interest and transmits it via the gatekeeper to the intended audience. You can try this for (a) a lecturer asking a student to present a paper to the class, (b) a newspaper reporter trying to inform the public of an event which has a strong emotional significance for the reporter, or (c) the manufacturer who employs a TV commercial firm to makes commercials for the product. Illustrate your presentation as much as possible as if it were to be displayed in a communications exhibition and give examples of the type of material used and the way in which feedback can be used.

Charles Osgood, an experimental psychologist, and professor of psychology at the University of Illinois, in 1957 dealt directly with the psychological processes of turning communication into transmittable form, encoding, and with decoding and interpretation. By leaving out any reference to noise and by housing decoder/destination/source/encoder in one mind, he achieves a much neater and simpler model than by just putting two Shannon and Weaver diagrams back-to-back to illustrate the two-way process.

By including the function 'interpreter', Osgood also suggests that the role of the receiver is an active one in terms of understanding, not just a passive reception of sensory input. As you know, it is possible for the decoding part of the brain to 'hear' or 'read' a message without being able to understand it. For example, a tourist may address you in

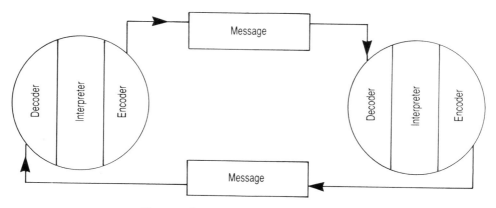

Figure 54   Osgood's two-way communication model

Japanese. You hear the utterance, you recognise speech, but the message defies interpretation. Has communication taken place? In a limited way it has.

In 1960, David Berlo, a lecturer in communication arts at Michigan State University, published a six-part communication model:

1   the communication source
2   the encoder

3   the message
4   the channel
5   the decoder
6   the communication receiver and, additionally, feedback.

To focus attention on the main parts, he lists the ingredients which have to be taken into account.

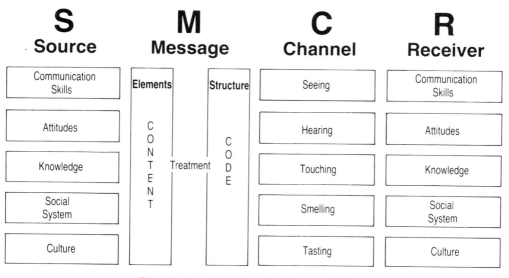

Figure 55   A model of the ingredients in communication.

Influenced strongly by stimulus-response theory in psychology, he examines the processes of learning and interpreting, showing how a person acts as receiver and source all the time so that learning becomes a process of interpreting a stimulus and responding to it and then acting on the consequences of the response.

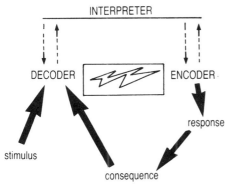

INTERPRETER

DECODER   ENCODER

response

stimulus

consequence

Figure 56

He says that stimulus-response connections can be strengthened or weakened by the use of repetition and frequency so that if a response is rewarded, habit will be strengthened, but if the response is not rewarded the habit will weaken and eventually die out. Explicit in his search for effective communication is Berlo's concept of the *purpose* of all communication. He says all communication behaviour has as its purpose the eliciting of a specific response from a specific person (or group of persons) and he believes that communication will be effective if we can reduce the effort required by the receiver to make the desired response. He gives five principles of effective communication:

1 The frequency of presentation of the message – with reward and without reward.
2 The competition of a given stimulus with other stimuli and responses.

3 The amount of reward which was perceived as a consequence of the response.
4 The time-lag between the making of the response and the reward which was received.
5 The amount of effort which the receiver perceived as necessary to make the desired response.

He elaborates his model to show the relationship between communication and meaning. He stresses that 'the elements of structure of a language do not themselves have meaning. They are only symbols, sets of symbols, cues that cause us to bring our own meanings into play, to think about them, to rearrange them, etc. Communication does not consist of the transmission of meaning. Meanings are not transmittable and not transferable. Only messages are transmittable, and meanings are not in the message, they are in the message-users.'

Exercise 10
Using Berlo's list of ingredients for Sender, Message, Channel and Receiver, predict the likely sources of difficulty in the following situations:
(a) A sighted person wishes to convey to a blind person information about a journey that the two of them will be embarking on.
    Try this (i) by post, and (ii) face to face.
(b) Asian parents with very little English are anxious about their child's progress at school and have asked for an interview with the headteacher.
    Try this (i) for a face-to-face interview, (ii) by telephone.

In 1973 Wilbur Schramm of Stanford University put forward a new kind of model which stresses the active involvement of the receiver. Schramm rejects the 1950s and 1960s idea that all mass communication and much interpersonal communication take place because the sender wants to change the receiver in some way, and that the poor receiver is just a passive sponge soaking up communications and being changed by it regardless of his or her own will. He suggests that listening and reading are active processes that the receiver takes part in because he or she wishes to. Schramm's model shows how the sender puts out a signal, making it available for someone to take notice of, and the receiver pays attention to it and makes use of it. The direction of the arrow *from* the receiver *to* the message is important, showing this active involvement. At the same time, Schramm points out that both sender and receiver are changed in some way by the act of communication so that by the time the next signal is sent, each has moved on a little. The changes may be very slight or they can be significant mental shifts in attitude, knowledge and emotions, etc. An extreme example might be the case of a nervous teenager making a declaration of love to a person of the opposite sex. The very act of saying the words produces profound emotional attitude changes in both the speaker and the listener.

In Figure 57, A and B are two participants. A is initially the sender and B the receiver. Sending a signal is labelled as a type A activity and receiving a signal is labelled as type B. S is the sign or signal which one participant puts out and the other makes use of. The vertical line between A and A' and between B and B' shows the shift to a new position before the next activity takes place.

Other models to look out for are those of Smith, Tracey, Jakobson (1958), Broadbent's Y model (1957), Dance's helical spiral model (1967).

For each model you can ask yourself the following questions:

1 What elements or ingredients are involved?
2 Has the model grouped the elements in a meaningful way which assists in understanding and remembering?
3 Does the model help you to identify (i) the signs and codes, (ii) the conditions and processes, or (iii) the purposes and effects?
4 Can you use the model to *describe* conditions in observable situations?
5 Does the model help you to *predict* what will happen as conditions change?
6 Does the model help you to *design* effective communications? What general idea of the *process* of communication does the theorist have?

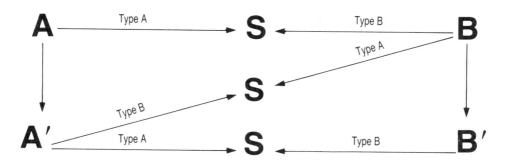

Figure 57 Schramm's model showing equally active sender and receiver

7   Is *purpose* important in the model, either in terms of the intentions of the communicators (both sender and receiver), the needs of the communicators, or the effects on the communicators or anybody else?

8   Is the direction of communication shown as one-way, two-way or a network?

9   Is there provision for feedback, either simultaneous or delayed?

10 Is interference referred to?

11 How does each model compare with each of the other models?

12 Is it a general model or only useful for particular situations?

13 Is it more useful for interpersonal, group or mass communication?

Before you attempt to answer these questions, you should try to look at the original articles as well as other authors' accounts of them.

References

The following books and articles are available on request from the British Library.

Berlo, D. K., *The Process of Communication: an Introduction to Theory and Practice* (London: Holt, Rinehart and Winston, 1960)

Dance, F. E. X., 'Towards a theory of human communication', in F. E. X. Dance (ed.), *Human Communication: Original Essays* (New York: Holt, Rinehart and Winston, 1976, pp. 288–309)

Gerbner, G., 'Toward a general model of communication', *Audio Visual Communication Review*, 1956, IV:3, pp. 171–99

Jakobson, R., 'Closing Statement: linguistics and poetics', in Seboek, T. (ed.), *Style and Language* (Cambridge, Mass.: MIT Press, 1960).

Lasswell, H. D., 'The structure and function of communication in society', in Bryson, L. (ed.), *The Communication of Ideas* (New York: Harper and Row, 1948)

Newcomb, T., 'An approach to the study of communication acts', *Psychological Review*, 1953, 60, pp. 393–404

Osgood, C., Suci, G. J. and Tannenbau, P. H., *The Measurement of Meaning* (Urbana, Ill.: University of Illinois Press, ninth printing 1957)

Schramm, W., *Men, Women, Messages and Media: a look at human communication* (New York: Harper and Row, second edition, 1982)

Shannon, C. E. and Weaver, W., *The Mathematical Theory of Communication* (Urbana, Ill.: University of Illinois Press, 1949).

Smith, A. G. (ed.), *Communication and Culture* (London: Holt, Rinehart and Winston, 1966

Westley, B. H. and MacLean, M. S., 'A Conceptual Model for Communication Research', *Journalism Quarterly*, 1957, 34, pp. 31–8.

INDEX

Items in **bold** type are main headings in the text.